The Long Short Walk

Diary of a Traffic Police Family Liaison Officer

Steve Woodward

Shield Crest

ISBN 978-1-910176-48-1

MMXIV

Published by
ShieldCrest
Aylesbury, Buckinghamshire, HP22 5RR
England
www.shieldcrest.co.uk

DEDICATION

I dedicate this book to all the victims and their loved ones. Without their full cooperation this book would not have been possible.

In some of the cases the fall out following the crash is so traumatic that I have had to change the names to protect those involved and have not included photos of the deceased. It will become obvious as to why when you read their particular story. Although I have stated at the start of those particular chapters that the names have been changed, rest assured they are all genuine cases.

In one or two cases I have not been able to make contact with the family concerned but, as much of their story is already in the public domain via the media and inquest hearings, I have included it within this book.

INTRODUCTION

Steve Woodward was a Police officer in Hampshire for more than 30 years, most of it on the Traffic Department dealing with countless road traffic accidents, many of them fatalities.

For the last seven years of his service he took on the extra role as a Family Liaison Officer to assist bereaved families through the trauma of losing a loved one.

There are a number of reasons why he felt compelled to write a book on a subject that has never been brought to the public's attention before now. He wanted to highlight the trauma that families go through, not just on the day he had to break the awful news to them, but for months, even years afterwards.

He also wanted to show how inadequate the judicial system is in bringing justice and solace to the families and finally to show that not all police work is about catching burglars, big car chases and pub fights. It's about helping people at the very lowest point in their lives.

CONTENTS

FOREWORD

Most of us go through life not expecting tragic events to happen to us, we then quietly think 'thank God' it happened to someone else and then the unthinkable does happen and instantly life is changed forever.

Our daughter died on the road in 2004 aged 25 and the aftershocks impacted on those who loved and knew her in so many unfathomable ways.

This book is essentially about the sheer force of what really happens (don't believe everything you read in the newspapers) and how this changes people's lives. There is no closure, only a strange evolvement into learning how to cope with this most dreadful event on a daily basis. It is true to say we are changed people but not in a good way, think of us more as damaged.

That is why this book is so important. Its purpose is to dig deep into the many different ways that people deal with their own personal grief and struggle to understand what has happened. Additionally this book helps to expose the systems that are in place to ensure that there is justice but do not always deliver. There are no clever answers as to why the systems don't always help, it's just that in the midst of all the emotional turmoil it is difficult for other people to understand or recognise how that loss takes over your reasoning and ability to understand the processes that need to take place in order to satisfy the judicial systems.

We can only say 'Thank God' for all the FLO's and in particular Steve Woodward who became our true support and metaphorically held our hands as he guided us through firstly being told about our daughters death, what will happen to the person who caused her death, the complexities of the various charges that would be made, the court proceedings and finally through the coroners inquest.

Steve was a constant source of honesty and empathy during the times of confusion for us as a family; he was always there at the end of the telephone line no matter what time of the day or night, never too busy to be there for us. Often he would share our frustrations when things became difficult and would unfailingly answer questions that we had probably asked many times before. At this point we would also like to say a special 'thank you' to Trish, Steve's wife who we know has quietly supported Steve in the background.

We believe that this book will help many people to understand the often complex ripples that arise from these devastating events and we are grateful that Steve has had the strength and tenacity to put into words what many of us cannot.

Mick, Tania and Mark Panormo

ABBREVIATIONS

FLO	Family Liaison Officer
FLO Coordinator	FLO Supervisor
FLO LOGS	Daily diary kept by the FLO of all contact between the FLO, the family and all other outside agencies
FLO Bereavement packs	Information packs given out to some families on certain procedures and other outside agencies
SIO	Senior Investigating Officer
PIO	Principal Investigating Officer
G28	Hampshire Police form used to enter deceased details for use by HM Coroner
RTA/RTI	Collision or crash
RPU	Roads Policing Unit (formerly Traffic Department)
CAT A ,B, C	Classification on the seriousness of the case to include level of criminality involved, number of casualties, level of media profile etc
CIU	Crash Investigation Unit
SOCO	Scenes of Crime Officer
Fatal	Police abbreviation for fatal RTA/RTI

All Services	Police abbreviation requesting that 'all Police resources' like SIO, PIO, CIU, FLO etc are sent to the scene immediately
ITU	Intensive Therapy Unit at hospital
PM	Post Mortem
ID	Police abbreviation for Identity
PNC	Police National Computer
BASICS Doctor	British Association for Immediate Care are emergency mobile doctors called to the scene by ambulance service
A&E	Accident and Emergency Unit (Casualty) at hospital
QA	Queen Alexandra Hospital, Portsmouth
RCH	Royal County Hospital, Winchester
CPS	Crown Prosecution Service
ROAD PEACE	Charity organisation that assists the families of those killed in road death
BRAKE	Charity organisation that assists the families of those killed in road death

LEGAL DEFINITIONS

Section 1 of the Road Traffic Act 1988 Death by Dangerous Driving

A person who causes the death of another person by driving a mechanically propelled vehicle dangerously on a road or other public place is guilty of an offence.

A person is to be regarded as driving dangerously for the purposes of sections 1 and 2 of the Road Traffic Act 1988 if;

1) The way he/she drives falls far below what would be expected of a competent and careful driver, and it would be obvious to a competent and careful driver that driving in that way would be dangerous; or

2) It would be obvious to a competent and careful driver that driving the vehicle in its current state (for the purpose of the determination of which regard may be to have anything attached to or carried on or in it, and to the manner in which it is attached or carried) would be dangerous.

Section 3 of the Road Traffic Act 1988 (as amended by the Road Traffic Act 1991) Careless Driving (often referred to as driving without due care and attention)

If a person drives a mechanically propelled vehicle on a road or other public place without due care and attention or without reasonable consideration for other persons using the road or public place, he is guilty of an offence.

A person is to be regarded as having driven carelessly for the purpose of Section 3 of the Roads Traffic Act 1988 if;

1) The way he/she drives falls below the standard of a careful and competent driver.

Section 3A of the Road Traffic Act 1988 Careless Driving Whilst Under the Influence of Drink or Drugs (as amended by the Road Traffic Act 1991)

2) If a person drives a mechanically propelled vehicle on a road or other public place without due care and attention whilst under the influence of drink or drugs shall be guilty of an offence.

PROLOGUE

"I couldn't do your job" are the words that Police officers hear all the time from members of the public.
"I couldn't do your job" are the words that Police Family Liaison Officers hear all the time from other Police Officers!

So on that basis does the role of the Family Liaison Officer rate as the worst job of all within the police service? Far from it in my experience, in fact I would go so far as to state that it was the best thing I ever did during my 32 year career. I met some of the most incredible people at the very lowest point in their lives and in most cases I think I was able to make the trauma of losing a loved one a little easier for them to contend with. But more of that later. Police officers have always been tasked with delivering the news that a your loved one has died, whether that be in a road traffic accident, a murder, an accident in the work place, a collapse in the street, a suicide or any other unexpected death, it's generally a police responsibility for which they have received virtually no training whatsoever other than a couple of hours role play whilst at training school. But it's the knock on the door from the Traffic cop wearing a yellow jacket and a white hat that the public identify with the most. If it happens at your door you know he hasn't come to deliver good news.

Every person who has ever joined the Police service has done so in the genuine belief that they want to make a difference, they want to help the public. However, within a very short time of coming out of training school you find yourself rolling around on the floor, fighting that same public and you very quickly lose sight of that ideology and those rose tinted glasses suddenly get all misted up. Cynicism is rife amongst police officers; some of them thrive on it. This has come about largely because that aforementioned wish to make a difference has been kicked in the bollocks by a drunken youth or his honesty and integrity has been publicly called into question by some snotty nosed lawyer in court or because his rest days have just been cancelled yet again, the list is endless and it doesn't take long for that dream to turn into a bit of a nightmare and the ideal is lost forever. I'm not saying that all police officers end up as candidates for a role in 'Grumpy Old Men' but finding a copper who has more than 20 years' service and is still genuinely enjoying his work is rare.

Whilst I would say that I can be extremely cynical and have been known to have the occasional rant, especially on early turn, because I don't do mornings (OK stop laughing those of you who worked with me!) I can also say that I am one of the lucky ones who enjoyed virtually his entire career. It may sound perverse at this point in the book to say that I enjoyed dealing with the relatives of people who had just lost a loved one but I hope to convey to you that my 'enjoyment' came from the satisfaction that I had done my absolute best for them, at a time when perhaps they couldn't help themselves, when without my help they would have been left in a pool of bureaucracy with little prospect of a life belt being tossed in their direction. In other words my pre-training school ideology was kept intact right up to the day I retired.

I have a small family and have never suffered the sudden loss of a close relative, so could never really appreciate the devastating effect that such bereavement might cause me personally. The closest I have ever come to experiencing such a loss came in April 2000 and again in 2007.

From about the summer of 1993 onwards I was crewed up with PC 1703 Kevin Angus, a larger than life character, who, like me loved his job. His wife Tina was a serving police officer and their two kids Matt and Cathy were very good friends with my three, in fact Cathy and my youngest daughter

Katie were seemingly joined at the hip, or by the lip, given the amount of time they'd spend talking (and still do). Kev and I had a very good working relationship, albeit we had completely different priorities and working practices. He was a big softy really and didn't have a confrontational bone in his body. I was the exact opposite. He was extremely methodical, especially when it came to doing his paperwork. I was the complete opposite. He would write in tiny print and underline a lot of his work with a ruler. If he made a single mistake he'd rip it up and start all over again.. If he hadn't finished a job come 10 o'clock booking off time he'd stay behind to finish it off and not claim a penny of the overtime he was due. I was the exact opposite. Perhaps that's why we hit it off and remained crew mates and good friends for nearly seven years. He drove me mad at times, I mean to the point where I could have cheerfully punched him, but I never did of course. It was a bit like having a second wife, I loved him dearly but there were times when he would frustrate me beyond all belief.

Then late one evening I received a phone call at home from a work colleague. Kev had died from a heart attack. He was 39 years old. It was like being punched really hard in the stomach. All the wind had been taken out of me in one sickening moment. I was completely numb. I couldn't think straight. It didn't make sense. I'd only spoken to him on the phone that morning. How could he have a heart attack for Christ's sake he's only 39? My wife Trish and I sat in the kitchen unable to move. We wanted to go and see Tina of course but there were complications to that.

Six weeks before his death Kev and I had been split up. Not because we had done anything wrong, far from it, but because two other colleagues just didn't get on with each other and our Sgt. had decided to split them up and on a temporary basis Kev and I would have to baby sit the pair of them until a more permanent arrangement could be sorted.

Unfortunately, despite his assurances, our Sgt. had

neglected to tell Kev of this enforced separation and due to the mischievous nature of one of the characters involved Kev was given the impression that I'd asked for a change of partner and this had caused some friction between us. Although he and I had sorted our differences Trish and I weren't sure if he had communicated that to Tina and so we decided that now probably wasn't the right time to find out.

In the days that followed Kevin's death I became even more distressed. It's traditional within the police service that your partner or very close work colleague will take on the mantle of liaison officer between 'the job' and the family. I naturally assumed this would be me. I was told in no uncertain terms that his temporary crew mate would be undertaking this role and not me. If the man had held any form of decency he would have understood this and stepped aside but he was an egotistical bastard and loved the attention it afforded him. He knew nothing of Kevin's family and made a number of significant mistakes that just made me very angry together with the rather malicious statement he conveyed from Tina towards me that we weren't welcome at her house because of the split.

Trish didn't believe this for one moment and so she phoned Tina. "Where have you been?" was Tina's first question "I expected you days ago". We drove straight over to the house and the relief was palpable. We all stayed in the kitchen, locked away from the prying ears of the so called family liaison officer who was ensconced on the settee, where he'd apparently been since day one almost permanently and to the obvious annoyance of Tina. When we got home I broke down for the first time. I've been described as an emotional cripple in the past and rarely cry or show much emotion. But on this occasion the flood gates opened and I realised just how much the silly old sod had meant to me.

Come the day of his funeral and it was much the same. We all gathered in the Traffic office in full dress uniform, six of us to be Kevs pall bearers. We had arranged for the Force's three Range Rovers to lead the funeral cortege (he'd have liked that because he loved his Range Rovers) and we then set off towards the house. Shortly after we arrived, the hearse glided silently into his road and the place fell silent as the reality of it hit us all. We proudly escorted the hearse the two miles from the house to the church and then the six of us had the responsibility of lifting Kevin's coffin from the hearse and into the church service. He was a heavy bugger; something to do with all the kebabs and burgers we ate on late turn I think! We bowed our heads after depositing the coffin onto its stand and as we did so I could feel myself welling up again. We'd done our official duty and managed to hold it altogether but I knew it wasn't going to last. As the service progressed outside to the burial site so I broke down again. It was made worse by the fact that I knew I wasn't the only one. Seeing hardened cops openly weeping in public just made it worse somehow. Saying goodbye to him at the grave side was truly terrible.

I made a huge error of judgment during all of this. As I've already said our kids all got along very well indeed and their relationship was close to that of siblings. They had almost known each other from birth and stayed at each other's houses for sleep over's, parties, BBQs and other social get-togethers. In my effort to protect my kids from the pain that their parents were suffering from I decided that it was probably better for them to stay at their grandparent's house on the day of the funeral and not to attend. Big mistake. Even though they were only 9, 13 and 15 I should have left the decision to them. They missed out on the opportunity to pay their respects to a man they loved too and more importantly to them they weren't there to support Matt and Cathy at a time when they needed it most.

The second time I experienced the very worst of emotions was in 2007. I'd been a FLO for more than five years by then and dealt with all manner of difficult situations, but nothing could have prepared me for the shock that I was about to go through.

Our eldest daughter Kelly was an outgoing and determined young lady. She'd been a dancer from the age of three and after progressing through the usual disciplines of tap, modern and ballet she took up Irish dancing after being transfixed by the River Dance phenomenon. And she was bloody good at it too, attending countless dance contests throughout the country, winning many of them outright and collecting numerous trophies and medals en route to the world finals in Dublin. At the age of 20 she decided she wanted to go and work in Disney World, Florida and got herself through a very tough interview and audition process to win a 12 month contract to go and work with Mickey Mouse. After that she returned home and eventually landed her dream job, as cabin crew for Virgin Atlantic. Seeing her at her passing out day in that bright red uniform was a very proud moment. Then she was off flying all over the world, but not before she'd bought herself a nice shiny black Audi TT. She had it all; Prestigious career, new sports car and the world at her feet.

She had returned home from the Orlando flight one morning complaining bitterly about being so tired. I mocked her and asked if she now understood what it was like to work the night shift as her father had done for many years. Two days later, we sat down for dinner and were chatting away about her latest in-flight experiences when in mid-sentence she suddenly reared up and backwards, her eyes rolling back. She was making a hideous choking noise and had gone completely stiff as she fell forwards towards the floor. The table and everything on it went flying as I managed to break her fall. There were fish fingers, chips and peas everywhere. I thought she was choking on her food as she seemed to be gasping for breath. There was white foam coming from the corner of her mouth and she wasn't responding to me at all. I tried to open her mouth in order to remove any food she might be choking on but she was so stiff I just couldn't release her jaw. Trish dialed 999 to get an ambulance and as I cradled Kelly in my arms she went from being completely rigid to limp. She seemed to have stopped breathing. In that very moment I thought she had died in my arms on the kitchen floor. I screamed out to Trish who was still on the phone "She's gone, she's gone" and I felt my stomach turn over and over. The feeling of utter despair is beyond mere words. And then she opened her eyes, took a breath and sat up right. She was cold and clammy and didn't know who she was, where she was or who I was. But frankly that didn't matter right now, she was alive. We got her up onto a chair and did our best to reassure her that she was safe. I think it was us that needed the reassurance not her! The ambulance crew and paramedics arrived, all of whom I knew and they were superb. Kelly was taken up to QA Hospital and in the months that followed she was diagnosed as epileptic. She lost her job, lost her driving licence and her car obviously but at least we still had her, which for a few brief seconds on that kitchen floor I didn't think I would. She handled it all very well considering, certainly better than her parents did I have to say.

Kevin's death and Kelly's episode (as we now call it) and several others she's had since have all given me an insight into how suddenly the course of the lives of the people closest to us can change forever. Kev's passing in particular made me revaluate my life and the way I lived it and made me understand just how quickly it can be snatched away and how valuable it is.

As a police officer, during my days as an inner city cop I attended and dealt with many deaths, mainly natural deaths, suicides and accidents at work. As a traffic officer for my last 20 years I attended and dealt with countless fatal and potentially fatal road traffic accidents (RTA's). Each and every one of them affected me in some way or another. Any police officer or other emergency service worker who says otherwise is a liar. After attending a fatal I would always drive home that little bit slower, having been reminded yet again how fragile life can be and that it's often a fine line between surviving an accident or not.

When I first went onto the Traffic Department in 1988 fatal RTAs were dealt with in a totally different manner to how they are now. The basic rule was this; if you were the first on the scene you dealt with it. And when I say dealt with it, I do mean all of it. Picture the scene. You arrive at the RTA; it's a head-on collision between two cars on a housing estate. The driver of one of the cars has died. The driver of the other car has allegedly overtaken another car just prior to the impact. There are eight independent witnesses who are all keen to provide statements. On the face of it the case looks relatively straight forward. At the scene you would be elected as the Officer-in-the-Case (OIC). The only tangible help you would receive would be from the force photographer who would take photos of the scene and send you a pile of albums a couple of weeks later. This would be followed by a report from the Vehicle Examiner who would take a very close look at any mechanical defects on the vehicles that might be contributory to the crash and an Accident Investigator who would attend to draw you a detailed plan of the scene and undertake some scientific calculations on speed and the braking efficiency of the vehicles involved. His report could take two or three months to compile.

Meanwhile I had several things to do. First I needed to find the family of the deceased and deliver the worst news in the world. This was done with little or no training, save what I had learned at training school more than 10 years before. And that training was brief to say the least. The basic rule of thumb was to get in there, tell them, without dilly-dallying and get the hell out. Obviously since leaving Ashford Police Training Centre in 1978 I'd gleaned a lot of first-hand experience and had developed a few methods of my own.

Once I'd delivered the death message then I needed to get the next of kin up to the mortuary to do the official identification and again there was no training given. Second only to being given the news, the official ID must rate as one of the very worst of experiences and it's only when viewing the body that the stark reality really hits home.

Then as soon as that odious task is completed I'd leave them to their own devices whilst I shot back to the station to commence an interview with the driver of the other car whose been sat in a cell now for about three hours. I'd ask him how the accident happened and write down everything he said, verbatim. Then he'd be released on bail for a few weeks to allow me the time to conduct my enquiries. The following day I would perhaps have to attend the Post Mortem examination and liaise with the Coroner's Officer. I'd talk to the press, maybe issue a plea for witnesses to come forward. Then I'd start ringing up my other witnesses to take lengthy written statements from them. I might have to go back to the deceased family's house to ask them a few questions or return some property to them. I would have to collect all the exhibits from the scene and make sure they were properly logged and recorded. Then I'd actually start visiting those witnesses, some of whom might live miles away from the scene, to write out their statements and gather the evidence I need to build a case against the other driver.

Then I might get a call from the Vehicle Examiner to tell me that he's found defects with the steering and two bald tyres on the offender's car. This might also have a bearing on the results of the calculations conducted by the Accident

Investigator. In between all this I'm still expected to go out on patrol, police the motorway during the rush hour, issue a few speeding tickets and attend other RTAs. Then as the reports come in from the other departments I'm expected to formally interview the offender when he answers his bail date. I might be a police officer with more than 10 years' experience but am I really qualified to interview a suspect who could be looking at a long stretch in prison and who obviously knows this so he's brought along a good solicitor who's champing at the bit to do battle with me across the interview table? Sometimes I'd arrive for the interview straight from the scene of another RTA or other incident having had no time to prepare.

Once all those witness statements had been obtained and the various specialist reports had landed in my box together with a number of impressive looking scene photos, nicely presented in bound folders then it was time to prepare the file for HM Coroner and if necessary the courts. Unlike standard crime files, fatal RTA files had a very specific structure and were presented in neat blue folders. They could take days to put together and once complete they were submitted to your Traffic Sgt. for him to scrutinise. In our case we had a Traffic Sgt. that most sections would kill for. Tony Larmour was a legend, pure and simple. He wasn't just incredibly efficient and ran our office single handed for many years but he was also a really nice guy, almost like the older brother you never had or your favourite uncle. You could go to him with any problem, whether it be professional or personal, and he always had the answer. Mind you if your fatal file wasn't up to his impeccable standards he would bounce it back until it was, he would never accept a sloppy file.

Over the years, I attended countless fatalities on the roads of Hampshire, mainly in and around the Portsmouth area, together with a huge number of potential fatal RTAs where by some miracle the victims survived, albeit with life changing injuries. And on the occasions I found myself knocking on the door I felt more and more compelled to do more than just deliver the message. Something inside of me was screaming out that merely doing that simply wasn't good enough. At the same time however I was reminded of a colleague's experience when he went above and beyond the call of duty in order to assist the wife of a man killed in a car accident. She lived close by to this officers house and out of compassion for her (and for absolutely no other reason) one morning helped fix her car so that she could make an important appointment. This was followed up shortly thereafter by him servicing the car properly in order to prevent it failing to start again in the future. Then there was a problem in the house with the boiler, then a shelf fell off the wall, then her computer malfunctioned and so it went on and on. In the end he realised that she was merely using him as a surrogate husband and he had to be cruel to be kind and tell her it had to stop. But it just goes to show how easy it is to cross the divide between being professional and perhaps becoming embroiled in something that could lead you into serious trouble, either at work or personally.

I recall attending a fatal on the Southampton Road at Cosham which really opened my eyes to just how awful such incidents can be for all those involved. Despite having attended many before this one and plenty more since, this particular incident had a profound effect upon me. The accident involved a ten year old boy and a 20 ton tipper truck and was witnessed by the boy's 11 year old friend. The accident had occurred when the boy and the young girl were racing each other along an alleyway known as Racecourse Lane on their bikes. The alleyway ran downhill from the nearby Paulsgrove housing estate and out onto the busy A27. At the end of the alleyway was one of those guard rail fences, deliberately placed to prevent people and kids in particular from running straight out of the alley and into the road. The boy overtook the girl at speed, couldn't stop in time, hit the guard rail and was catapulted over the handlebars and the fence and straight under the wheels of the passing truck. He died instantly.

When I arrived at the scene it was truly shocking. The pitiful sight of the boy under the rear of the truck was bad enough. The young girl was sat on the pavement completely traumatised. The truck driver, a man in his 50s was inconsolable. Although I wasn't first on the scene it was obvious that this was too much for one officer to deal with and so I volunteered to locate the boy's parents and deliver the awful news. I got down on the floor and spoke to the girl. She was very brave and managed to give me the boy's name and address. I then arranged for her to be taken by patrol car to the police station where she could be looked after until her parents came to collect her.

I drove up onto the Paulsgrove estate and located the house. I really didn't want to do this. My breathing was so heavy I could feel and hear every breath. I eventually plucked up the courage and knocked on the door. No reply. I knocked again. No reply. I went next door and tried the neighbours. Luckily they were friends, good friends as it transpired but that's not always the case. Once I'd ascertained that, I had to tell her what had happened so that she understood the gravity of my call and how urgent my getting hold of the parents was. She was really good and told me that the mother was at work, she didn't know the phone number but felt sure the number would be in a diary she kept in a drawer in the lounge. She led me straight to the side of the house and located the spare key under a dustbin. We entered the house and found the diary. I was just flicking through it when we heard a key in the front door. There was a long pause as the mother looked at me, dressed in my yellow jacket and white hat looking through her diary and then looked at her neighbour. She knew instantly. She screamed out loud and advanced towards me.

Within seconds she was flailing her arms backwards and forwards beating me on my chest and screaming in my face that it wasn't true. I tried to grab her wrists to prevent her from giving me a real pasting whilst her neighbour tried pulling her away from me but the poor woman was getting as distraught as the mother. It took me several minutes to calm her enough to sit her down on a chair and quietly explain what had happened. Within the hour we were at the QA Hospital where we met up with her husband and then went through the trauma of doing the ID. The death of a young child is about as bad as it gets and no-one should ever have to suffer that.

About two days later I was tasked with visiting the truck driver to interview him and obtain a witness statement if possible. His wife had said on the phone that he was in such a bad way she doubted very much if it would be possible to obtain such a statement at the moment. I thought I'd give it a try anyway and in my experience getting people to talk such things through can often help them. We sat at his kitchen table. He looked like he'd aged 10 years since the accident and was clearly a broken man. But I had no idea how broken or why. The story he then told me, chilled me to the bone.

He spoke in a very slow and deliberate manner, with tears streaming down his face. He held a soaked handkerchief in one hand as his wife gripped the other. When he was ten years old he and his eight year old brother were running down Racecourse Lane. This was in the days before the guard rail had been erected. He could run faster than his brother and was several feet ahead of him. He ran straight out onto the A27 and was more than half way across when he heard a screech of brakes. He turned around to see his younger brother being hit by a car and flying through the air. He was probably dead before he hit the road. Although he didn't actually say so I detected the burden of guilt had never left him. As a man he became a lorry driver and remained local to the area which necessitated him driving along the A27 several times a day and every time he passed Racecourse Lane so he would have a little thought about his brother.

He broke down and sobbed uncontrollably, apologising for being so silly. Both his wife and I told him that he wasn't being silly at all and that he had every right to cry. After a few minutes he regained some composure.

"I knew as soon as I saw them what was going to happen" he said "I could see two heads behind the hedge travelling fast down the hill and I just knew...........I just knew..........in fact I'd started braking before he came out the alleyway and hit the barrier."

He broke down again. This big working class man, with leathery hands the size of a dinner plate, just couldn't control the out flow of emotion. The hand of fate had dealt him a cruel blow, not once, but twice. To witness the death of your brother in such a violent manner had clearly scarred the boy and the man, but to be the driver of another vehicle that has killed a young boy of almost the same age at the exact same spot is surely too much for most of us to comprehend. All he kept saying after that was that he would never drive again and yet this tragic incident was never his fault, but he felt totally responsible. I thought this might just be an understandable reaction to the incident and that in time he would get back behind the wheel, but I heard a few weeks later that in fact he had sent his driving licence back to the DVLA.

It showed me that it's not just the victim's immediate family and friends who can be severely traumatised by a road death, but it can affect others not previously connected and can have a major impact on the rest of their lives too.

On average some 1000 people a year die in homicides in the UK. On average some 3500 people a year die on our roads, although that figure is steadily reducing. That's a huge number of human beings and it happens every year. 3500 deaths is the equivalent to seven fully laden Boeing 747 jumbo jets crashing in this country, every year, with total loss of life. If that were to happen none of us would ever fly again and there would be a national outcry and all manner of public enquiries. And yet we, as a society, treat road death in a rather blasé fashion. Its never going to happen to us is it? But those statistics hide an even bigger figure; that of the families left behind, whose lives have been destroyed forever.

In 2000 the Government introduced the Road Deaths Investigation Manual onto the statute books and it changed the way the Police dealt with road related deaths. In essence the Road Deaths Manual was based upon the Murder Investigation Manual that CID had been governed by for decades. It basically meant that every road death should be investigated as a homicide until proven otherwise and be dealt with by a team of specialist investigators and not by the first Traffic cop to arrive at the scene.

The RDIM formalised the manner in which the police investigated every fatal or potential fatal RTA. The officer actually dealing with the case, which previously would have been the first officer to arrive, would be referred to as the PIO or Principal Investigating Officer but from now on he/she would not be acting alone. Above him/her would be a Traffic Sgt. or Inspector, depending on the overall severity of the case who would be referred to as the SIO or Senior Investigating Officer. Every decision taken at the scene by everyone involved would be written down in the Incident Log or the Policy Log (or both) to ensure that transparent accountability could be accessed by those that needed to question certain decisions in the future.

Other RDIM initiatives included the mandatory use of Scenes of Crime Officers in circumstances where there might be a defendant involved and forensic evidence was required, Crash Investigation Units to undertake all their work at the scene and in the months that followed to produce mathematical calculations on things like speed, direction of travel before and after the collision and a whole host of other procedures that would eventually form part of a prosecution case or as evidence to put before the Coroner. For the first time ever a formula was laid down for the strategic interviewing of suspects undertaken by specially trained officers rather than the PIO and guidelines were issued on dealing with the press. And amongst it all came the need to train a number of FLO's who would deal almost exclusively with the family of the deceased and to act as the liaison between the family and the investigation team.

The two leading forces in the development of the FLO role were Merseyside Police and the Avon and Somerset Constabulary who had trialed the idea as the RDIM was being formulated. The Hampshire Constabulary has always had one of the most innovative and proactive Traffic Departments in the country and like every other force had no choice but to take on the RDIM. It came at a time when Michele Cook, a newly promoted Sgt. on the Traffic Department in Hampshire became more than interested in the RDIM and in particular the newly formed role of the FLO.

Prior to her move onto Traffic she had attended an RTA in Southampton where a young girl on a pedal cycle had died after a collision with a bus. With no formal training and very little idea about what she was doing she and a young male colleague attended the home address to deliver the worst news in the world. Right from the start it went horribly wrong and both officers couldn't get out of there quick enough. The situation haunted Michele for some considerable time.

She and PC Martin Vine, from the Traffic Training department attended meetings at Bramshill Police College, with various other senior officers from Hampshire's Traffic Department to discuss and formulate Hampshire's policy on the RDIM. They were then tasked with developing the training package for Hampshire's FLO's. Martin was dispatched down to Avon and Somerset and underwent the very first FLO course that they had devised. That then set the standard for the Hampshire course which Martin then developed further.

One of the things Michele wanted to introduce was a package of information that the FLO could hand over to a bereaved family that would contain information on other professional organisations that could help them as and when required. Police officers are not trained to be counsellors, therapists, social workers, clergy, accountants, insurance assessors or qualified to answer many of the myriad of tasks and requests that often befall them during their everyday duties but they somehow manage to offer sound advice on all of these topics and many more. But when it comes to dealing with the bereaved it's not quite so easy to give such brief advice especially if you end up dealing with that family over a protracted period of time.

So Michele went back to the mother of the young cyclist and asked her help to develop what became known as 'FLO packs'. They contained leaflets and contact details for organisations like Road Peace, Brake, Victim Support, booklets to assist parents with very young surviving siblings which helped explain why a family member was no longer with them, a note book for them to write down questions in the middle of the night (rather than phone their FLO at 3am) and a whole host of other really useful information that a family could make use of where their FLO just couldn't realistically help. Creating these FLO packs not only helped Michele ease the guilt she felt when dealing with that family but it also helped them come to terms with a badly handled death notification and they felt that the FLO packs were a fitting tribute to their young daughter.

Michele and Martin also developed a categorisation of

fatalities whereby the level of police response would be governed at a fairly early stage by the overall severity of the incident. For example there is a huge difference between a car leaving the road and colliding with a lamppost because the driver had a heart attack and died at the wheel and a drunk driver who swerves into a cyclist, kills him and then drives off. The level of police response at the very early stages is the same but once the circumstances become established then the incident will become either a Category A, B or C with A being the most serious and requiring the maximum amount of resources. These categories were eventually rolled out nationwide and adopted as policy into the RDIM. Around 2004 each fatality was also granted an Operation name in much the same way that all murders had been. These names were taken from a Home Office listing and were used to make identifying an incident by a single name e.g. Operation Neptune rather than saying "that fatal on the High Street in 1997, you know the one, where the car and the lorry collided head-on".

In 2001 when the job first advertised the fact that they were looking for volunteers to take on the role of FLO I have to admit that I was rather sceptical about the whole thing. Coppers hate change, although I've often wondered why they do. No other profession has had to endure a veritable tsunami of changes brought about by successive Governments since the early 1980s and indeed that constant change 'to modernise and make the Police more accountable' is still going on today. Make the Police more accountable? No single organisation in the UK has ever been more accountable than the British Police. So you'd think we'd have got used to the idea of change and perhaps embraced it? Not really. And so I viewed the Road Deaths Investigation Manual and the FLO role contained within it as little more than a passing fad that would soon evaporate and get replaced with yet another ill thought out scheme. So I ignored the plea for volunteers. But plenty of my colleagues didn't; in fact some 30 of them took the plunge, went on the FLO course at Netley Training Centre and qualified in the newly established role. My crew mate at the time, PC Alan Price was one of the volunteers and within minutes of him returning from the course his infectious enthusiasm for the FLO role had me thinking that perhaps I'd missed the boat.

By early 2002 the force was struggling to retain the number of FLO's it required as a fair percentage of them had found it didn't suit them for one reason or another and the numbers had plummeted by almost 50%. So they started looking for a second wave to train. I thought seriously about it for a couple of days and then had a long chat with Al Price about it.

Al was a big character and respected by all. He was always positive, had an infectious laugh and a big smile on his face. He convinced me that I had the right attitude and character to take on the role and that he would endorse my application if I decided to pursue it. I went home and discussed it with Trish. She agreed with Al and said I should go for it. In her I knew I had someone I could lean on if things got a bit tough. She was a psychiatric nurse who could read me like a book and if I had any issues with my job she could tell the minute I walked through the door. So I submitted my application forms and got recommended by my Sgt., my Inspector and Chief Inspector and so at the end of May 2002 I attended a one week Family Liaison Officer course at Netley.

There were 12 of us on the course, although only four of us were from Hampshire with the other eight from the neighbouring Dorset Police. These eight officers were to be the first FLO's for that force. Our course instructors were Inspector Pete Hughes, Sgt. Michele Cook and PC Martin Vine and on day one they outlined the course objectives and said that being an FLO would be like walking on egg shells.

They added that there would be a large number of guest speakers including a couple of those officers who had been undertaking the role since the first course and a number of relatives of those who had been killed in road accidents to convey their thoughts and feelings on the manner in which the Police had dealt with their particular incident. Martin warned us in advance that some of their stories would be quite harrowing.

After morning coffee it was time to get down to the first part of our learning and it was a one hour video made by the Metropolitan Police. It focused on three families who had each lost a relative in a road crash and it looked closely at the manner in which they had been informed by the Police and how they had or had not been kept in the loop during the subsequent investigation. I wasn't the only one sat there with my jaw wide open as the mother of one victim told how she and her husband had returned home after an evening at the cinema to find a hand written note pushed through their letter box that read;

"Your son was killed in a car accident earlier tonight. Please phone Hammersmith Hospital and they will give you the full details, signed PC Smith, Met Police".

I'm not going to make any further comment about this because words fail me. Suffice to say that had that been my son and I'd been told of his death in that manner then I'd have hunted down PC Smith and probably rendered him some serious damage!

The father of another victim whose teenage daughter lost her life in a motorway crash whilst her boyfriend survived unscathed told how his attitude towards the Police had completely changed. He was severely unimpressed with the manner in which the Police had investigated the crash and ended up making an official complaint. He cited all manner of investigative cock ups and missed opportunities to convict the man responsible for his daughter's untimely death. He knew exactly how the Police should have conducted their enquiries because he himself was a serving Detective Sgt. It made embarrassing viewing.

It was a sobering start to the course and later that same day we listened intently as the mothers of two more crash victims sat in front of us with framed photos of their respective son and daughter to tell us their stories. You could have heard a pin drop in that room. It wasn't the big issues that caused the most upset either it was always the little things, like the Police not returning a certain photo or not listening to a request or taking their concerns, albeit minor ones seriously.

The lack of information was also a big concern, like learning certain things about the investigation via the media was clearly an upsetting item.

During the rest of the course we were introduced to people from Victims Support Service, Road Peace (www.roadpeace.org) and Brake (www.brake.org.uk/) the latter two organisations doing tremendous work with families bereaved through road death. We were encouraged to promote both organisations to any of the families we came into contact with.

We listened to north Hampshire's Coroner Mr. David Bradley who was brilliant. As an officer who had always worked in the Portsmouth area I'd heard about the legendary Mr. Bradley from those who operated in the north of the county and this was the first time I'd met him. He was a superb speaker and spent two hours firing stories at us from all angles from the truly awful to the absolutely hilarious and about both good and bad Police practice from his view point.

By Wednesday afternoon we were at a local crematorium to watch and learn about the process of cremations so that in the event of us being asked certain questions by a bereaved family we might be able to answer them. We were invited to look through the furnace window to watch a body being incinerated, followed by the crematorium staff sweeping out the ash, separating certain metals like the gold from teeth or metal medical plates or joints and then placing the ash into urns to present to the family. The whole process was undertaken with the utmost dignity towards the deceased and it was pleasing to witness such professionalism from an industry that is rarely talked about.

There was a lot of input about the press with several of my class mates spitting feathers about journalists and how they had quite literally made up stories that wouldn't have been out of place on Jackanory. One by one we were asked to recount a bad experience we'd had with the press and there was only one that sprang to mind for me. A couple of years previously I'd dealt with a fatal accident on a quiet country road where a motorcycle had left the road on a right hand bend, entered the large adjacent ditch before colliding with a tree where the female passenger sustained fatal head injuries. The rider (we'll call him Mr A) broke his collar bone and arm and was detained in hospital. The only details released to the press the following morning were the riders name and address, which was a mistake made by someone in our office.

A reporter from the Portsmouth News was dispatched to the address in Gosport. He got no reply from the house so he started knocking on the neighbours doors. Had they heard about the accident? No. Well Mrs A was sadly killed and Mr A is in hospital with serious injuries. What our reporter didn't know was that the neighbours were all very good friends and within minutes most of the street knew and had gathered outside the house, some crying, all of them stunned at this tragic news whilst the hack was busily lapping up all the juicy bits he could muster. Then a taxi pulled up and out stepped Mrs A. I'm not sure whose jaw hit the ground first, the neighbours or the reporter but I wish I'd been there with a camera just to capture the moment. The friends and neighbours gathered around Mrs A to check that she and Mr A were indeed alive and to ascertain exactly what was going on. Mrs A then had to explain, as best she could, that the female passenger who had died was in fact the woman that Mr A was having an affair with! I've always imagined at this point that the neighbours' heads then all turned as one towards our reporter who then turned and fled in a cloud of mortified dust.

Personally I'd always enjoyed a good relationship with the press and found them more than useful when it came to appeals for witnesses or to get some toe-rags photo splashed across the front page following his/her conviction for a serious offence. By working together both our professional interests were served and the result was usually positive.

However under the auspices of the RDIM a set press policy had to be recorded in the Policy Log for each incident. This policy would be a joint decision between the PIO/SIO and the FLO with assistance at times given by the forces Media Services people who would, where required deal directly with the press. This policy would govern when the details of the deceased could be released and where applicable that family statements and photos of the deceased could be given to the press. This was usually done on the strict understanding that they would not then go and knock on the family's door looking for further information.

Towards the end of the week we were looking at procedural issues like the filling out of FLO logs. These A4 sized carbon copied books were to become the diaries for each incident we dealt with. Every meeting with the family, every phone call made or received, all dealings with the press, the SIO/PIO, with any other outside organisation, in fact anything and everything connected with that case was to go into the FLO log. It could mean hours of writing but everything needed to be recorded on a daily basis to protect me, the family and others in the event of any complications or complaints.

On the final day we learned that we would become a human sponge, able to soak up large amounts of emotional trauma but not be affected by it too much. Our welfare was now at the very top of the forces concerns. What? That's never happened before. Why the concern now? It was obvious when you thought about it. Here we were about to embark upon a new path in our careers, except that it wasn't really a new path, more an officially mapped out route with rules and guidelines laid down by statute and force policy, which meant that the force was now officially responsible for my welfare because of it.

We were told in no uncertain terms that we would not be allowed to take on more than five FLO deployments at any one time. This was to ensure that we didn't soak up too much trauma and thus over load that sponge because what happens to a sponge when it can't hold any more water? Exactly. To ensure we were monitored effectively a number of Traffic Sgt.s. were installed as FLO Coordinators. They included Michele Cook, Wayne Voller, Alison West, Mick Streeter and John Geden. They were trained in the same manner we had been but with a greater emphasis on looking after our welfare out in the field. To back up the FLO Coordinators every FLO was to attend an all-day FLO Conference at Netley every month with no exceptions. These bean-bag sessions had us gathered around a large conference table as one by one we gave graphic, in depth accounts of our latest deployments. Everyone was then allowed to ask you questions or perhaps give guidance on something you could have done better. It was fascinating listening to other officer's stories and the situations some of them found themselves embroiled in, from family rows to acts of amazing courage or kindness. Some of the stories were horrific whilst others were simply hilarious. You were allowed to level criticism of the investigation team, of senior officers, in fact anything and everyone because what was said in that room remained in that room, it was strictly confidential but more importantly it was a method of release for us, to squeeze out that sponge and it really worked.

In one final act of concern for our welfare the force insisted that once a year you went for an MOT. Not your car but you personally. Another trip to Netley had you sitting in front of Quita Jones, the force psychiatrist on a one to one basis. She would listen intently to some of those same stories and then ask you some quite in depth and personal questions about how it had affected you and your family. She had the power to either reduce your work load or have you removed from the FLO role on a temporary or even permanent basis if she thought you weren't coping.

On the final afternoon having passed the course we were given our new Nokia 6310 phones complete with the number we would have to give out to the families we were to come into contact with. I'm pretty good at memorising numbers and I didn't think I'd have a problem remembering this one – 07879 888891 was probably the easiest mobile phone number I'd ever clapped eyes on. Then we were given instructions and details about the call-out system whereby we would be placed on a rota to be called out from home at night if there wasn't a FLO already on duty. There was no extra payment for this or for being a FLO in general, it was all undertaken with a huge dose of goodwill and the desire to ensure that the job was done in the best possible way.

The final two acts of the week were the obligatory course

photograph and the promise from Michele Cook that we wouldn't get deployed for at least a fortnight to give us all time to read the vast amount of literature they had dumped on us and to allow the systems within the Force concerning the call out rota to go live. So that was it, I was now a fully qualified Family Liaison Officer and with some trepidation I awaited my first deployment.

STEPHEN BARRON

Category C
Sunday 2nd June 2002

2002 Hampshire fatalities = 96
2002 Nationally fatalities = 3431

My family and I had been invited to a neighbours' house for a big BBQ to help celebrate the Queens Golden Jubilee. The garden was packed with lots of other people from our neighbourhood and our hosts had been very generous with the food and drink and it wasn't long before a good party atmosphere was in full swing. Well it's not every day we get to celebrate the Monarch sitting on the throne for 50 years is it!

It was a very warm summer's afternoon and it was perfect weather for this type of celebration, the sort of day where in years to come people will reminisce about the street party they went to or the fancy dress party they took part in and the good weather certainly played its part.

As we sat around tables in the garden some of my neighbours started asking policing type questions, as they invariably do on such social occasions. Most of the time I don't mind, people are naturally inquisitive and without doubt a large percentage of the public are fascinated by police work, whether they are in awe of the job we do or just want to

1

moan about the lack of justice, it seems that many like to have an input if they get the chance. The subject somehow got around to the police being awarded the Queens Golden Jubilee medal to mark the occasion and unlike some of my colleagues who received theirs with a touch of disdain, which I thought was sad, I was actually rather proud of mine. And I was pleased that every serving officer with more than five years' service got the medal rather than the select few very senior officers who were awarded the Queens Silver Jubilee medal back in 1977. I was a 17 year old Police Cadet then and was based down on Thorney Island for a whole week looking after about 200 other police officers and a large number of RAF crew from the fly past squadron. We worked nights for the entire week guarding the base and I had a serious dose of man-flu and have always felt that I should have been awarded that medal for my devotion to duty!

It was late afternoon and the party was going great when my mobile rang. It was Michele Cook and she apologised straight away for phoning me on my day off, followed by a second apology for breaking her promise at the end of the FLO course when she had stated that we wouldn't get deployed for at least a fortnight. This was clearly leading somewhere. And it was.

There had been a possible double fatal on Portsdown Hill and another one north of the county somewhere, so the lates Traffic shift were now really stretched. But of course they needed two FLO's to assist at the Portsdown Hill crash, so could I go? Do I have any choice? Luckily I hadn't been drinking so that excuse was out, although in hind sight I suppose I could have lied about it. But within the emergency services there is a huge amount of goodwill devoted by the staff that goes virtually unnoticed, unrewarded and unrecognised by the management and certainly by the public.

In many other jobs, especially the more unionised

professions wouldn't dream of doing more than a minute of overtime without proper remuneration. And to have their day off cancelled, interrupted or disturbed in any way whatsoever would be unthinkable. This is especially true of CPS lawyers, magistrates, judges and others in the legal profession who would think nothing of dragging a police officer into court to give evidence on the most trivial of matters when he was in the middle of his leave or having only been in bed two hours after a night shift. But hold court cases in the evening or at weekends? Heaven forbid.

I don't think Trish was too impressed as I made my excuses and walked back to our house where I quickly got changed into my uniform and then drove the three miles up to Cosham nick. On entering the office my mobile rang again and it was the control room asking for my e.t.a at the scene. I grabbed the keys to a patrol car, got all my FLO kit together and drove up to Portsdown Hill. The scene was actually on James Callaghan Drive and as I made my way towards it I wondered just how many fatals I'd been to over the years up here on Portsdown Hill. I think I'd counted to about a dozen when I reached the roundabout with the road closure on it. I got let through and then drove slowly towards the scene itself.

A gold coloured Vauxhall Calibra was upside down on its roof. It had clearly hit the embankment on the northern side of the road as there were huge chunks of mud and grass strewn everywhere. It had traveled a long way since hitting the embankment and had overturned several times looking at the huge amount of damage to the car and the large number of fresh scrape marks on the road surface. Scattered all around the car, in amongst the shattered windscreen glass were various bandages, swabs, syringes and other medical paraphernalia left by the ambulance crews. There was an eerie silence about the scene with only the Swallows darting about in the summer skies to bring any movement to the place. I liaised with Sgt. John Geden who was the SIO and was told that the Calibra was apparently the only car involved and that all four male occupants had been ejected out of the windows as the car overturned. Three were in a serious condition, two of them with life threatening injuries. Another FLO had been brought down from Farnborough and had recently arrived at QA Hospital which was less than a mile from the scene.

I drove back down the hill to the QA and saw another patrol car outside A&E. There seemed to be a large number of people gathered around outside the entrance to the hospital. The weekends are always the busiest days at A&E and it quite often resembles a war zone with waiting times of six hours or more. Even though I was quite used to seeing it busy I have to confess I was taken aback by the number of people, there must have been about 50 of them. I got into the other patrol car to liaise with the other FLO. I told him that this was my first official deployment since my FLO course. He laughed and said that this probably wasn't the best one to start off with because all these people gathered outside were friends and relatives of the four males from the car and that there were more on their way up from Gosport where they all lived. He said that so far all he had were two names, 22 year old Stephen Barron and 21 year old Matthew Mason. I took Barron and he'd take Mason.

We walked into A&E and it was bedlam, there were people everywhere, some crying, others on mobile phones, some of the lads shouting out stupid things and swearing at one another. The nursing staff were already having a busy day prior to this lot arriving and had seemingly given up on trying to keep some sort of order. I walked into the relative's room, which was packed with about 30 people, which made it about 200% over its capacity. A woman in her early 50s with jet black hair grabbed my arm and said she was Stephen Barron's mother Vicky and could she have a word with me outside. We walked out into the corridor and back around to the entrance foyer.

"Are you going to be our liaison chap?" she enquired.

"Yes I am."

"I needs to 'ave a word with you about my Ash, he's my husband," she went on.

"OK," said I. There was something a bit threatening about this, I could tell.

She took hold of my arm again and pulled it downwards so that I leant forward and she could whisper in my ear.

"The trouble is, my Ash is a schizophrenic and e hates the Old Bill. I mean e *really* hates the Police, cos e's had a lot of bad dealings with you lot in the past so I just thought I ought ta warn ya in advance" she said before letting out a rasping cough.

With that she scampered off back to the relative's room. What a great start I thought. I went and found one of the A&E Doctors to try and ascertain an update on the lads condition to be told that he had been taken up to the operating theatre for emergency surgery and that in his opinion it was unlikely he would survive.

I went back to the car to make some phone calls to update the SIO and to give myself a chance to catch my breath and to risk assess the prospect of dealing with Mr Barron when and if the time arose. There were still taxi's arriving with more Gosport residents whilst others darted in and out of the main reception area to have a quick fag before going back inside again. Some of the girls just stood there hugging each other whilst the lads stood in groups or sat against the wall. It was now about quarter to ten and it was starting to get dark. I decided to get another update from the staff and if things were the same then I'd resume back to the office and go home. No sooner had I walked into reception than a nurse asked if she could have a quick word; Stephen Barron had died on the operating table and the doctor had just told his family. I left them to it and went back outside to the patrol car and phoned the SIO again. As I sat in the car which was facing the entrance to A&E so I saw the raw emotion spread through this group of mainly teenagers, like wildfire. The realisation that one of their mates had now died hit them like a steam train. Shouts of "No" followed by hands over faces, some reeling away to be on their own, before coming back and flinging their arms around each other. Some took to their mobiles to make frantic phone calls to other mates whilst girls just sobbed uncontrollably. It was a surreal scene played out via my cars windscreen as if I were watching it on TV.

There was a huge explosion behind and above me. The earth shook and I literally jumped out of the car. There was another massive bang that made me jump again. I looked up. It was fireworks. Not your ordinary household rockets and roman candles oh no, these were industrial strength display fireworks being launched from one of the posh houses on the estate directly opposite the QA. The sky was lit up with reds and golds, greens and blues in celebration of the Golden Jubilee. I looked back at the crowds of people stood outside the hospital entrance, all of them seemingly oblivious of the irony. It was bizarre. Here I was standing directly in between two groups of people. To my left a number of human beings celebrating Her Majesty's 50 years on the throne whilst to my right another group mourning the loss of a friend. The booms and the bangs continued to shake the ground we stood on and I actually found myself getting really annoyed about it. How dare they do this I thought? Don't they know that people are suffering over here? It even crossed my mind to go over to the house that was hosting this equivalent to the nightly displays at Disney World and under the provisions of the Portsmouth City Police Act (which is completely fictitious but I've seen it used on a number of occasions by older, slightly wiser officers than myself in circumstances where no real Act of Parliament would fit) demand that they cease forthwith.

They must have used several thousand pounds worth of

fireworks during that half hour display and as the gunpowder smoke started to clear so I went back inside the hospital, expecting more fireworks if I met up with Mr Barron. However he was no-where to be found and I made arrangements with Mrs Barron to see them at their house in the morning where we could go through a few procedural things in relative peace, which we certainly couldn't do here.

I came into the office the next morning and spoke to John Geden and it had been decided from an early stage that this was likely to be a Cat C incident. Two out of the three passengers were still in hospital, with Matthew Mason on life support.

I drove across to the rather grandly named San Diego Road in Gosport, which is anything but grand frankly. Gosport is one of the more deprived parts of the greater Portsmouth area with row upon row of terraced housing set amongst some small industrial units and MOD and Naval establishments. It's a poor area and under privileged with an above average unemployment rate. It has a rather depressed reputation.

I arrived at the mid terrace house and was rather dreading my face to face meeting with Mr. Barron. Vicky opened the door and she looked exhausted. She was still in her dressing gown with a fag in her hand. She beckoned me in and I found the house was almost full of visitors, with most of them standing in the kitchen. The air was thick with cigarette smoke and it seemed that everyone in there was a smoker except me. I was ushered into the front room and then we were joined by Ash. He shook me by the hand and then asked me what I was doing there. I explained what my role was and that I would do everything I could to ensure that they got the answers they were looking for and that I would keep them fully up to date with the police investigation. But first I needed to fill out a load of paperwork on behalf of the Coroner.

I have to say that Ash was extremely pleasant towards me and wasn't confrontational in any way whatsoever, which was a relief. He did have a lot of questions about how and where the crash took place and so I offered to take them up to the scene as it would be easier for me to explain if they could actually see where it took place. He agreed but Vicky wasn't keen, besides which she had a house full of people to look after. Its often struck me in such circumstances how rather unfair it is that friends and relatives descend upon the immediate family and they then have to busy themselves with making tea and coffee at a time when perhaps somebody else should be doing it for them.

I drove Ash and a friend of his up to James Callaghan Drive and parked in a lay-by. The huge gouge marks in the grass embankments still dominated the scene, as did the scrape marks on the tarmac from where the Vauxhall Calibras roof had come into contact with it. I explained to Ash the circumstances as we understood them so far and he stood there in complete silence for a while staring at the damage to the grass and the road. He couldn't quite comprehend the distance between the two as it appeared that the car had travelled more than 150 yards from the point of initial impact to its final resting place.

"He must have been really motoring then?" he enquired.

"Well that's something that the Crash Investigation Unit and any witnesses might be able to shed some light on as the investigation progresses" I replied.

He walked the entire length of the crash scene twice more before thanking me and stating he'd seen enough. We drove back to Gosport in virtual silence.

The house was still full when we got back but Vicky and Ash showed me into the front room again so that we could have some privacy in order that I could go through a couple more things with them including the press policy and a statement about Stephens last known movements. As we sat and drank a second cup of tea so Vicky started to tell me more about Stephen. It transpired that Stephens brother was engaged to Matthew Mason's sister. So they were all very closely knit. After completing all the necessary paperwork I gave them my card and phone number and told them to ring me if they had any questions at all and that as soon as I found out anything about the crash then I'd be in touch with them.

Four days later Matthew Mason lost his fight for life and died at the QA Hospital.

I hadn't heard anything from the Barron family for a couple of days until Vicky phoned me one afternoon to let me know about a war of words that had been brewing between members of her family and the Mason family, who were blaming Stephen for killing Matthew. As the animosity between them grew, so it spread amongst that large group of friends throughout Gosport until eventually there were two distinct camps. It had quickly reached the stage where a number of individuals were openly talking about physical attacks upon each other. Emotions were clearly running very high and so I reassured Vicky that we would monitor things very closely. I phoned the other FLO who had just heard similar stories from his contact with the Mason family and it became apparent that things were likely to come to a head that Friday night in some of the pubs in the Gosport area. The potential for serious public disorder was obvious.

I passed on my concerns to John Geden and it was quickly agreed that a PSU (Police Support Unit) would be drafted into Gosport that night to back up the local Gosport units in the event of any trouble. The other FLO and I made contact with the two families to advise them to spread the word amongst their family and friends that any such disorder would be swiftly dealt with. It seemed to have the desired effect because thankfully that Friday night and the rest of the weekend passed without any real problems.

The rear seat passenger Paul Spooner, who had been thrown out of the car via the back window as it over turned had sustained serious but not life threatening injuries and within a fortnight of the crash was fit enough to be interviewed by the investigation team. He stated that the four of them had been drinking for much of the day and were in very high spirits. After leaving the pub they decided to drive up onto Portsdown Hill. He said that Stephen was driving really fast as Matthew sat on the window sill with his upper body fully out of the car as he shouted and screamed at everyone they passed. As the car travelled up the hill so Stephen continued accelerating and then started shouting out his speed as "85…..90…..a ton…..a ton ten" and that was the last thing Paul Spooner could remember as the car hit the nearside embankment and overturned.

At the same time reports started coming in from various specialist departments including the Vehicle Examination Unit who found that the Calibra had two completely bald tyres and no MOT. The investigation team also discovered that none of the four occupants was wearing a seat belt at the time and was the reason they had been ejected from the vehicle as it over turned. So a combination of alcohol, excessive speed, dangerous driving, no seat belts and defective tyres conspired to bring about the deaths of two young men. It was now my job to go back to the Barron family and tell them before it became public knowledge at the inquest.

Being told your son is dead is hard enough, but to tell his parents that it was 100% his fault and it was completely avoidable is something else. Thankfully it wasn't actually going to be me that rubbed salt into the wound but John Geden. I was there as his back up really, not in a physical sense but more for moral support. John was a great communicator and

I felt confident that he would be able to put the facts across in a compassionate manner but even so I can't say I was looking forward to this and felt rather nervous as we stood knocking at their door once more. It was three months since the crash. We sat in the front room and John outlined all the facts.

At first Vicky and Ash just sat there in silence. Then Vicky said she didn't believe the bit about the bald tyres because Stephen often took his baby daughter out in that car and there is no way he'd have risked her life by having bald tyres. Then she disputed the fact that the car had no MOT, then that Stephen had been drinking and driving and that he always wore his seat belt. She got more and more upset and said she didn't believe any of it, that it was a police stitch up and that we had come down on the side of the Mason family.

In the end Ash interrupted her. He reminded her that he had been up to the scene with me the next day and he'd seen the damage to the embankment and the road surface and that the evidence that Paul Spooner had supplied was first hand evidence, he was there, why would he lie about it? He managed to pacify her enough and thanked us for being open and honest with them.

John and I sat back in the patrol car and together let out a big exhale of air.

The inquest was held at Portsmouth Coroners Court on 22nd October before HM Coroner James Kenroy. Although witness statements had been obtained that stated they had all been drinking during the day it wasn't possible to obtain accurate toxicology reports on Stephen because of the drugs he had been given at the scene and in A&E. However the combination of excessive speed and dangerous driving meant that the Coroner reached a verdict of accidental death on both men. He concluded by saying;

"A car can be a lethal weapon when not used properly. The way in which this car was being driven did, I am sorry to say, court disaster and sure enough that tragedy did occur."

The following day The Daily Echo put a photo of the battered remains of the Vauxhall Calibra on their front page with the banner headline 'DON'T END UP LIKE THIS' with a sub title below stating 'Families issue warning after high speed car tragedy claims lives of their sons'

The two page article urged other young men in the area not to drive at high speeds or they too could end up dead.

Ash was quoted as saying "My advice is just don't chance your arm or your luck will just eventually run out".

Whilst Vicky was quoted as saying "Don't end up like Stephen. Don't lark about at the wheel of a car and wear your seat belt. It isn't worth risking your life for. It is just too short".

So in the end I think Vicky came to accept the facts and wanted to warn other young men. For my part it was a fairly simple start to my life as an FLO and apart from the tensions between the families during the early stages things had gone relatively smoothly.

At least I thought they had. Whilst writing this book I have made contact with the families I have highlighted to gain their approval to use their story and to ascertain certain facts from the aftermath of the event. When talking to Vicky I was somewhat taken aback at her memory of the incident that claimed the life of her son. She now claims that Stephen wasn't the driver and that Paul Pond was. She went on to state that he and Paul Spooner had conspired together with Matthew Masons father to make compensation claims against Stephen's insurance. She also reverted back to her insistence that the police investigation had sided with the Mason family because Sgt. Geden was, in her opinion, a member of the Masonic Lodge, as was Mr. Mason senior, allegedly. I reassured her that John Geden was not a member of the Masonic Lodge and even if he had been it would not have made the slightest difference to the investigation because he was one of the most honest officers I had ever come across and his integrity was bomb proof.

But the ripple effect went much further than that. Her two other sons, one of whom was now married to Matthew Mason's sister didn't talk to Vicky for more than eight years after the crash. The accusations, the rumour and speculation have done a lot of damage and it would appear that tensions are still running high. This has had an adverse affect on Vicky and Ash's health and is further proof that as the parents or close relatives of the deceased in such cases, you don't ever just get over it.

CHRISTOPHER HAMMOND

(All names changed to protect family)
Category C
28th July 2002

2002 Hampshire fatalities = 96
2002 Nationally fatalities = 3431

It was a baking hot Sunday morning and I was on a day shift, busily sorting out paperwork and other issues when an RTA came in for the A34 southbound at Sutton Scotney Services. Nothing to do with me, not my area I thought and so I carried on sifting the mountains of paper. How I hated paperwork, it was the bane of every coppers' life but mine in particular it seemed. I never got to the bottom of the pile before somebody threw a load more on top of it. Every job you get sent to gives the green light to some Brazilian lumberjack to fire up his chain saw and fell another tree in the rain forest, just so I can write somebody's name, date of birth and address onto 15 different forms that all relate to the same incident.

One by one the northern Traffic units arrived at the scene. It was a confirmed double fatal with two other serious injuries; could they have all services please.

Mike Control to Mike Charlie 01
Mike Charlie 01 go ahead
You are the only FLO on duty at the moment; can you head north to this fatal and assist please?
Mike Charlie 01 Roger

Yet again the paperwork would have to wait. I took a

large gulp of coffee, grabbed my kit and jumped into the BMW X5 and headed west along the M27, up the M3 to junction 9 and then north up the A34. It was a long way really and whilst en route I got a basic idea from the radio traffic that a Vauxhall Nova had left the road to the nearside and overturned into a field with the two deceased and two other youths having been ejected from the vehicle as it overturned, much like the Calibra had done on Portsdown Hill only a month before.

By the time I arrived the Crash Investigation Unit were busy setting up their equipment and various other officers were gathering information from witnesses. I spoke to the SIO who took me to the inner cordon where the bodies of two young males lay in the long meadow grass, close to the car which was lying on its side. Apart from the paramedics who'd tried in vain to save them, no-one had yet gone near them to ascertain any ID. That was my job. At the same time I was told that PC Pete Haywood was on his way up to the scene having been dragged out from home, to act as the other FLO.

I donned one of those all in one disposable blue paper suits, which are almost impossible to put on over the top of your uniform. It's a bit like putting on a rubber wet suit and no matter how hard you try you aren't ever really comfortable in it. Add a pair of vinyl gloves and I was ready to do something I really wasn't that keen on doing but it came with the territory I suppose.

I knelt down beside one of the bodies which was lying on its side. There were very few visible signs of injury and he looked so small. Searching the pockets of a deceased person always feels so invasive, so very personal, so I always did it with the utmost respect and would often find myself talking to them, asking their permission and apologising for having to do it. I found his wallet which contained his driving licence which gave me the name of Christopher Hammond aged 18 years and from the village of Bramdean just a few miles from the scene. I sat back on my haunches. 18 years old, what a waste. As I sat there a Red Admiral butterfly landed on the young lads' leg and sat there for a few moments before fluttering off.

I left the scene and travelled to Bramdean, a small village on the A272. I found the detached bungalow on my left opposite a childrens' play area. My heart was now pounding as I plucked up the courage to go and knock at the door. I walked across the small driveway and rang the door bell. God it was hot. There was no reply except for a dog inside that was barking frantically. I rang again. No reply. Maybe they are sunning themselves in the back garden I thought, so I shouted over the side gate but got no response. I rang the door bell again. No reply. So I went next door to the neighbours on the right. No reply. Then I tried the neighbours to the left. An elderly gent answered the door but he was useless. He didn't know anything about his neighbours at all, so it was back to square one. I knew I was likely to be here for a long time so I shot off to a petrol station a few miles down the road and grabbed myself a sandwich and a bottle of water. I'd hoped that by the time I got back to the house someone may have returned home but I was sadly disappointed. In the end I ran out of ideas and so reversed the patrol car up onto the driveway and waited. It must have been the hottest day of the year and I had to keep the engine running to keep the air conditioning ticking over otherwise I was going to melt. I sat there for almost two hours.

Suddenly a 16 year old lad appeared on the driveway. He looked towards me as he walked towards the house. I got out of the patrol car and we met by the front door. I ascertained that he was Christopher's younger brother Robert and that his parents were out somewhere.

"What's this all about? he enquired.

"I can't really say without your parents being here," I

nervously replied.

"It's about Chris isn't it," he said looking straight into my eyes.

"Yes it is," I wasn't going to lie to him if he asked me a direct question.

"He's dead isn't he?"

'Yes Robert he is, I'm sorry."

Quite how he had reached that conclusion in such a short space of time is beyond me, but he obviously knew his brother better than I did so maybe there was something about Chris that I was yet to learn.

Robert leant against the front of the house and slid slowly downwards and sat on the ground and said nothing. I took a huge breath and could feel myself shaking. I wasn't sure if I'd broken some kind of rule on telling a juvenile without his parents being present but it was too late now, I'd done it and I'll have to live with the consequences if the shit hits the fan over it. We eventually went into the house but not before Robert had put the dog, who was still going bananas, into the front room and shut the door. He found his father's mobile number and I insisted it was me who rang him. He answered it almost straight away and said he and his wife were shopping in Guildford. I told him I was at his house with Robert and requested he return immediately but obviously wouldn't tell him what it was about.

I sat in the spacious lounge whilst Robert busied himself in the kitchen and tried pacifying the dog that was still barking and jumping about in the other room. He said he dare not let it out because it didn't like strangers. That's fine with me. Half an hour later and Mr and Mrs Hammond arrived home. I stood up and felt myself starting to shake again. They entered the lounge and Mr Hammond looked straight at Robert and rather aggressively said to him.

"What have you been up to this time then?"

He'd clearly put two and two together and made five,

understandably as it was only Robert and I who stood on his front room carpet. I think I'd have jumped to the same conclusion if it had been my son stood next to a Police officer.

"No, no" I said quickly "It's not Robert I'm here about but Chris"

"What about Chris, what's he been up to?" said Mr Hammond.

"There's no easy way to tell you this but there's been a bad accident on the A34 and I'm afraid Christopher has died in the crash".

There was a long silence. Mrs Hammond then ran from the lounge and disappeared upstairs and I could hear her crying as she did so. Mr Hammond sort of collapsed in a deflated heap on the settee. Robert just stood like a statue in the middle of the room and even the dog seemed to have gone quiet. It's always been my experience that once you've delivered the worst news in the world you then shut up and say absolutely nothing, allow them to absorb what you've just told them in their own time, don't start firing other statements or asking questions of them right now because they just won't hear you. After a couple of minutes Mr Hammond started to ask questions like where, when and how together with the usual "Are you sure it's Chris"?

"No we aren't 100% certain which is why I need you to come to the hospital with me to do an ID. There's absolutely no rush, whenever you are ready" I said.

He went upstairs to talk to his wife returning a few minutes later to say they would both come with me and that his wife was going to find this particularly difficult because she was a theatre nurse at the Royal Hampshire County Hospital in Winchester, which is where we were going. He went on to explain that Chris and some friends had been up to Stratford for the weekend to the Gods Kitchen music festival and had met his sister Heather up there. I then had to explain that it wasn't just Chris who had died but one of his friends too. He asked which one and when I told him it was possibly Gavin Underwood he shook his head in disbelief and then told me that Gavin's father was a Police officer.

I went straight out to the patrol car to update the SIO on the news I had ascertained so that he could pass the information onto Pete Haywood. By the time I'd finished Mr and Mrs Hammond were ready to join me and within a few minutes we were leaving their driveway and heading the five or six miles along the A272 towards Winchester. I drove as slowly and carefully as I could often looking in my rear view mirror and seeing the faces of two parents whose lives had just been completely torn apart. We made the journey in total silence.

The RCH in Winchester is one of those old Victorian hospitals built on the side of a steep hill with an infrastructure that was never intended for 21st century efficiency. After negotiating a maze of tiny roadways at the rear of the hospital we arrived at the mortuary. I left them in the car whilst I quickly went in to ensure that the staff were ready for us. I met Ruth and Laura the Pathology assistants and their calm and professional approach was always a comfort to me and the other FLOs they looked after. They somehow made our jobs a little bit easier, not by taking over but by being brilliant with the newly bereaved relatives we brought in and by the calm manner in which they explained things to them.

I brought Mr and Mrs Hammond in through the side door, across the hallway and out into the neatly laid out garden area which led directly to the entrance of the viewing room. Ruth led Mrs Hammond in first and then quietly spoke to them about the procedures that would follow. We all sat in the inner waiting area until they had composed themselves and were ready to do what no parent should ever have to do. We entered the viewing room and Mr Hammond made a positive ID that it was indeed his son Christopher. Ruth and I then left the room to allow them all some privacy.

A few minutes later Mr Hammond came back out.

"I don't envy you and your job I really don't" he whispered quietly "It must be awful" he continued.

"Well right now Mr. Hammond I'd rather be me than you" I replied and he sort of nodded a nod of appreciation before returning to the viewing room.

The journey back to their house was as silent as before, both of them staring straight ahead. When we got back to the house Mrs. Hammond went upstairs and I sat on the settee to talk to her husband, John. He was as helpful as any parent could be in the circumstances and gave me all the information I needed for the G28, ID statement and other paperwork. We went through the press policy and thought it likely that they would opt for doing a family statement. He also expressed an interest in visiting the scene as he thought that might help him understand better how his son's car ended up in a field. After a while he popped upstairs to check on Marie and whilst he was gone I glanced towards the patio door at the other end of the lounge and noticed the perfect imprint of a bird about the size of a Blackbird or Thrush with its wings outspread. It had obviously flown into the window and left a perfect print of itself on the glass. I'm sure it wasn't there before we went up to the mortuary.

We went through the circumstances leading up to the crash again. I didn't have too much information but it would appear at this stage that Chris's Vauxhall Nova was in the outside lane when it drifted into the central barrier, lost control and then as it came across the carriageway it clipped the front of another car before over turning into the field.

"He didn't drink and drive you know" said Marie as she came down the stairs.

I then explained that toxicology tests would be done as a matter of routine during the PM. Marie was more concerned about contacting their daughter Heather and other relatives and so I said I'd leave them in peace for now and would pop back tomorrow to collect the family statement and maybe take them to the scene if they were up to it.

I drove to the Traffic office at Winchester to complete the G28 and start a new FLO log. I met the PIO and we went through a few things, including the return of Christopher's property to his parents and doing a scene visit. He said they'd managed to talk to one of the two rear seat passengers and he said that the three of them were asleep because they'd been up all night at the gig and had basically left Chris to drive them home. He said he was all right to drive but maybe he'd drifted off to sleep as well. That would concur with what the other witnesses had said and with the physical evidence at the scene with the damage to the barrier and the car. It wasn't heavy impact damage it was scraping to the bodywork on the off-side of the car.

The following day I drove back to the house and picked John and Marie up to take them to the scene. Marie had a small bunch of flowers with her. We parked in the car park at Sutton Scotney Services and then had to walk from there quite a distance along the exit slip road from the services back out towards the main A34. It was too dangerous to undertake this without some form of protection and so I'd arranged for a patrol car to follow us out with its lights on so that we were a little safer. Just as we got to the end of the slip road, by a large bush, we turned left and into the adjacent field. I took them to where Chris had landed and you could still see where all the activity had been because of the flattened meadow grass. Marie laid the flowers down on the ground and John put his arm around her. They stared at the ground for some considerable time before John asked me to go through how the crash happened again and to point out the sequence of events and where the car ended up. We were only there for about five minutes I suppose but it certainly helped them understand things a little better.

When we got back to the house we had a cup of tea and talked in general terms about young lads and their cars and how they all think that they are indestructible. I told John I really couldn't say too much on the subject because as a teenager I was terrible once I'd got my first wheels. I look back now at some of the things I got up to and it makes me shudder.

Over the next few days I visited them a couple more times to return some of Chris's personal effects and I built up a good rapport with John in particular. A date had now been set for the funeral and he asked me if I would attend. It was a highly unusual request but he specifically wanted me there in full uniform in a marked patrol car so that everyone, especially Chris's young friends who were just starting out on their driving careers, could see that if they mucked about in cars then they too would get a copper at their funeral. I could see his point but I was a bit uneasy about going to the funeral of a person I'd not actually met. But that said, for John's sake I'd do it.

I arrived at the church and managed to find a parking space on the approach road, so that everyone could see the patrol car just as John had requested. No yellow jacket for me today, it was the old tunic which always looks so much smarter anyway. I did feel like an intruder though. There must have been 150 people there I suppose, many of them youngsters of Chris's age and a few of them asked if I'd been to the crash scene. I told them what they wanted to hear and John was right, it did seem to have the desired effect on them. So although it was a rather strange experience for me personally I think it made a few of his friends sit up and take notice.

Several weeks passed by and I hadn't had any contact with the family at all. I then got a call from Inspector Dave

Watkins at Whitchurch Traffic. He was the SIO and said he wanted to meet the family to go through the file with them prior to the inquest. He then told me why this was particularly important and my heart sank. I phoned John to make the arrangements and we convened at their house two nights later.

John, Marie and Heather sat on one settee whilst Robert sat on the floor as Dave and I took up position on another settee. Dave went through the evidence piece by piece and concluded by stating that the car had indeed just drifted into the central barrier before losing control and ending up in the field. He said that neither Chris nor Gavin had been wearing their seat belt which is why they had been ejected from the car as it over turned. There was no doubt about this as certain tests had been conducted on the seat belts and they weren't in operation at the time. But the reason Dave needed to talk to John and Marie was because of the results of the toxicology tests that had been carried out during the PM. Large quantities of ecstasy had been found in Christopher's system and had they been aware that he took drugs? It was a shocking revelation and Marie erupted, shouting at Dave that it was bad enough that her son had died and what right did we have to come into her house and rub salt into the wound. We had no proof that her son was taking drugs and if he did then it was a one-off incident.

Dave tried to intervene but Marie was having none of it. It's only natural for a parent to protect their child especially if they aren't in a position to do so themselves. John calmed her down a little. Dave then told them that actually this wasn't the first time that Chris had been associated with illegal drugs. He then produced two items of paper; one was a HORT/1 driving document form that Chris had been issued with a couple of months prior to the crash. It bore his signature and the second form was a Police disclaimer form for the small amount of cannabis that had been found on him during a search on the same night. It also bore his signature. Marie was still in denial and started shouting at Dave again until Heather interrupted and told her mum to stop it. She was crying and told her mum that Dave was telling them the truth.

"What do you know about this Heather?" asked Dave

"I know he had ecstasy tablets with him up at Gods Kitchen because he asked me if I wanted some" she blurted out.

"And did you?" asked John.

"Yes but only a couple, everyone does at these things," she revealed.

John and Marie looked crushed. It was bad enough that their son had died and that his friend had been killed as well but to find out that he was full of illegal drugs and that his sister probably knew was the final blow. Dave also told them that Gavin had almost as much in his system. I felt really sorry for them, because their son, whom they'd put on a pedestal since his death was actually partly responsible for his own downfall and it was all so unnecessary.

A few weeks later we attended Winchester Coroner's Court where the Coroner recorded verdicts of accidental death on both young men.

CAROL PARSONS, ROSE FORTUN AND ARCHIE WHITEAR

Category B
Tuesday 7th January 2003

2003 Hampshire fatalities = 108
2003 Nationally fatalities = 3508

I've never liked early turn. By early turn I mean starting before 6am and not finishing until two or three in the afternoon. It does all manner of nasty things to my internal system. I eat more, I drink more, I'm grumpier than normal and by mid-afternoon I could literally sleep until the alarm goes off at 5am the next morning. In the days when we did what was commonly called 'straight sevens' i.e. seven earlies on the trot I was fit for absolutely nothing by the end. It was worse during the winter months when it was still dark outside and I could hear the rain beating against the bedroom window with the wind howling like a wolf. The mere thought of climbing from my warm pit to face the world was not something I relished.

It was the first week of a new year and it was bitterly cold. Temperatures were falling well below zero every night and barely rising above one degree all day with a biting north easterly wind giving the chill factor extra bite. These were the times you didn't want anything to happen, but if it did you'd have to wrap up with the inner liner buttoned onto your water proof jacket, a scarf, gloves and thermals if you were so inclined. I attended a couple of minor accidents during the morning rush hour but nothing out of the ordinary thankfully. Breakfast took longer than usual just because none of us wanted to go back out and for once I was quite keen to do some paperwork! It was still barely above freezing outside by mid-morning.

Mike Control to Mike Charlie 01
Mike Charlie 01 go ahead
RTA M275 on the J carriageway single vehicle into central barrier, lane 3 blocked
Mike Charlie 01 Roger

The rest of the office mocked my having to go out and brave the elements and told me not to bother calling them to back me up because they were warm and toasty and had no intention of getting cold again. Bastards!

I arrived at the scene five minutes later and sure enough there was a Renault Clio broadside across lane 3 with debris everywhere. The young girl driver was sat on the barrier wearing jeans, open toed sandals and a cardigan. She was close to being hypothermic. The wind was coming in across Portsmouth harbour and was doing its best to make the temperature even colder. I sat the girl in the patrol car, sorted out some of the debris and then jumped back into the X5 to await the recovery truck, with the heater on full blast. As we sat there so I heard another RTA come in from the local control room at Charlie-One.

Charlie-One to any Mike Charlie units available for an RTA on the B2177 Southwick Road, believed to be a head on collision.

I smirked as I heard the rest of the office volunteering to turn out; that'll teach them to take the piss out of me I thought! Then the radio traffic started to get serious.

Charlie-One to those units attending the RTA we are getting further reports that the vehicles are on fire and that there are persons trapped. Hampshire Fire and Rescue are also en route

One by one they arrived and within a minute or two it was being declared a double fatal and they were calling it an all services. There was frantic radio traffic about the fire, something about a baby and the need for further ambulances. It really did sound like a big one and here was I stuck on the M275 babysitting a teenage ice berg.

Mike Control to Mike Charlie 01
Mike Charlie 01 go ahead
Once you've finished on the M275 can you make your way up to this double fatal at Southwick to act as the FLO please?
Mike Charlie 01 Roger

Thankfully the recovery truck arrived a couple of minutes later and he kindly agreed to take the young lady home and so within 10 minutes I was on my way and as I drove up Southwick Hill Road past the QA Hospital and onto B2177 Southwick Road towards Wickham I could see the smoke up ahead rising above the trees.

The B2177 used to be classified as an A road so it's fairly big and wide in comparison with other B class roads. It has a couple of long sweeping bends on it and it's subject to the national speed limit so it's quite a fast piece of road.

The scene that greeted me upon my arrival was bedlam. It looked like two vehicles were involved; a silver Mazda 626 saloon and a Ford Transit pick-up truck. Both vehicles had sustained major frontal damage consistent with the report of it being a head-on crash but both were strangely positioned one behind the other and both facing towards Wickham. Both vehicles had sustained fire damage with the front of the Transit badly damaged and the rear of the Mazda having lost all its paint as far forward as the front doors. The flames were out but there were still wisps of smoke rising from both vehicles as the fire service sprayed the occasional jet of water over the vehicles to damp them down.

As I surveyed the scene the Hampshire Fire and Rescue

Service Crash Tender arrived to join the other two fire engines, three ambulances and half a dozen Traffic cars. One of the ambulances then left the scene under Police escort to the QA with a 13 month old baby boy on board who had been plucked from the burning Mazda by two off duty Police officers and a Royal Navy Rating. The baby was apparently in a bad way with two broken legs and serious head injuries.

After we had been given the all clear by the fire service I was joined by PC Andy Faulkner, a Traffic motorcyclist who had come down from the north of the county as the second FLO. Our job now was to approach the car and search the two bodies inside it together with the car itself to see if we could ascertain some idea as to the identity of both the ladies trapped in the wreckage.

I took the driver whilst Andy looked after the rear seat passenger. I was somewhat relieved that neither of them had suffered any kind of burns as that is doubly hard for the relatives to deal with. Both of us found the ladies handbags and within minutes had a pretty good idea who they were.

Whilst searching the car I kept looking at the baby seat that was positioned on the front passenger seat. The impact was so severe that the baby seat was crushed up hard against the mangled dashboard and the top of the windscreen had popped out to reveal a six inch gap along the front of the roof. It seemed impossible to think that the baby had survived the initial impact or that anyone had managed to get him out. There was a baby's milk bottle and dummy rolling about in what was left of the passenger foot well. It was only after I got back out of the car that I realised just how bloody cold it was. In fact the north side of Portsdown Hill was still covered in ice and frost as the temperature was still below zero at this location, but we'd all been so busy we hadn't noticed.

Andy and I sat in the Police Crash Tender with a cup of hot chocolate as we sifted through the contents of the two hand bags, as the fire service got to work on cutting the bodies from the wreckage. The driver was Carol Parsons aged 56 from Wickham whilst the passenger was Rose Fortun aged 66 from the nearby village of North Boarhunt. We did all the usual identity checks via PNC, Voters Register etc. before setting off towards our respective deceased addresses to locate the next of kin.

Within ten minutes I was pulling up outside the address in Wickham. It was set amongst a row of very small semi-detached bungalows, the sort of thing that used to be built for railway workers or coal miners. I suppose that as we were right next to the old railway line there was every chance that these were once the houses supplied to those who worked there.

It was now just gone midday as I walked across the still very crisp white grass towards the house. I took a deep breath as I knocked on the door. No reply. I knocked again, no reply. Why does this always happen to me I thought? So I went to the neighbours and after some confusion about the names ascertained that Carol Parsons wasn't married but that her partner of some 30 plus years was Ian Reid, but he was at work as a wood cutter the other side of Wickham.

It took me ages to find him and his place of work but eventually I caught up with Mr. Reid who was obviously the outdoor type. His office was contained inside a small wooden hut on the edge of the woods and it was little more than a glorified shed really. He stood there in his boots and woollen hat with bright red cheeks and cold blue hands. I got him to confirm that he was Carol Parsons partner and next of kin and then broke the news to him. He just stood there in complete silence for a minute or two.

"Was her sister with her?' he asked.

"Do you mean Rose Fortun?' I replied.

"Yeah that's her sister, is she alright?"

I then told him that she had also died. His eyes then widened and there was panic written all across his face.

"What about the baby, please tell me they didn't have the

baby in the car," he gasped.

"Well yes they did and although he survived he is in a bad way, who does the baby belong to"? I asked.

"He's our grandson, I need to get hold of Ian" his voice now quite panicky.

"Who's Ian"? I asked.

"My son" he replied.

"And where is he do you know"?

"Erm…I think he's working on a site in London somewhere today, he's a scaffolder"

"Can you contact him at all"? I asked.

"Yeah but the numbers back at the house" he said.

With that we got back into the X5 and headed back towards the house. He didn't say much during the short journey. As we entered the house he started sifting through various bits of paper looking for his son's mobile phone number. After five minutes he found it and I asked him if he wanted me to phone Ian. He said it was OK and that he would do it. I told him quite firmly that he wasn't to tell Ian that his mother was dead and that his baby son was seriously injured because I didn't want him racing back from London and possibly putting himself at risk. Just tell him to get home as soon as possible but don't tell him why. Is that understood Mr. Reid? Yes perfectly.

I stood in the doorway to the tiny front lounge as Mr. Reid dialled the number and then spoke to his son.

"Ian, its dad, your mums been killed in a car crash and Bradley's been badly hurt so get your arse home as quick as you can, alright" and with that he put the phone down.

I stood there open mouthed, unable to comprehend what I'd just heard. He seemed oblivious to what he'd said and when I asked him if his son had responded he just said that he had and was on his way home. Then he remembered that Carol was probably supposed to be picking up their 8 year old granddaughter from school this afternoon so was there any chance we could do it? Yes of course, no problem at all, which school is she at? He didn't know other than it was in nearby Bishops Waltham somewhere. I phoned the control room to get an idea on the number, names and locations of the junior schools in the Bishops Waltham area, maybe if I confront him with the name it might jog his memory. There were only two schools and the control room came up with the idea that if I gave them the child's name then they'd phone the schools on my behalf to ascertain which school she was at, which would save me a lot of time. So I asked Ian what his granddaughters surname was. He didn't know. Because his son Ian wasn't actually married to his partner he didn't know whether she used the Reid name or the mother's surname, which he didn't know either. I couldn't work out whether he was just in a state of severe shock or if this was normal behaviour for him.

I then got a call from Andy Faulkner who said he was having real difficulty tracking down Rose Fortuns husband and was there any possibility that Mr. Reid might be able to help out? I doubted it somehow but I'll ask.

Ian replied that he and Patrick Fortun never got on, in fact they hated each other and although the two women were very close the families certainly weren't. If he did know anything that might help he certainly wasn't forthcoming with the information. Andy went on to confess that riding a bike today was too much even for him and could we meet up at Fareham nick so that he could jump in with me? So I packed Mr. Reid into the back of the X5 and headed into Fareham, picked up Andy and then drove out towards Bishops Waltham. As we did so we got a phone call from the control room who had somehow tracked the girl down to Bishops Waltham Junior School and they had contact details for the girl's mother who they said they would ring in order to get her to meet us at the school.

We arrived just as a couple of dozen mums arrived at the

31

school gates. It seemed like they all knew what was going on even before we did. I left Andy in the car with Ian and found the Head Mistresses office and explained the situation to her. She was great and said that she would remove the little girl from her class five minutes before the bell went and bring her to her office, then get a member of her staff to bring the mother in when she arrived. I went back out to the patrol car to update Andy and ten minutes later saw a teacher beckoning me over to the school gates. I went with her to the office where I met Sandra, the girl's mother. I took her outside to the hallway and broke the news to her, including the injuries to her baby son. She put her hands to her mouth and gasped. I said I'd arranged for another Police car to attend the school in five minutes time so that they could drive her and her daughter straight down to the QA Hospital.

I thought I'd done everything I could given the circumstances but nothing prepared me for what happened next. I didn't think I needed to tell this young woman that it probably wasn't a good idea to tell her eight year old daughter that her grandma and aunty were dead and that her little brother was in a critical condition in hospital. I thought she might save that for a more appropriate time. I'd just got back to the patrol car when I heard the most horrendous screaming coming from a child inside the Head Mistresses office. She was screaming "No, no, no" over and over again. I stood by the patrol car door with my hands on my head probably looking as incredulous as I had been when Ian put the phone down. Then I started seeing that a lot of the mums gathered outside the school gates were now crying. Some were hugging each other whilst a few pulled their offspring a bit closer. A lump swelled up in my throat as this raw emotion really got to me and as I looked towards Andy we both just shook our heads in disbelief.

The screaming seemed to go on for ages and just as it died down the other patrol car arrived. I quickly updated them on the situation we now had whilst Andy went into the school to collect mum and daughter. They came out a few minutes later, both of them still crying. I told her I'd be down to the QA later once I'd sorted a few other things out first.

An hour later and we were pulling into the mortuary car park at the QA. Ian was very quiet and had been almost from the moment we'd met. It's understandable, everybody reacts in a different way and there are no rules in this game. He hadn't asked me any questions about the crash or how it happened or anything, but then some people just don't want to know whilst others insist on knowing every last detail. I went into the mortuary and met the staff there who had prepared Carol for viewing. I went back out to the car and gave Ian the instructions he needed to do the I.D properly. We entered the viewing room and I stood behind Ian as he confirmed that it was Carol. I then left him in private and waited outside for him. It was now dark.

He was back out within a minute and stood out in the cold with me taking in deep breaths. We took him home and I went through the G28 paperwork and I.D statement with him whilst he tried to find son Ian's phone number again to see if he had got to the QA yet. There was no reply so it was likely that he was now at the hospital so I agreed to drive him back to the QA to see how his family was doing.

We arrived at the Paediatrics Unit to find Ian and Sandra stood out in the corridor. Father and son hugged each other and both burst into tears. Ian junior was a big lad, a typical scaffolder it has to be said but a thoroughly likeable bloke. He thanked me for looking after the "old man" and for helping Sandra get to the hospital. He told me that young Bradley had a fractured skull and two broken ankles and a lot of cuts and bruising but they thought he was going to be OK which was a huge relief. He said he wanted to see his mum and so I agreed to get that sorted out tomorrow morning and I'd be in touch just as soon as I could arrange it. With that Andy and I left to return to Boarhunt to see if we could try and locate Mr. Fortun.

It was bitterly cold, probably minus two or three degrees already and it was only about six o'clock. We arrived at the house and the lights were on which was a good sign. Andy got out and knocked on the door which was answered straight away and in he went. Within half an hour he phoned me to ask if I could make arrangements with the mortuary to get the staff there to do an out of hours viewing for I.D purposes. So I contacted the control room and within 10 minutes it was sorted and then we were off back down the road to the mortuary again with Mr Fortun. I left them to it as I wrote a few pages of notes in my FLO log.

Half an hour later and with the I.D of Rose Fortun completed we drove Mr. Fortun back towards Boarhunt. Andy took him back indoors to complete the G28 and I.D statement which he said wouldn't take more than half an hour or so. I wrote some more notes in my FLO log and then reclined the seat a bit and took five minutes to lay back and reflect on the day's events.

Almost an hour later Andy called me up on the radio and gave me directions to another house about 100 yards away, behind the house that he was in. I was curious to say the least and wondered quite why he had moved location. It transpired that the house belonged to the 84 year old mother of our two victims and no-one had told us about her and therefore she was completely unaware that her only two daughters had died earlier that day. Except that wasn't quite the case.

When Andy and Mr. Fortun arrived at the house there was a reporter by the name of Jeff Reines from The Portsmouth News standing in her kitchen having just delivered the shocking truth to her himself! The poor lady was confused and understandably very upset by what she had been told, most of which we suspect was wholly inaccurate and Andy quite rightly confronted the man about it. He was apparently quite pleased with himself that he had beaten the police to the address and questioned why it had taken us so long to contact the victim's next of kin and that perhaps we'd been more than a little lax in our duties towards her. Andy not very gently placed Mr. Reines against the kitchen wall and told him he had five seconds to vacate the premises or he'd get nicked. Leaving immediately was probably the wisest move he'd made all year.

Mr. Fortun said he would stay with his mother in law to calm her down and look after her as Andy and I waited outside fuming that some rogue reporter had barged into an 84 year olds house just so that he could be the one to tell her that both her daughters had died and then ask her how she felt about it? We decided that his Editor would be receiving a personal visit from me in the morning.

I dropped Andy off at Fareham and then drove back to Cosham. By the time I'd typed up the G28 for the Coroner, sorted out some information for the SIO/PIO and Media Services it was gone midnight. I'd been on duty for more than 18 hours and it had been a bitch of a day, most of which was never covered on my FLO course.

I was back in the office for 6am and recounting the story of the reporter when I got dragged into the Sgt.s office by Simon Goss who had a favour to ask. Apparently whilst we were all busy yesterday dealing with the double fatal at Southwick there was another fatality involving a dustbin lorry up on Port Solent municipal tip whereby one of the crew had been run over by his own truck. Although it didn't happen on a road and therefore doesn't fall under the remit of the RDIM it had come down from upon high that there had to be some Police involvement on behalf of HM Coroner, even though the Health and Safety Executive were investigating the circumstances. So it was felt that an FLO needed to be involved to liaise with the family and the Coroner.

'I know you're busy with yesterday's carnage mate but

any chance you could take a look at this one too"? He asked.

I agreed but only if he phoned The News to arrange a meeting with the Editor and that he accompanies me to that meeting to ensure that I don't overstep the mark and say too much! It sounded like a fair deal to me.

So I started to make some enquiries into the death of 60 year old Archie Whitear and by 8.30am I was at his house in The Crossways at Portchester where I met his wife Pat. I immediately felt that something wasn't quite right, for a start she was on her own in the house and secondly there were cards and flowers everywhere. It transpired that Archie's accident didn't happen yesterday but on Monday, two days previously and this was the first time anybody had spoken to her about it. She was very nice about it all and thought that was just the way things were done.

We sat down with a cuppa and I started to explain some of the formal things that needed to be gone through but I was stopped in my tracks when she told me that she hadn't even seen Archie since he died because by the time she had arrived at QA his body had been taken to the mortuary and it was too late for her to go and see him. I popped outside and phoned the mortuary at QA and arranged to get a viewing done within the next hour. As I was doing so Archie's son arrived followed by a couple of family friends. By the time I'd got back indoors they were asking if they could go and visit the scene of the accident after we had been to the mortuary.

An hour later Pat and her son climbed aboard the X5 with me and we drove to the mortuary where they both identified Archie. I then went outside to leave them with him for a while and as I did so I got a phone call from Simon Goss. Our meeting with the Editor of the Portsmouth News is scheduled for 2pm this afternoon. No sooner had I finished taking that call it rang again. This time it was Ian Reid junior who wanted to visit his mum and had I arranged it yet? I said I'd get back to him once I'd spoken to the mortuary staff and between us all we settled on a 4pm visit and that I'd meet Ian outside A&E as he was obviously going to be at the hospital anyway visiting Bradley.

I then drove Pat and her son to the tip at Port Solent. This vast area of reclaimed land was now a series of hills, having been used as a landfill site and then covered with various layers of soil. However the last remaining section was still being used by the waste collection services to dump tons of household rubbish onto and it was this area where Archie had had his accident. He was apparently standing on the foot plate by the passenger door as his crew mate started to drive away from the spot where they had dumped their load when Archie lost his footing and fell beneath the front wheels and was crushed. I stopped by the office at the entrance to the tip and went in to speak to the site foreman to explain that we wished to visit the scene. He said that the refuse truck was still in situ and had been cordoned off with scene tape by the Health and Safety Executive but I was welcome to drive up there if that's what the family wanted. He said he would stop any further trucks from going up there until we had finished which I thought was decent of him.

So I drove up the steep and muddy roadway towards the plateau at the top of the landfill site. Up ahead I could see the refuse truck, all taped off and sitting alone. There were sea gulls everywhere, bloody thousands of them, crapping all over the patrol car. The noise they made was incredible and as we got out of the car it was like a scene from Alfred Hitchcock's 'The Birds' as they swooped down amongst the three of us. We stood and looked at the truck and they stared intently at the front wheel. The wind whipped across from the sea as the gulls commenced their next dive bombing manoeuvres on us. I left Pat and her son to their thoughts as I rather cowardly got back into the car as another dollop of white stuff splattered across the windscreen. Pat placed a flower by the front wheel and they both returned to the car. As we started our descent down the muddy track her son said.

''My dad spent his whole life dealing with shit and ended up dying in shit. It's just not fair''.

It sounded like he was immensely proud of his dad but also frustrated at the hand he had been dealt in life as well as in death. I drove slowly down through the mud, with the wheels barely able to keep traction on the slippery surface. As we approached the office at the entrance I was amazed to see half a dozen refuse trucks had all stopped in a queue waiting to go up whilst all the crews were standing to attention in a line alongside their trucks and as we drove slowly past so they all took off their woollen hats and bowed their heads as a mark of respect to Archie. Two of them even saluted. It was a poignant moment and I nodded towards them as a thank you. I didn't know any of them but I was mighty proud of them for doing that.

We returned to the house and Pat was keen to show me their pond that contained a number of beautiful Koi Carp. I kept Koi myself and as we both sat on the wall at the edge of the pond with another cup of tea Pat told me how much pleasure she and Archie got from raising their fish and it seemed we had a lot in common.

In view of the issues we'd experienced less than 24 hours earlier I spoke to the family about the press and they opted to write out a family statement there and then and provided me with a great photo of Archie holding an enormous fish he had caught on one of his many fishing trips. The statement read;

"Archie was a very popular, outgoing man with many friends – a little man with a big heart. He was loved by all who knew him and will be sadly missed by all".

In truth there was little else I could do for them other than giving them my number so that in the event something cropped up that they needed my help or advice on then they were more than welcome to call me, but I suspected that they were the sort of family that probably wouldn't for fear of disturbing me.

It was rapidly approaching 2pm and I picked up Simon Goss and we headed into the Editors office at The News. I outlined the circumstances surrounding Mr. Reines intrusion and the manner in which he had allegedly broken the news to an 84 year old bereaved mother and although clearly uncomfortable with our complaint he stopped short of condemning his reporter's actions. He said he'd have a word with him and would try to "curb some of his enthusiasm". Simon very diplomatically reminded the Editor that we had a good working relationship with each other and that it would be a pity if one reporter were to jeopardise that. I felt that an uneasy truce had been reached as we left his office.

By 4pm I was back at the mortuary to meet Ian. He was livid having only just found out about the reporter and his grandmother. He was a big bloke with shoulders and biceps bigger than my legs and I pondered on the idea of arranging a one-on-one meeting between him and Jeff Reines! It took me a while to pacify him enough to enter the mortuary in a better frame of mind. After that I shot across to Boarhunt Garage where the Mazda was currently being kept in order to go through it and retrieve a number of items that Mr. Reid had asked me to look for including a couple of photos that he thought Carol kept in the car. The car didn't have the tidiest interior I'd ever seen and there were personal effects strewn everywhere but some of it was literally wedged in between folded panels of metal crushed during the impact. I managed to find one of the photos and a few other items which I placed in a small cardboard box and returned them to Ian by mid-evening. Then it was back to the nick where I had to spend over an hour and a half washing the BMW X5 down and trying to scrape off a thousand lumps of sea gull shit and a ton of mud from the tyres and underside. After that I spent another couple of hours writing several more pages in the two FLO logs I now had on the go before I booked off duty at 11pm having done another 17 hour shift. It had been a very emotional and challenging two days.

In the days that followed both Andy and I received information that the feud between the two families might boil over at the funeral plus Ian Reid junior was adamant he didn't want the press there and if any reporters or photographers were seen at the funeral then he wasn't going to be held responsible for his actions.

Part of the underlying current of tension came about because Patrick Fortun had been interviewed by Jeff Reines of all people a couple of times since the accident and there were two whole page articles paying tribute to Rose but virtually nothing about Carol.

Both Ian senior and Ian junior asked if I would attend the joint funeral on January 25th at Portchester Crematorium just in case there was any trouble. I'd never had to police a funeral before but agreed to the request, if only to help keep the peace and ward off a certain reporter. As I stood close to the main entrance to the crematorium I looked to my left and saw the funeral cortège enter the grounds and as I did so I could see a photographer lurking behind the trees by the gate. He was photographing the hearses as they came in and so I started to make my way towards him some 100 yards away but without making it look too obvious so as not to arouse suspicion with the people attending. The last thing I wanted was to spark some kind of riot. The photographer saw me coming and scarpered! The service was packed with more than 300 mourners from both villages and despite the obvious tension between the two families things passed off peacefully.

In the weeks that followed we were all pleased to learn that little Bradley had made a full recovery and no doubt his dad will one day tell him just how lucky he was to escape with his life. And we all learned just how close he came to becoming the third victim when details of his incredible rescue started to emerge.

Three genuine heroes were thankfully amongst the first to stop at the scene. Two off duty Police officers and a civilian driver from nearby HMS Dryad Naval Base could hear Bradley screaming in the wreckage. They had already ascertained that both Carol and Rose were probably dead but how were they going to get the baby out of the car?

The flames from the Transit were now coming over the rear of the Mazda and were starting to engulf it. They had literally seconds to react. The damage to the car was so severe that none of the doors would open. PC David Edwards then saw that the top section of the windscreen frame had come away from the body of the car and with super human strength he managed to prise the frame away further, reach into the car with both hands, undo the baby seat buckles, push the seat back away from the dashboard that it was crushed against and lift Bradley out of the car whilst the flames licked David's head and face causing him some minor burns. Meanwhile PC Peter Phillips and the Naval driver Dave Kenward hooked up his van to the Mazda with a tow rope and pulled it away from the burning Transit thus preventing the tragedy from becoming any worse.

Without doubt their actions saved Bradley's life and

prevented Rose and Carol from being burned. David Edwards was rightly awarded a Royal Humane Society bronze medal for bravery by the Lord Lieutenant of Hampshire in an awards ceremony later that year but I was saddened and angered to hear that some moron at Winchester nick had scrawled a load of expletives across the newspaper cutting reporting on that ceremony when the article had been pinned to the notice board in the canteen.

The inquest was held at Winchester on August 6th and we were all stunned to hear the Transit drivers evidence when he confessed that he had upwards of 15 seconds in which to react when he saw the Mazda come across onto his side of the road after negotiating a long right hand bend but he hadn't done anything to avoid the collision because he thought that the other driver would swerve out of the way! The Crash Investigation Unit could find no mechanical defects with either vehicle or any evidential reason why Carol Parsons's car was on the wrong side of the road. There was supposition that maybe she had bent down to pick up Bradley's dummy or his bottle and had drifted across the road as she did so but there was no firm evidence to support that. In the end the Deputy Coroner for Central Hampshire Mr. Simon Burge recorded a verdict of accidental death.

DEAN FOSTER & BRIDGETTE PANORMO

Category A
Tuesday 17th February 2004

2004 Hampshire fatalities = 63
2004 Nationally fatalities = 3221

On 16th February 2004 I was on late turn with a probationer on board when we were directed to the scene of a quite horrific RTA on Elm Grove in Southsea. A young motorcyclist by the name of Dean Foster was minding his own business riding in a responsible manner and crossing the traffic light controlled crossroads with Grove Road South, when a BMW 330 came through the red light on the left and hit him

broadside at high speed. Deans left leg took the full force of the impact and it was virtually severed mid-way down his calf. I helped hold the shattered remains of his leg together whilst the paramedics made him as comfortable as they could before transferring him to the QA.

Although Deans injuries were incredibly serious they

weren't life threatening but I was absolutely determined to catch the driver responsible because he had driven off immediately after the impact. But all I had was a description of the car, a silver 3 series BMW convertible. The impact had left items of headlamp glass behind together with the front number plate bracket but no number plate. It had to be at the scene somewhere and after searching all of the obvious places in the immediate vicinity with no result I looked upwards to the flat roofs above the nearby shops. My probie and I then gained access to the roofs and searched in vain for another half an hour but still couldn't find the actual number plate. It was frustrating to say the least. There was nothing for it but to contact The News and make a plea for witnesses in the vain hope that someone may have written the number down.

The following afternoon I was back on late turn and in my work box was a note stating that a Mr. Yeganeh wanted to talk to me about yesterday's hit and run. I phoned him and to my amazement he stated that his son Mark had stolen his BMW 330i convertible yesterday afternoon during a blazing row about Marks drug taking. He gave me the registration number and said that he may have gone to London where his ex-girlfriend was living, although he had no idea where exactly that might be. But the registration number was a great start, at least I could circulate it as stolen on PNC and hopefully it would pop up somewhere and he would be arrested. I drove straight down to the large hotel that Mr. Yeganeh owned on Southsea seafront and took a written theft report and statement from him before he changed his mind. Mr. Yeganeh was of Egyptian origin and not short of a bob or two.

As soon as I'd finished that I went straight up to the QA to check on Dean to give him the good news. I met Dean's father outside and his news was anything but good. He'd just been told that Dean would probably have to have his lower leg amputated. I entered the room and saw him lying in the bed with both his legs in traction and a massive open wound to his left shin that ran from his knee to his ankle. His young girlfriend was sat beside him and he looked a pitiful sight but to his credit was trying to put on a brave face.

As I was talking to them I became aware of radio traffic concerning another RTA some 10 miles away in Fareham. At first I didn't take too much notice but as the first couple of Traffic units arrived so it became obvious that it was serious and within a couple of minutes it was being referred to as a potential fatal and they called it in as an all services. As such I knew that other Traffic units would need to be utilised very quickly and so I bid Dean and his father goodbye and said I'd be in touch as soon as I had any further news. As I started my way down the stairs I got the call.

Mike Control to Mike Charlie 01
Mike Charlie 01 go ahead
Don't know if you've been monitoring this but there is a potential fatal at Quay Street roundabout, Fareham and they are asking for an FLO. Are you able to attend?
Answer yes, en route, traveling time from QA.

As I travelled west along the M27 my mind started to race with all the usual concerns about what I was about to face. I'd always found that there was a distinct difference between how I felt attending a serious incident and dealing with it upon my arrival and being asked to attend as a specialist and coming in to undertake that specific role.

As the first arrival you go into automatic pilot and undertake the role of officer in charge, often running on pure adrenalin, making snap decisions and ensuring that everything is done by the book so that come the day of the Crown Court trial maybe 18 months from now that you have done everything possible to ensure that the person responsible for another human beings death faces justice. But as the specialist your approach was somewhat different. By the time you get there most of the immediate decision making has already been done and although your role is just as important and that aim for justice just as focused you can invariably slow your approach down both physically and mentally.

As I continued towards the scene I heard over the radio that it was now a confirmed fatal of a young woman who had been riding a pedal cycle when she was in collision with a bus. Her body had been removed from the scene by ambulance and conveyed to the QA Hospital and now other units, including a Traffic Sgt. and the Crash Investigation Unit were also being called in.

I arrived at the scene a few minutes later. Quay Street roundabout sits at the junction of the A27 that skirts Fareham town centre and the A32 that is the main arterial route into Gosport, a peninsular town another 5 miles south. It is a bottleneck at the best of times with queues of traffic trying to get into and out of Gosport on a daily basis and now the Police had shut the roundabout completely it was going to cause chaos, no other word for it. But that was somebody else's problem today.

I looked at the scene and as ever there was an eerie silence about it. A large single decker bus belonging to the First Bus Company was positioned mid-way between the two minor junctions that lead from the town centre and Quay Street, the road that gives access to Fareham nick, which virtually overlooks the roundabout. A pedal cycle lay under the front of the bus. I spoke to the Traffic Sgt. to ascertain a brief synopsis of the circumstances. It appeared from very early initial inquiries that the bus had emerged from the side road and followed the cyclist out onto the roundabout and then collided with the rear of the bike, knocking the female rider to the ground as the bus then ran over her before stopping. Although people had done their best for her at the scene it appeared she had died almost instantly. However the ambulance crews continued working on her all the way to the hospital, but she was pronounced dead on arrival. No-one knew who she was at this stage. It was my job now to obtain her identity and locate her family as soon as possible.

I got back into the BMW X5 and headed straight back to QA some five miles away. I entered A&E and went straight into Room 1, which was a hive of frenetic energy as usual with nursing staff and doctors doing their best for another dying patient in cubical two, as two other nurses were tidying up in cubical one, where the body of the young woman was laying on the trolley. After confirming that this was the woman from the Fareham RTA I asked if they had managed to obtain any ID from her yet. One of the nurses handed me a purse that had a wealth of information in it, like a driving licence and bank cards all in the name of Bridgette Panormo from Gosport. She was just 25 years old. I stood there and looked at her. She just looked like she was asleep with no visible signs of damage save for a very small graze on the side of her forehead. When I passed comment about this, Mr Carr, the A&E Consultant, whom I had a huge amount of respect for sighed deeply and said that her injuries all appeared to be internal, as if she had been crushed to death.

I took the purse and made all the usual checks, on the voters register, PNC etc and when I was as sure as I could be I left A&E and got back into the patrol car to head towards Gosport. It was now about 5pm and I couldn't believe my ears when I heard on the radio that there had just been a second serious RTA between a bus and another cyclist in Gosport town centre and that this was also likely to be a fatality. Every Traffic unit in the county was now being dragged south to help. Well they can't have me I mused, I'm busy.

As I reached Eastern Way, the A27 dual carriageway that links the M27 to Quay Street roundabout I met the traffic. It was at a stand still. I put the siren on and worked my way through it all, back past the scene and onto the A32 into Gosport which was also completely solid with stationary traffic in both directions. I fought my way about three miles south, slowly but very noisily picking my way through the traffic to Wych Lane where I turned off to find the address. After a couple of minutes I located it. It was a small mid terrace property in a quiet residential street. My heart was now pounding as it had done on so many previous occasions. I took a deep breath and then took the long, short walk towards the house. I opened the old wooden gate and slowly closed it behind me. I knocked on the door and coughed a nervous little cough. No reply. I knocked again. The door was opened, but only slightly by a young man who just looked at me.

"Hello, are you Mr Panormo?" I asked

"No" replied the male who I could now see was probably only about 18 years old.

"Is Mr Panormo in please?" I asked.

With that the door was shut in my face. I wasn't expecting that. It threw me a bit I have to confess and as I stood there wondering what my next move might be so the door opened again and a hand came out with a piece of paper attached to it. I took the paper and no sooner had I done so than the door was shut again. The piece of paper had a mobile phone number on it. I went back to the car and phoned the number, taking another deep breath as I did so. This time I got Mr Panormo but obviously I wasn't going to tell him over the phone and merely requested he return home immediately, which he said he would be able to do in about ten minutes or so.

I sat in the car for what seemed like hours, listening to the radio and all the frantic goings-on at both RTAs. A car pulled into the residents parking area and a man in his late 40s got out and looked straight at me. This had to be Mr Panormo. He started to come over towards the car. I got out and he spoke first.

"What's this all about officer, it's obviously serious?" he asked.

I didn't want to tell him in the street so asked if we could go into the house. He ushered me into the front room and I sat in an arm chair as he sat on the adjacent settee. I told him the terrible news. He sat there in complete silence, head bowed. After a few seconds he switched into protective husband and father mode. He needed to get hold of his wife. I stood up as Mr. Panormo went out into the kitchen. I could hear him talking to someone and assumed it was the young man I had seen earlier. I looked around the front room and on a nearby chair was a cat that just stared at me. Cats and me have never seen eye to eye and they invariably dig their claws into my leg in unprovoked attacks of feline savagery whenever one of them deems my lap to be comfortable enough to squat on, so I rarely, if ever go out of my way to make friends with them. I could hear a small dog barking out in the garden too.

Mr. Panormo came back into the front room. He beckoned me to sit down again and as I did so I saw the cat make its move towards me. He said his wife was on her way home. He'd done the same as I had and just told her to get home and hadn't told her anything on the phone. I was concerned that it might take her a very long time to get here because of the traffic but as we waited he started to ask me questions, with the obvious one being, how did it happen? I could only give him the briefest of details because that's all I had at this stage but he was caught between seeking further details and constantly looking at his watch and wondering where his wife was. He kept getting up and pacing about, looking out of the lounge window. It was then that I noticed he walked with a very pronounced limp. He was quite small and slim in stature and his hair was tied back in a ponytail. His mobile rang. It was his wife, stuck in the traffic on the A32 and clearly distressed. I told him to tell her to pull over somewhere and that we would come to her in the patrol car because I could use the blues and twos to get through the traffic again.

Mr Panormo went back into the kitchen and when he returned so the other young man followed him and he introduced him to me as his son Mark. We got into the X5 and headed back out onto the still grid locked A32 and south towards Gosport. Again I fought my way down through the middle of the traffic until Mr Panormo shouted out that his wife was parked over on the left outside an industrial unit. I pulled over and we got out. Once she'd seen me, her husband and then Mark she knew this was about Bridgette.

Mr Panormo stood in front of her and put both his hands on her shoulders and quietly told her that Bridgette had died in an accident. Mrs Panormo shook her head and said "no, please, no" as her husband pulled her towards him and they held onto each other. I looked at Mark and he seemed really uncomfortable, his head was down and he was shuffling from side to side. His dad pulled Mark towards him and they just stood there hugging each other. This was a moment of pure emotion that I felt I was intruding upon and so I turned away and looked out onto the passing traffic that was inching its way passed us. I looked at the occupants of each car, all of them without fail were staring at the scene beside them, of three people in the throes of the most awful moment in their lives and yet none of these people had a clue what was happening. I made myself as big as possible and stood there with my big yellow jacket on, hands on hips, trying to shield the Panormo family from the gawping masses as they crawled by just a few feet away.

"Can we go and see her?" Mr Panormo asked.

"Of course we can," I replied and ushered them back into the X5.

The three of them sat on the back seat with Mr Panormo sat in the middle, his arms around both his wife and son, pulling them all tightly together. Then a terrible thought struck me. The only route to QA from here was via the scene of the crash at Quay Street roundabout, where the Crash

Investigation Unit was busy doing their work. I called up on the radio and my worst fears were confirmed. I obviously couldn't go the right way around the roundabout because that would mean driving right through the scene so I got permission to drive around the roundabout the wrong way and then enter Eastern Way from there. I decided not to tell the Panormo's anything about this and hoped that they might not see anything as we passed.

The A32 was still at a standstill in both directions as I pulled back out into the traffic, switched the lights and siren back on and fed my way back north towards Quay Street roundabout. As I approached the old brick viaduct that frames the approach to the roundabout I could see blue lights ahead at the scene. Thankfully the roundabout is placed on quite a steep incline and contains a few trees and lots of vegetation that shrouded much of the scene on the far side. I entered the roundabout and turned right against what would have been the normal flow of traffic, but there wasn't any of course because it had all been diverted onto the flyover above us. But as I turned right I could see the crash scene straight ahead of me. As quick as I could do so I turned right again onto Eastern Way and then floored the throttle as hard as I could. As I did so I caught a glimpse of Mr Panormo staring intently at the scene. A shudder went down my spine.

A few minutes later and we arrived at QA Hospital and I took the Panormo family into the relative's room. I did my usual and showed them where the toilet was, the kettle, the box of tissues and explained about dialling 9 to get an outside line on the phone should they need to use it. I then left to go and find myself a member of the nursing staff to let them know we were here and to find out where they had put Bridgette so that I could do the formal ID. She had been moved to the side room directly opposite the relative's room and it was agreed I would do the ID first and then Mr Carr and a nurse would come and see them in the relative's room to explain a few things.

Second only to being told your loved one is dead is having it confirmed by viewing the body. It's then that the total realisation hits home. Before I went back into the relative's room I entered the side room just to double check that it was in fact Bridgette there and not somebody else. Can you imagine anything worse after being briefed and psyching yourself up to enter that room only for it be somebody else or worse, nobody in there at all? It was a small, bland room and I made sure there were a couple of chairs there and that the blind was down and secure before I went back into the relatives room. They had already decided that Mark would stay in the room until after they had been to see Bridgette and then if he wanted to they would bring him in. We walked across the corridor and entered the room. I quietly shut the door and stood behind them as Mr. Panormo confirmed that yes, this was his daughter. I then left the room in order to give them the time and privacy they needed to be alone with her. I popped back into the relative's room and tried to make small talk with Mark. He didn't really reply to anything I said other than giving the occasional nod or shake of the head. A few minutes later Mr Panormo came back in and took Mark over to see his sister.

After about five minutes they all came back and I summoned the medical people to come and talk to them. Mr. Carr was his usual calm, sympathetic and professional self and he told them that Bridgette had sustained massive internal injuries to the abdominal area consistent with being run over by a heavy vehicle and stated that she would have known very little about it. All things considered they took it very well. Mr. Panormo then asked about organ donation because Bridgette had been very keen on this and that they had actually talked it over fairly recently. The nurse shot off to go and obtain the services of the organ donation unit and within a few minutes a rather bouncy young lady with a pony tail and a clip board returned and she asked a lot of questions about Bridgette and her personal life which Mr. and Mrs. Panormo seemed quite happy to answer. In fact the atmosphere had lightened considerably as it seemed that something positive might come out of Bridgette's death and that this is what she would have wanted given the circumstances. The organ donation lady left to go and make some inquiries with the medical team. In the meantime other members of the Panormo family started to arrive in the relative's room.

The lady returned about half an hour later with the sad news that owing to Bridgette's internal injuries they wouldn't be able to use organs like the heart, lungs, liver etc but they could perhaps harvest her eyes. What a bloody awful expression that is.........harvest her eyes..........as if it were akin to gathering in the wheat in time for Harvest Sunday. Again the Panormo's spirits lifted as they agreed to give their permission in the hope that Bridgette's eyes might give another human being the gift of sight.

We waited another half an hour or more until the lady returned with one more question. When did Bridgette get her eye brow piercing done? About two weeks ago, why? The lady disappeared again, returning ten minutes later with more bad news. Because the piercing is less than a month old and very close to the eyes it wouldn't be possible to harvest her organs and therefore they were sorry to say that they wouldn't be carrying out any procedures. The family looked devastated.

Before we left the hospital the family visited Bridgette again to say their goodbyes. Leaving her there as we made our way back to their house in Gosport must have been extremely difficult. But this was only the start for them because now I needed to do the formal paperwork and I personally found this difficult at times because you are asking personal questions about somebody who has literally only just died and you really do feel like you are intruding at this point. Most of the paperwork isn't for police benefit but for HM Coroner and that paperwork has to be on his desk by the following morning or else.

We sat in their front room. Mr. Panormo was a very up-front sort of man, if he had a question to ask, no matter how difficult, he'd ask it, which I rather liked, I have to admit. His name was Mick and his wife's name was Tania. Their son Mark suffered from Aspergers Syndrome and he found one on one communication with new people rather difficult, which explained his virtual zero interaction with me. At least I understood why now. Mark had disappeared upstairs to be on his own as Mick explained that Marks best friend in the entire world was Bridgette and he was now fearful for his son's future and wondered how he might cope without his sister there beside him. Bridgette was so good with him because she made him do things he just wouldn't do on his own, like shopping, going to the pub or to the gigs she went to. She was even looking for a flat for the pair of them to rent in order for Mark to gain a bit of independence and help boost his self-confidence. She didn't have to do that, but that was just the type of person she was. I sat there and just let them talk. And talk they did. They were immensely proud of Bridgette, especially Mick and it was quite obvious very early on that she was a daddy's girl. She was also a very good musician. I don't just mean she could strum a guitar or sing a few notes, she clearly had talent and was the bass guitarist in a local group called Rolling Dog, who it seemed were on the cusp of great things, having just released their second CD.

All this talk was constantly interrupted by the phone ringing. Friends and relatives phoning in, having only just heard the news on the grape vine meant that either Mick or Tania would get side lined for five minutes as they briefly explained how Bridgette had died. Tania in particular found this really difficult and try as she might, she just couldn't stop the tears. Every time Mick would do his best to comfort her and then she'd apologise to me for "being silly". I quickly understood that Mick and Tania were incredibly lovely people.

We went through the paperwork for the Coroner and got that out of way first. Then I explained my role to them and the fact that they were going to have to get used to seeing my face around here because, given the circumstances, it was likely that we would be seeing rather a lot of each other. Straight away Mick queried why. I then explained the technical differences between Section 1 Death by Dangerous Driving and Section 3 Careless Driving to them.

"It's quite simple from where I'm sitting that it was death by dangerous driving surely, how could it be anything but, he followed her out onto the roundabout and then ran her over" exclaimed Mick.

I told him that at this very early stage it was impossible for me to comment further because I hadn't received any update from the investigation team. But I needed them to fully understand the legal differences between the two possible offences and that if it was deemed to be death by dangerous driving then that would throw up all manner of things I doubt they had ever contemplated.

"Such as?" Mick enquired.

I then explained that there would have to be a Post Mortem to ascertain the actual cause of death. As usual this was met with further tears. The very thought of your daughter being subjected to such treatment is gut wrenching. Once the two of them had regained a little composure so I had to hit them with the fact that the man responsible for her death could actually demand a second independent Post Mortem if he was looking at a charge of causing death by dangerous driving and that he had up to 28 days in which to demand it.

"What possible right has he got to do that?" Mick blasted, his voice now filled with anger.

This also threw up the fact that Bridgette's funeral might well be delayed if the driver of the bus decided to go down this path. Mick and Tania found this incredible. I then tried to explain that everything the police investigation team were doing, from the moment they arrived at the scene was done in the Panormo families best interests and in particular Bridgette. As difficult as it might be to fathom right now our aim was to obtain justice for all of them and that the road ahead was likely to be very difficult. I had no idea at this stage just how difficult though.

We then moved onto the press.

"What about them?" asked Mick "I don't want them involved".

I explained as best I could that actually they had no choice in the matter because once you die your name becomes public property and because of the nature of Bridgette's death there would inevitably be local press interest. They sat there, heads bowed for a moment, this was clearly something they hadn't considered and why would they? We all read the papers and watch the TV news but do any of us really take that much notice of the people involved in these 'stories'? I then gave them my now familiar speech about taking control of the situation and to use the press in order to gain something positive out of this. My favoured approach with the media has always been the cooperative one. Far too many cops dismiss the press as intrusive vultures with blood on their claws, but actually I'd always had a very good relationship with them and really used *them* to further my investigations and I have to say it worked most of the time.

The family basically had three choices; first to ignore the press altogether. However if they chose to do that then without doubt a reporter would knock on their door uninvited. I always thought me knocking on the door was hard enough but can you imagine cold calling on a house to ask questions about the violent death of a person just to sell newspapers? Callous beyond words. If that reporter fails to get an answer from your door then they start knocking on your neighbours door, then the corner shop, the pub, the post office or if that fails they just make it up. The bottom line is, you have no control over what gets printed and invariably this causes you and your family further distress.

Your second choice is to invite them in and get 'interviewed' by some inexperienced but deeply ambitious young hack who probably isn't really that interested in what you've got to say and is only doing this because his editor told him to and because he feels totally uncomfortable in your presence he'll be out the door faster than Road Runner being chased by the Wylie Coyote. Again you have little or no control over what gets printed.

Thirdly you write out a family statement, complete with a photo of the person we are referring to and you hand it to me and I submit it to the press via our Media Services people, under the very clear understanding that if the family do this then that should satisfy the media and they don't come knocking on your door or try to make contact by some other means. 99% of the time the press will abide by those rules. At least that way you take control of what is printed, they will be your words, not theirs and it will be as accurate and as personal as you want it to be. I could even hold them off for about 48 hours but I would need a decision sooner, rather than later. We agreed to give them until tomorrow to think it over.

We then talked about Bridgette's personal property and the fact that I would be able to hand back most, if not all of her personal belongings like her purse, jewellery and the contents of the bag from her bike within the next 24 hours. However her bike and possibly her clothing would be subject to intense examination by the Crash Investigation Unit, the Photographic Department and Scenes of Crime Officers, plus her bike would be examined for mechanical defects by the Vehicle Examination Unit. Mick was quite sure that Bridgette's bike was in perfect working order as this was something he undertook personally on her behalf.

It was now close to midnight and they were exhausted. We agreed to meet again the following morning and I bid them goodnight, but not before I'd given them my mobile number and told them they could contact me anytime they wished as I kept it on 24/7. I drove slowly back towards the office at Cosham, mulling over the unfairness of it all, that yet another decent family had been destroyed in a moment of apparent gross neglect. By the time I'd written several pages in my FLO log it was close to 2am and I made my way home, drained again by the emotion of it all. As usual Trish was waiting up for me and as usual she listened to me as I told her of today's tragedy.

I was back in the office for 8 o'clock and spoke to Inspector Howard Marrs who was the SIO. I'd known Howard since we were 16 year old Cadets together and we had a good working relationship. He explained how the investigation was going but it wasn't good news, we had virtually no witnesses, except for three passengers from the bus itself. At present there didn't appear to be any totally independent witnesses who might have seen the crash from outside. The only CCTV camera in the vicinity was of course doing the obligatory looking-the-other-way-routine and hadn't captured anything remotely useful. The press coverage with witness appeals was therefore going to be crucial. Howard was leaning towards this being a Section 1 but needed the evidence to secure it. The driver of the bus, 63 year old Dennis Sharp had apparently declined to comment in his first and very brief interview and had been released on police bail pending further enquiries.

I drove over to Gosport for about 10 am. Mick and Tania looked exhausted and had clearly had little or no sleep. There were several friends and relatives in the tiny house and one by one I was introduced to them, including Mick's parents Joy and Stuart. Eventually Tania moved everyone out into the kitchen whilst Mick and I sat down in the front room and he showed me the family statement he and Tania had compiled, together with a lovely photo of Bridgette playing her guitar. The brief statement read;

Bridgette loved life, people and animals. She would help anyone out. She was bright, caring, funny and a talented musician. She lived for music and made many friends and fans. Bridgette was a strong minded person with a deep sense of justice and honesty which she has shown over the years by how she took care of people. She was much loved for her spontaneity and zany sense of fun and will be so sadly missed by her family and all those who knew her.

It was brief but to the point but above all it was their words and not some anonymous reporter. The cat slinked into the room and stopped in front of me. It turned its head towards me and I could see it eying up my leg. He made a move towards me which I sort of brushed to one side. Thankfully he took the hint.

I had Bridgette's purse and other personal property in the regulation zipped poly bag. God I hated this bit, it's just so impersonal, but what's the practical alternative? I handed Mick the bag and he took it from me, looking at it as if it was somehow contagious. He paused for a moment and I knew what he was thinking. He stood up and placed it on a book shelf and covered it up with a magazine and said he and Tania would deal with that later once they were on their own.

I then revealed the issues surrounding the lack of witnesses and the fact that we would have to rely on the press quite a bit and make witness appeals through them, which he was OK about; in fact he was quite prepared for anything if it meant helping the investigation.

On returning to Cosham I scanned the photo in and e mailed that and the family statement up to Media Services at Winchester, although it was too late for today's editions. Later that afternoon I got a copy of the Portsmouth News and the crash took up the whole of the front page. But I was horrified to see that the reporter was Jeff Reines, whom we'd had trouble with at the double fatal at Southwick just over a year before. I also knew that colleagues from Fareham Traffic had had problems with him on a number of other occasions and he had received some kind of Police warning about his behaviour. It seemed he hadn't heeded the advice his Editor supposedly gave him following my complaint then. I'd never spoken to him personally but I was instantly uneasy about it. Inside the same edition was a decent sized column about Dean's accident in Elm Grove with a further appeal for witnesses.

I drove back over to Gosport and returned the photo. We sat down with a cuppa and Tania was horrified to see me stirring my tea with a pen. Because I'm diabetic I always ask for tea with just milk, no sugar but then add a sweetener from the little dispenser I always carry in my pocket, but because I've asked for it without sugar people invariably don't give me a spoon so I just use my pen. For the first time both Mick and Tania laughed a little bit. They were such lovely people, so very caring of everyone else's feelings rather than their own. They talked some more about Bridgette and her work with homeless people at the Two Saints hostel in Fareham, which is where she had been on the afternoon of her death. Its often the case of course that relatives will start to reminisce about what a good person the deceased was, especially parents, but the more I learned about Bridgette the more I wish I'd met her. During our chat the conversation somehow got around to young Deans accident and the damage he had sustained to his legs. Mick then rolled up his trousers to reveal a prosthetic leg. It transpired he'd lost his leg below the knee in a motorcycle accident several years ago. The pair of them then cracked a couple of personal jokes about Mick's life since then but Mick told me to tell Dean to keep his chin up and that the hospital staff would do all they could to help him.

No sooner had I left them I received a call on my mobile from Tania's sister Diane. Could she meet me in private somewhere to discuss what had happened to Bridgette? She was coming down from London but didn't want to ask me certain questions in front of Mick and Tania. We agreed to meet at Fareham nick at 2pm.

Within seconds my phone rang again, only this time it was the Metropolitan Police. They had arrested Mark Yeganeh after a brief pursuit in the stolen BMW. He apparently crashed the car into some railings in Lewisham, got out and did a runner. After a hundred yards or so he fell into a phone box and burst into tears. The arresting officer's statement then read that Yeganeh cried out;

"I'm in big trouble".

"You're fucking right you are sonny, now get up" which sounded like a line from the script of The Sweeney and made me laugh out loud.

It was agreed that Hampshire Police would arrange an escort to travel up to the Met overnight to collect Yeganeh and return him to Portsmouth for interview. I punched the air in delight "yes, yes, yes, got him" I shouted out.

By 2pm I was at Fareham nick where I met Tania's sister who was armed with a note book and pen. I ushered her into a side room where she explained that she and Bridgette were more like sisters than aunty and niece and that she was finding it really difficult to come to terms with what had happened. However she worked for the London Ambulance Service and wanted to know exactly how Bridgette had died. She said that I could probably tell her certain facts that perhaps I hadn't been able to tell Mick and Tania so far. There were alarm bells ringing in my head and my instincts immediately put me on the defensive. This just didn't feel right.

In truth I couldn't tell her much more than I'd told Mick and Tania even if I'd wanted to. Mick was so probing in the questions he'd asked me so far that I'd told them everything that the investigation team had told me and I hadn't held anything back. So I think she left a little disappointed and I was left a little confused about her motives.

I picked up my copy of the Portsmouth News later that evening to find a full page article about Bridgette on page three. Written by Jeff Reines it contained the family statement and the photo together with quotes from the lead singer with Rolling Dog. There was a Police appeal for witnesses together with quotes from local residents telling the world just how dangerous Quay Street roundabout was. It was well written and I hoped the appeal for witnesses might do the trick.

The next morning I was in bright and early because it was time to meet Mark Yeganeh. Armed with all the witness statements I drove across to the Custody Centre at Portsmouth Central where I met his brief Stephen Tricker. He and I hadn't exactly seen eye to eye on previous meetings, either during the interview process with one of his clients or later in court. Whilst Mr Yeganeh finished off his breakfast in his cell I disclosed all the evidence to Mr Tricker. He didn't ask me any questions and just handed them back.

"What are you looking at charging him with then?" he asked.

"TWC, dangerous driving, failing to stop after an RTA" I replied.

He then went down to the cells to have a word with his client before returning with him to the interview room. I was quite taken aback by Yeganeh's demeanour. He was a big lad with jet black wavy hair, brushed back with a slightly eastern look about him but he cut a dejected and pathetic look as he took his seat at the table. His head stayed bowed and he shuffled his feet a lot. I was surprised about how open he was when I started to question him. We talked about his chronic drug addiction, with heroin and cocaine being his downfall and the cause of the split from his long term girlfriend and of course the furious rows with his father. He admitted stealing the BMW and then whilst under the influence of cocaine driving like a maniac through the streets of Portsmouth. However when it came to overtaking the line of stationary traffic sat at the red light and then colliding with Dean on his bike his mind went conveniently blank. But he did remember the actual collision and what happened immediately afterwards. He said he saw Dean lying in the road and knew it was serious.

"How serious did you think his injuries were?" I asked.

"I thought he was dead" he replied.

"So what happened next?" I asked.

"I thought "*fuck this, I'm off*" he said and for the first time he sat up and looked me straight in the eye.

I heard Stephen Tricker let out a sort of whimper!

"So you hit the lad on the motorcycle and you think you've killed him is that right?" I asked.

"Yes"

"So what did you do next?" I asked.

"Drove off to London as fast as I could" came his reply.

The interview took over an hour at the end of which Mark Yeganeh was charged with three of the most serious offences possible under the Road Traffic Act and not once during my time with him did he ask how Dean was which summed him up perfectly for me. He did however answer one question that had baffled me from the moment I attended the crash; what happened to the front number plate on the BMW? Simple, it had come off in a previous car park bump and he'd put on the dashboard. No wonder I couldn't find it then. I phoned Deans father to update him. I said I'd try and pop up to the QA and pay him a visit later in the week.

Over the next few days the investigation team tried everything they could think of to secure some kind of independent witness evidence, trawling through CCTV footage from nearby premises, questioning residents, putting up the usual Witness Appeal notices but all to no avail. Nothing. Not a peep. How can that be? It was the start of the rush hour and Quay Street roundabout is packed with traffic almost 24 hours a day, how can nobody outside of a few bus passengers have seen nothing? It was frustrating to say the least. As the first week anniversary of the crash loomed it was decided to do a TV appeal in an effort to reach a wider audience than the local paper.

I spoke to Mick and Tania and they were very supportive of the idea, anything they could do to help even if it meant them being interviewed on camera. And so one week to the day I met Mick, Tania, Mark and several other family members in the front office at Fareham nick together with the Meridian TV reporter. Although I'd seen him on TV countless times I had no idea just how tall he was. I mean I'm six feet two and he towered above me. He had already been sent a brief outline of the circumstances and to my relief he had at least read it through and didn't ask any crass questions of the family. He and the cameraman then went outside to film some footage of the scene with Mick and Tania in the background. He interviewed the PIO PC Mark Foster who actually made the appeal. Fingers crossed it would work.

Over the next couple of days we all waited for that vital phone call. It didn't arrive. Then my mobile rang; it was Jeff Reines. Could we arrange an interview with the Panormo family?

"No, absolutely not" was my blunt reply.

"Why not"? Came his response.

"Because you have a bloody awful reputation Mr Reines and I'm not having you bulldoze your way into this family's grief right now."

"How's about tomorrow then"?

"Are you serious, are you really that thick skinned"? I said incredulously.

He knew we were struggling for witnesses and he said he

could help by keeping the story, as he kept calling it, in the public domain rather than just letting it fizzle out. His American accent was very persuasive and my sensible head was telling me to stay true to my principles in that I had always used the press to further the investigations I was involved in, but I was still very uneasy about bringing him on board. He asked me a lot of probing questions about the crash that I wasn't prepared to answer right now. I said I'd consult the SIO first and then the family and only if they agreed would I even consider allowing him anywhere near them.

"But understand this Mr Reines, if you go anywhere near them before I've given you the green light I will personally come and arrest you and I'll make sure you never work in the Portsmouth area again, do we understand one another?"

"Hey, I'm only trying to help"

Sure you are.

I went back to see Mick and Tania to explain that no new witnesses had come forward from the TV appeal and that Jeff Reines wanted to interview them and take their photos and perhaps obtain new photos of Bridgette to illustrate the article. I told them of my concerns about the man and some of his ethics but Mick was quite philosophical about it all really and said that if Mr Reines got under peoples skin then maybe, in these circumstances it might be a good thing. And if it meant that the witness we were seeking read it and came forward then it had to be worth it. However they didn't want him coming to their house and we agreed that the interview would take place at Mick's parent's house in a couple of days' time.

The interview was the least of my concerns right now because I had to tell them that the bus driver was dragging his feet over whether or not he wanted a second PM. It was difficult to ascertain whether it was actually Dennis Sharp or his solicitor who was playing politics. The scenario went like this. Sharp was on bail pending the result of the police investigation which might take three months, at which time he would be brought back to the police station to face a formal interview under caution. Only then would he be charged with either Section 1 death by dangerous driving or Section 3 careless driving (there was no offence of death by careless driving at this time although it was coming onto the statute books shortly).

So whilst Sharp was on bail his solicitor kept asking the question "What offence is my client likely to be charged with?" to which the Police would reply "Until our investigations are complete we cannot comment" to which the solicitor stated "Well if it's going to be Section 1 we will of course require a second PM and until the police make their decision I'm afraid we can't commit ourselves one way or the other"

It was an absurd and frankly obscene and cruel situation. All the Panormo family wanted to do was lay their daughter to rest.

I met Mick, Tania and Mark at Joy and Stuart's house in Gosport. It was now two weeks since the crash. I saw Jeff Reines pull up outside and I went out to talk to him. I reiterated the ground rules and he promised me that all he wanted to do was help the family find a witness or two that might lead to justice for Bridgette. I was still concerned about the outcome but I had to trust him right now. I made the introductions and they all rather nervously started to talk to each other whilst I stood there like some kind of Premier League referee waiting to show Jeff Reines a red card. Then a photographer arrived and within minutes he'd taken a couple of photos of the family, which they were clearly uncomfortable with and then promptly left. Jeff Reines finished up and promised them he would do all he could to help. Mick and Tania let out a large sigh of relief as he left the house.

With some trepidation I picked up my copy of the Portsmouth News the next evening to find a full two page spread written by Jeff Reines with quotes from Mick, Tania, Mark, me and several other people. There were a couple of new photos of Bridgette to help keep the item fresh and I have to confess I was impressed with the depth and the accuracy of the article. Let's hope it works I said to myself.

The following week there was another full page article about Bridgette which this time focused on a story that until now I was completely unaware of. She had worked with a lady called Dawn Blackman at the hostel. Now I knew Dawn personally and had also worked with her husband Martin who had been on our department until he retired in 1999. A couple of years previous to that Trish and I had taken in French students on exchange visits (not because we liked French students but because we were skint!). Anyway Dawn was the co-ordinator for the Portsmouth area and we got to know her very well. But in 2000 their 34 year old son Lawrence was murdered in Copenhagen, beaten to death by two assailants. When Dawn eventually returned to work Bridgette was there to help her through the grieving process, talking to her and just being there for her. Dawn described her as her "rock".

Jeff Reines had put another appeal for witnesses in the article and this had kept it in the public domain just as he promised.

Witness appeals aside I knew that the thing hurting them most was not being able to lay Bridgette to rest. This had gone on long enough. I met Howard Marrs and raised my concerns with him. Dennis Sharps defence team were taking the piss out of the system and it was about time we did something to counter that. Howard agreed and sympathised but said our hands were tied. Now I'm not one to lose my temper all that often but on this occasion I did. I'd known Howard for many years and knew I could say anything I liked to him without dropping myself in the shit. I hate smart arse lawyers especially when in collusion with arrogant defendants who then manipulate the system to suit themselves, it makes my blood boil. We had a frank exchange of views and in the end I asked him how he'd feel if it was his daughter being kept in a fridge in perpetuity whilst others played cat and mouse? We both sat there in silence for a few moments, probably both visualising the same thing.

"Leave it with me Steve and I'll start putting the pressure on" he said "You are right; this has gone on long enough".

We then started to talk through the investigation to date and he was determined that Dennis Sharp should be looking at a Section 1 but was as frustrated as the rest of us by the lack of independent witnesses and he doubted that CPS would entertain anything but a Section 3 unless we could come up with something else. He suggested I start to prime the family for that possibility.

It was now approaching a month since the crash and Jeff Reines who was obviously now in direct contact with the family, penned another two one page articles with new photos, quotes and the now familiar plea for witnesses. Mick and Tania said that their lives were in limbo because they didn't have the answers they were looking for and couldn't lay Bridgette to rest because of the post mortem, although it was never revealed to the press just what that PM situation was. I suspect it would have made the front page headlines if they'd been made fully aware of the facts.

Howard phoned me at home, he'd spoken to the Coroner and he agreed that he would arrange for a second PM to be conducted independently, that he would pay for it and the results sealed in his safe. If Dennis Sharps solicitors wanted the results they'd have to pay him. He was hopeful that the PM could be concluded within the next couple of days and then I'd get a call informing me that Bridgette's body could be released back to her family. It was a highly unusual, possibly unique solution that might ruffle a few feathers but frankly I couldn't care less about that.

He also said that a lady had come forward as a direct result of the appeals in the Portsmouth News to state that she had arrived on the scene almost immediately after the crash and had spoken to a man who was driving a black Ford Focus who said he'd witnessed the incident but then he disappeared shortly afterwards. It wasn't much but it might prove invaluable if we can trace the car.

I phoned Mick from home and gave him the news they had been waiting for. He sighed as if a huge weight had been lifted from his shoulders somehow or maybe it was the prospect of having to attend his daughter's funeral. Either way it would give them something to focus on. I said I'd call him just as soon as I heard from the Coroner's office.

Two days later I got the call and within seconds I'd phoned Mick who said he'd also just received a call from the Coroner's office. He said they had already been in contact with the undertakers and had a provisional date of April 2nd for the funeral.

I phoned Jeff Reines to get the details of this black Ford Focus splashed over the papers. By the next day on Saturday 20th March he'd done another piece on Bridgette with yet another new photo of her playing her bass guitar and had managed to obtain the date for her funeral. It was a couple of days before I got to read it because on that day Portsmouth were playing Southampton in a Premier League match, the first time the teams had met for a number of years. I was on the Support Group and tasked with driving one of the personnel carriers. I've seen plenty of football violence over the years but never have I seen such anarchy on our streets. Before the match I witnessed a number of Pompey's better known hooligan element from the 1980s aka the '657 Crew' who were now all in their mid to late 30s or older, openly 'educating' their off spring, whom they had dragged to the match about how it was their duty to kill the scummers (Southampton fans). The pubs were packed and large groups of these sub species lined the streets waiting to attack. We pulled up beside one particular group, many of whom I recognised from previous encounters. One of them recognised me and smiled.

"This is just like the old days Mr Woodward" he beamed.

"I sincerely hope not" I said "I trust you lot are going to behave yourselves today"

"You know us" he smirked.

Yes I do know you and that's what I'm afraid of.

Pompey won 4-1 so you'd think the fans would be happy with that alone. Well the real fans undoubtedly were but the mindless morons still wanted to kill the scum, so they set about it in their attempt to get at the opposing fans, but were thwarted by huge numbers of determined police officers backed up by mounted officers from Thames Valley Police. We had running battles with about 500 of them for three hours or more afterwards and I've never seen such orchestrated violence. Bricks, lumps of concrete, bottles, scaffold poles and planks of wood rained down on us in Fratton Road as we charged at them time and time again. I used the carrier as a bettering ram to smash down the barricades they'd put up as more bricks and stones smashed into my windscreen. Every shop window for half a mile was smashed with some of the shops having been looted with terrified staff cowering for cover. Had it not been for the horses I think we might have lost. And they have the cheek to call the opposition scum?

Mick phoned me on Monday morning. He and Tania had come up with an idea which he wanted to run past me. Could they put up a load of appeal notices in Fareham town centre, Gosport, even Portsmouth to see if it might jog someone's memory? I certainly couldn't see a problem with it but did advise him that some jumped up council clerk might threaten him with prosecution for fly posting of course but if that did happen then he could refer them to me and I'd deal with it. Mick just felt the fatherly need to do something more proactive, anything that might help out. I could feel his pain. He got Jeff Reines involved again and by the following Friday another half page article with a nice photo of Mick and Tania standing on the footbridge that overlooked the scene holding some of their appeal notices. The following Monday there was another article, this time announcing that they had set up a memorial fund called 'Play for Brijj'. They hoped that the fund might allow them to buy musical instruments for the kids at Bridgette's former junior school.

On Friday 2nd April, more than seven weeks after the crash, the Panormo family and some 250 mourners attend Portchester Crematorium to finally lay Bridgette to rest. It was standing room only during the service and Mick said afterwards that he was genuinely touched by the sheer number of tributes and the lovely things that people he had never met before said about his daughter. The following days full page article in the Portsmouth News covered the funeral in depth and still contained further appeals for witnesses and the driver of that black Ford Focus to come forward.

A couple of weeks went by and I had recently picked up another FLO commitment following another fatality and one morning as I climbed out of the shower I could hear Trish talking on the phone. As I came downstairs I could see she was talking on my mobile and as I listened in it was clear that it was either Mick or Tania she was talking to. One or two of my FLO trainers have probably just taken a collective sharp intake of breath right now. But I trust my wife implicitly; she's a bloody good listener and an even better talker and she and Mick talked for over half an hour whilst I made the tea.

It was early August and Mark Yeganeh's Crown Court appearance was looming. I got a visit from his father who wanted to withdraw the theft allegation against his son. What? They had reconciled their differences and he thought he deserved another chance on the promise that he would attend further drug rehab courses. I was furious and explained to him that he would end up being prosecuted himself for permitting his son to drive without insurance and that given the severity of Deans injuries it was likely to cost him a fortune in compensation. He just shrugged his shoulders and said he was prepared for that.

In truth it didn't actually affect the trial itself because the circumstances surrounding Yeganeh taking the car could still be brought to the jury's attention. Oh yes did I forget to mention he was pleading not guilty? Despite his full and very frank confession during interview he had decided to change his plea. It had been a while since I'd seen Dean and I visited him at his bed-sit with his girlfriend so that I could take a Victim Impact Statement from him, outlining the injuries he had sustained and exactly how the crash had impacted upon his life. It took me a couple of hours to squeeze out of him just how bad things had been over the last six months and that he wasn't out of the woods yet. His left leg just wasn't healing properly and the external fixator; a 12 inch tubular bar bolted to his tibia was about the only thing physically holding him together right now. The deep indentation, complete lack of tissue to the front of his leg looked awful and there was every possibility that he might still lose his foot because of it all.

Dean was determined to attend every minute of Yeganeh's trial and I have to confess I encouraged him to do so because it certainly helps a jury to actually see the victim in such cases, especially one that is still on crutches. I'd also spoken to one of my contacts at the Portsmouth News, not Jeff Reines this time but Khushwant Sachdave who could be as forthright as Mr Reines. She had followed the story from day one and I knew she'd do a good job if we got the right result.

And so we hobbled into Court 4 at Portsmouth Crown Court. There was Mark Yeganeh resplendent in his sharp suit clinging onto his fathers coat tails like a lost nine year old. He sat in the dock with his head bowed. The jury was sworn in and took their seats; four men and eight women. There was some legal argument then as Yeganeh's defence claimed that there was insufficient evidence to try his client for dangerous driving and so in order to save the courts valuable time he would graciously plead guilty to careless driving. Yeah I bet he would. Thankfully Judge Gareth Cowling rejected this and so the trial began. It was a fairly short lived affair really, only taking one day.

Dean's evidence was accepted by the defence and so his witness statement was merely read out to the court rather than him actually having to give physical evidence. Then after I'd read out the interview notes it was time for Yeganeh to enter the box. It's at this point in proceedings that I always look at the jury to gauge their initial reaction when the defendant opens his mouth for the first time. As soon as he started to speak the eight women all folded their arms and pulled a face reminiscent of that Les Dawson character, the one with the curlers and the false teeth. You're doomed mate; I thought to myself, you haven't got a chance. If the women don't like you, well you may as well just give up now.

He came across as uncaring and arrogant but in truth I don't think he actually meant to. He refused to answer a lot of the prosecutions questions which didn't help and at no time did he offer an apology towards Dean, which if I'd been his brief I'd have insisted he do, even if he didn't mean it.

By mid-afternoon the trial was over and the jury was sent out to consider its verdict. They took twelve minutes. We didn't even have time to drink a cup of coffee. Twelve minutes; that's got to be some kind of record?

Mark Yeganeh was convicted of dangerous driving, no insurance and failing to stop at the scene of an accident. He showed no emotion at all. He had a number of previous driving related matters on his record including driving whilst under the influence of drugs and had been disqualified twice before. The prosecutor then read out Deans Victim Impact Statement to a hushed court room.

My name is Dean Foster and I want to tell you how this accident has affected my life. Ever since I can remember I have wanted to join the Army, to do my bit for Queen and country. I don't know why but it's just what I wanted to do. My application forms arrived on the morning of February 16th.

You know all the facts surrounding the crash but let me tell you what it was like for me. As I rode my bike along Elm Grove that afternoon I was as happy as anyone could be. Then out the corner of my left eye I saw a car and within a split second it had hit my left leg. I remember flying through the air and landing on the other side of road and I knew immediately that I was in serious trouble. I couldn't move and the pain was excruciating. I really thought I was going to die there in the middle of the road. A man came over to help me and I begged him not to leave me. But this was only the start of my problems.

I spent two months in hospital during which time I had five operations in an effort to save my leg. I lost a large amount of flesh and tissue which I'll never get back so the massive indentation and scar tissue is something I'm going to have to live with for life. Even now my long term prognosis is not good. I have a heavy external fixator bolted to the bones in my left leg to try and keep it stable and aid the bone growth but the Doctors continue to warn me that if the bones don't heal then in all likely hood they will have to amputate my left foot.

I still have nightmares about what happened. I keep feeling the car hitting my leg, which makes my panic attacks worse. When I have the nightmares I often wet the bed. Can you imagine how that feels? This has turned me from a placid, happy-go-lucky young man into an angry and stressed out person that my girlfriend and family just don't recognise.

I will never understand why the man responsible for all of this didn't stop and help me. I would have done if the roles had been reversed.

Reluctantly the Judge adjourned the case for a month for pre-sentencing reports because of Yeganeh's drug issues, which was a shame because I always think that the jury want to see the punishment fit the crime and they somehow miss out when adjournments are made. However he did let Yeganeh know in very plain English that a lengthy custodial sentence was likely.

Khushwant had a long chat with Dean afterwards and said she'd send a photographer to his place tomorrow because she wanted a photo of his injuries. Dean had a huge smile on his face and his dad shook me firmly by the hand and thanked me for everything that we had done.

The following day's edition of the Portsmouth News had Yeganeh's face splashed all over the front page and on page three it carried the full article with a cracking photo of Dean showing off his battle scars. It left no-one who read it in any doubt about the arrogance of the man responsible and I felt more than satisfied that my relationship with a number of journalists could reap excellent results when required. Without their help in publicising the crash in the first place I would not have reached Mr Yeganeh senior and so it was only right that come the day of the trial that the favour was returned and they got a good front page story out of it. Vultures? It's not always the case. It can be and should be a two-way street where both parties benefit.

A month later and Mark Yeganeh was jailed for nine months and disqualified from driving for three years and ordered to sit an extended driving test once his ban was over. In sentencing him Judge Cowling said "Even when faced with the evidence in this case you couldn't bring yourself to accept you had driven dangerously. You have a terrible record of driving offences. This offence and all the other offences demonstrate your lack of regard for motoring laws and your willingness to put other members of the public at risk and your inability to face up to your responsibilities. Just look at the consequences for that young man; a young man at 19 who has had his life changed forever.

As the maximum sentence at this time was two years imprisonment I was quite satisfied with the result. He deserved prison time, albeit he would probably only do six months inside, whereas Dean had a life sentence.

Howard Marrs called me into his office. It wasn't good news and I knew what was coming. The CPS had decided that there was insufficient evidence to charge Dennis Sharp with Section 1 Death by Dangerous Driving and therefore the charge would be Section 3 Careless Driving. My heart sank; this was going to kill Mick and Tania. Howard suggested a meeting with them, so that he and the PIO could spell out exactly why that decision had been reached and left it to me to make the necessary arrangements.

I drove across to Gosport that evening and I think I was more nervous about telling them this than I was on the day of the crash. It was made worse because Mick was in a very buoyant mood because the 'Play for Brijj' fund had just topped the £5000 mark and they were over the moon with the response from the public, most of whom they had never met. It was a fantastic achievement on their part at a time when quite frankly many people in similar circumstances wouldn't have been able to cope let alone do something as positive as raising money to provide musical instruments for other kids. But then not everybody are Mick and Tania Panormo.

I broke the news to them and just like me they weren't surprised but nonetheless were still incredulous that a professional bus driver could fail to have seen Bridgette in these circumstances. I offered them the opportunity to meet the SIO and PIO which they readily agreed to and between us we settled on a date in a few days time.

So the evening arrived and I collected them both and drove to Fareham Police Station where we met Howard and Mark Foster and sat around a small table with a cup of tea. Howard was his usual firm but fair self and told them why this case had been so difficult to conclude with the lack of physical evidence being key. The bus only had three passengers on board and they were the prime witnesses but the CPS had stated that they couldn't be classed as totally independent, unlike a witness who may have seen the crash from outside the parameters of the bus. But of course therein lay the problem; we didn't have such a witness. There was also a lack of forensic evidence. In almost every crash there is an exchange of material to connect the two vehicles. If two cars have collided even at fairly low impact both are likely to be damaged or to have left some kind of mark. But in this case there was nothing. The Crash Investigator Stan Gibbs, who was the most experienced investigator in Hampshire, could find no trace of any exchange of material. At the very least he had expected to find a black tyre mark at the front of the bus, but there was nothing. This brought into question whether or not there had ever actually been a collision or had Bridgette just fallen off her bike of her own accord and then tragically been run over by a bus that couldn't stop in time? The CPS had therefore based their decision on the facts as presented to them and not on supposition and emotion.

Mick started asking probing questions, good ones to. He wasn't prepared to accept the CPS decision and couldn't grasp why they wouldn't take a chance on charging Sharp with Section 1. He was fighting Bridgette's corner and I had nothing but sympathy and a big dose of admiration for him for doing so. Mark Foster interrupted him and in a manner that I can only describe as somewhat hostile towards Mick, tried to reinforce the issue. He showed a complete lack of empathy and I squirmed in my seat with embarrassment. I think Howard sensed the growing tension within the room and managed to calm things down a little by stating that as the SIO in this case he had to shoulder some of the responsibility and said that on the basis of the evidence alone, he had to agree with the CPS decision., but as a father himself he fully sympathised with them.

Mick slumped back in his chair and looked defeated. A court date of November 12th had been set and all the indications were that Dennis Sharp intended pleading 'not guilty' even to the lesser Section 3 charge.

That information proved to be correct and so more than nine months after the crash we attended Portsmouth Magistrates Court for the trial of Dennis Sharp. Mick, Tania and Mark were there together with another dozen or so friends and family. Sharp arrived with several members of his family and it was quite obvious to me that by the time all the relatives, police officers, journalists and other members of the public had crammed into Court 3 that there just wouldn't be enough room. However I was very pleased to find out that our case would be heard by non other than District Judge John Wollard, known to the local yob element (who were terrified of him) as 'Well-ard Woollard' because of his no nonsense approach. Its seems that he agreed about the lack of room and so there was a significant delay until we were eventually moved next door to the full sized Court 2.

I ushered the Panormo family into court and settled them down on one side of the court room as Sharps family filed in behind us and took up their positions on the other side of the room. I was struck by an atmosphere of hostility almost immediately, not from the Panormo's but by a couple of members of the Sharp family, in particular his daughter, an extremely fat, ginger haired woman who kept on staring intently towards Mick and Tania in a very threatening manner, whilst muttering what I took to be either threats or insults towards them. I decided at this stage to leave it as proceedings were at last about to begin but I would keep a very close eye on the situation.

The Prosecutor then outlined the case by stating that Bridgette had cycled from work in Fareham town centre the short distance along Portland Street and past Fareham bus station where Dennis Sharp was just starting his journey in the number 86 single decker bus. He pulled out of the bus station, turned left into Portland Street and then drove the 50 yards or so to the junction with Quay Street roundabout where Bridgette had stopped. Sharp pulled up and stopped right behind her. The design of the bus meant that it had a flat frontage and so once it had stopped Sharp was physically less than three feet away from Bridgette, with a clear view of at least her head, shoulders and upper torso. She was wearing a cycle helmet and a reflective yellow jacket, the weather and visibility were good. Quay Street roundabout is notoriously difficult to get onto from any of its five exits even in a car let alone a pedal cycle and so Bridgette had to wait quite a while until there was a gap big enough for her to pull out.

The Prosecutor then called the first witness, 19 year old James Bagley who was sat towards the rear of the bus on the slightly elevated section of seating. He said he had a clear view through the front windscreen and could see Bridgette sat on her bike at the junction. He saw her cycle out onto the roundabout and said that the bus pulled out at almost the same time. It accelerated and Mr Bagley became very concerned and thought to himself "Is he going to slow down or go around her?" He said that everything then seemed to go into slow motion and he became frightened as the bus got ever closer to the rear of the bike. He said that the bike then disappeared from view and all he could hear was a scraping noise from underneath. I looked towards Mick and Tania. He was looking at the floor and she had tears streaming down her face.

The next witness was another young man by the name of Alan Ruff. He was also sat towards the rear of the bus on the elevated section but on the other side of the aisle from James Bagley. He also had a good view out the front windscreen although at times, depending on the angle of the bus, his view was partially obscured by the cab itself. Like Mr Bagley he saw Bridgette on her bike waiting at the junction and saw her cycle out onto the roundabout. As the bus got really close to Bridgette he was so concerned for her safety that he actually shouted out "Mind the bike, mind the bike" but then it disappeared from his view. He couldn't actually say whether or not there had been a collision but like James Bagley heard the hideous metallic scraping sounds underneath the bus and shouted at Sharp to stop. He said it seemed to take him ages to do so and when he got off the bus he could see Bridgette behind the front wheels and knew she was dead. The court was completely hushed, except for Sharps daughter whom I saw shaking her head and uttering the words "Rubbish".

The court then adjourned for lunch and as we all filed out so I caught Sharps daughter glaring at the Panormo's again but I got side tracked by someone else and wasn't able to deal with it before she left the building. Tania's sister had noticed as well and asked me if I had seen what she was up to, so I wasn't the only one to witness it.

The family seemed quite pleased with how things were going overall, although Tania seemed to be in a rather subdued state. It must be so very hard to have to listen to complete strangers talking about your daughter in open court like she was some kind of inanimate object.

An hour later we were all called back in but not before I took Sharps daughter to one side and told her in no uncertain terms that if she continued with her behavior then I'd have no hesitation in nicking her and taking straight downstairs to the cells. She denied it and said she didn't know what I was talking about but I think my warning shook her up a little. I made sure that she knew I was watching her like a hawk.

Our third bus witness entered the witness box. She was a young lady with blonde hair, quite tall and of large build. She wasn't very bright and that's putting it mildly. Every question she was asked she just replied "I dunno". Even simple questions like "Where were you sitting?"

"I dunno."

"What did you see?"

"I dunno."

Everyone got very frustrated with her until something within her triggered a startling fact that until now we were unaware of. She eventually revealed that she might have been standing next to the driver and talking to him, although she wasn't entirely sure because she knew him, being a regular on his bus and might have confused it with a previous journey. But surely this crash is a major event and that you must be able to recall whether or not you were or were not standing next to the driver at the time of the crash she was asked?

"I dunno."

Her testimony, whilst possibly revealing a significant and hitherto unknown fact couldn't exactly be relied upon and after more than two hours grilling by the prosecution, the defence and by Judge Woollard himself the woman left the court with most of us more confused now than ever before. Stan Gibbs then brought some clarity to proceedings and did his best to convince the court that in his expert opinion Sharp had ample opportunity to have seen the cycle even after it left Portland Street and really should have been aware of its existence. The defence made great play on the fact that there was no physical evidence to suggest that there had even been contact between the two vehicles. I have to confess that things were not looking good for us; the evidence wasn't exactly over whelming.

The defence then called Dennis Sharp to give evidence. Mick and Tania's grip on each other's hands tightened. This was the moment they would hear at first hand from the man accused of killing their daughter. This bespectacled, grey haired 62 year old bus driver had an air of confidence about him that took me by surprise I have to say. Maybe his defence team had told him that he had little to worry about because the evidence was weak. He answered all the questions from his defence barrister confidently and those of the Prosecutor in the same vein until it came to the finer detail. He said he remembered seeing the cycle in front of him at the junction and that after it emerged onto the roundabout he had to wait for two cars to pass before he pulled out. Shortly after that he heard a scraping noise and because it persisted he then stopped. He was vague on detail when pushed and then Judge Woollard asked him a question.

"Whose fault do you think this crash was?" he asked.

Sharp literally shrugged his shoulders and muttered "No idea………it wasn't mine though".

"Well if it wasn't your fault Mr Sharp am I to assume that you think it was the cyclists fault?" enquired the Judge.

"Well that's for you to decide isn't it," replied Sharp, looking away from the Judge and towards the floor in an act of petulance.

He was arrogance personified. I heard Judge Woollard let out a sort of "Hmmnn" under his breath. All of a sudden I felt somewhat lifted by this brief exchange. Had Sharps apparent indifference towards the victim been enough to convince the Judge that he might not be telling the truth?

Time was getting on and so the case was adjourned, not until tomorrow morning but for two weeks! There wasn't sufficient court space to allow the trial to continue and the earliest we could reconvene was on November 23rd. It was a ridiculous situation and my concern was that by the time the rest of the case was heard certain key elements that we'd learned today might well have been forgotten about.

The family all gathered together in the hallway outside Court 2 and we all compared notes on Sharp and that female witness. Mick was clearly seething inside, he just couldn't understand why Sharp just didn't own up to his guilt to save his family the trauma of having to wait another two weeks before they found out whether or not, in the eyes of the law, Sharp was guilty. Jeff Reines was there of course and he scribbled various quotes into his note book. I stood next to him and whispered in his ear.

"I trust you're going to splash Dennis Sharps picture all over the front page?" I asked through gritted teeth.

"Already taken care of Steve" he smiled.

And so it proved. The following day's copy of The News had a full colour photo of Sharp leaving the court building with all the details of the day's proceedings throughout the whole page article.

Just over two weeks later we were back in Court 2, all the same people were there and further evidence was heard including that of an expert crash investigator on behalf of the defence. He tried baffling everyone with science over photographs he'd taken from inside a similar bus, not the actual bus and started waffling on about depth of vision, field of vision, anything he could think of to rubbish the two key witnesses who'd seen everything from the rear of the bus. In the end Judge Woollard basically said he'd heard enough and accused him of deliberately trying to confuse everyone. With the evidence concluded and final addresses made by both the

Prosecutor and Defence Barrister it was time for Judge Woollard to retire and consider his verdict. I'm usually pretty good at reading court situations but I couldn't call this one at all and I was all the more concerned because of it. If Sharp was found not guilty I'm not sure that Mick and Tania would ever come to terms with it.

I then spoke to the Prosecutor about the Victim Impact Statement and asked him (in the event that Sharp was convicted of course) if he wanted me to read it out or if he was happy to.

"Oh I don't think we need bother with that do you? Came his rather curt reply.

"But this is the family's opportunity to tell the court exactly what impact Bridgette's death has had on them, it's important" I said.

"I think the Court has heard enough don't you and Judge Woollard is no mug, he doesn't need to hear about how it's affected the family, he can see it for himself"

"I don't think you quite understand, I know these victim impact statements are a new concept and that you personally might not agree with their introduction but the family want their voice heard" I pleaded.

But there was no swaying the man. I actually think the emotion of it all had got the better of him. He wasn't the best Prosecutor I'd seen in action and he certainly didn't put Sharp under enough pressure in my opinion. I was livid that he refused point blank to allow it to be read out but what more could I say?

I think we were out for about 45 minutes before being called back in. The court was completely silent as we patiently waited for the Judge to enter. We all kept looking at one another, lips pursed, eye brows raised, fingers crossed.

"Court rise" bellowed the Court Usher as Judge Woollard breezed in. Sharp remained standing in the dock as instructed by his Brief.

The Judge then précised the evidence he had heard and in particular praised the compelling evidence from both James Bagley and Alan Ruff who, despite being several feet further back inside the bus had seen everything that Dennis Sharp should have seen. He went on to examine Sharps testimony in detail and found it difficult to comprehend that a professional driver of more than 30 years' experience just couldn't remember the finer and most important detail of this accident. He therefore had no doubt that Sharp had driven carelessly and found him guilty accordingly.

There was a sharp intake of breath from everyone around me. I looked at Mick and Tania and the relief on Mick's face was palpable. Dennis Sharp was guilty in law of killing his daughter and in no way was Bridgette to blame. That's all he wanted to hear really.

Sharp was disqualified from driving for six months and fined £250. Not the harshest of sentences but then you have to remember here that he was convicted of careless driving only; there was no offence of causing death by careless driving at that time so the law could only be concerned with a driver's actions and not the consequences. But the family wasn't concerned with his sentence, it was the fact that he and not Bridgette had been found to be the cause of the crash. Sharp showed not one ounce of emotion as he was convicted, nothing. I've met and dealt with a good number of arrogant people in my time but he is without doubt one of the worst I've ever come across and the worst aspect of his arrogance is the fact that he never said sorry, he didn't show any remorse towards the Panormo family at all. In my experience if the person that possibly caused the death of another in a road crash just says sorry at an early stage and in a genuine manner then it really, really helps the victim's family in coming to terms with their loss. But when that same person publicly just shrugs his shoulders and says "wasn't my fault" then they deserve everything that's coming to them.

Before Judge Woollard released Sharp he turned towards the Panormo family to offer his sincere condolences for their loss and to thank them for the truly dignified manner in which they had conducted themselves throughout the trial. I couldn't help but nod in agreement with him, they were an exceptionally nice family and it had been my privilege to have helped them in some small way. We all gathered outside the Court building once more. There were tears, smiles, hugs all around as one by one Mick and Tania's family thanked me and my colleagues for everything we had done. Mark smiled at me briefly. I put my hand on his shoulder and asked him if he was happy with the result. He said he was and then said "thank you". Those two simple words meant a great deal to me because I knew how much Bridgette had meant to him.

I saw Jeff Reines taking notes again. I thanked him for everything he'd done to ensure that Bridgette's death was kept at the forefront of everyone's mind during the nine months it had taken to get Sharp to Court. I couldn't recollect a higher profile case locally that involved a road death and despite my initial reservations about him he proved beyond doubt that he had been worthy of my trust and I was very grateful.

"I haven't finished with him yet" he smirked "Make sure you get your copy of The News tomorrow".

But this wasn't the end of my involvement with Mick and Tania; we still had the trauma of a Coroners Inquest to come yet, but for now we parted company.

Jeff Reines did a real hatchet job on Sharp the next day, putting his face on the front page and writing another full page spread on the conclusion of the court case. A month later he picked up on the fact that Sharp had been sacked by First Bus and quoted some union official saying he'd been unfairly treated and had been made a scape goat, which was factually incorrect of course. Mick was quoted as saying he was relieved that Sharp would no longer be driving a bus and that as far as he was concerned this was an early Christmas present for him and his family.

In January Jeff Reines continued to keep things in the public domain by writing a big article on Mick and Tania's fund raising efforts for the 'Play for Brijj' Fund. They'd raised an incredible £5000 and were pictured back at Bridgette's old junior school with the 18 guitars, amplifiers and carry cases that the money had paid for. Together with members of one of Bridgette's bands an impromptu gig was performed and the seven and eight year olds loved it. Without doubt it helped Mick and Tania in that some good had come from her death and who knows, maybe one of those kids will be just as inspired by music as Bridgette was and may go onto great things.

It was fast approaching the first anniversary of the crash and Mick phoned me to ask a favour. On February 17th could I possibly stop the traffic at Quay Street roundabout so that the family could walk across to the grassed area inside the roundabout to lay a few flowers? I'll be there.

The Panormo family and a few friends gathered on the pavement at 4pm on February 17th, exactly one year since the crash. It had been a long and arduous twelve months for all of them and their mood was sombre as I stepped off the pavement and out into the road to halt three lanes of traffic. Once it had stopped and I was sure it was safe I beckoned them across to the safety of the roundabout itself. They laid flowers and Mark hammered in a sign from the charity Road Peace that said 'Remember Me'. At 4.15pm and in a quirk of fate whilst we were all gathered on the island the number 86 bus emerged from Portland Street and made its way around the roundabout before heading down the A32 towards Gosport. A shudder went down my spine. No one anything; we just stared at it.

On July 20th we were all back at Portsmouth Court for the Inquest. The trial had only concentrated on the facts leading up to Bridgette's crash and not the aftermath including the actual medical cause of her death. By their very nature they are emotional formal public hearings that conclude with HM Coroner recording the cause of death. Witnesses that hadn't been called to give evidence at the trial would be brought in together with a number of those who had previously given evidence including Sharp himself. Although held within the main Court building the Coroners Court is one of the smaller Courts and everyone sits a lot closer to each other than we did in Court 2.

A few weeks prior to the Inquest Mick and Tania had asked me to pop over to the house for a chat about the procedures involved. Once done Mick had one of his questions for me. He wanted to know if the hydraulic system that lowers the bus to kerb height at bus stops had been operated once Sharp had stopped the bus following the collision and if once he had realised that Bridgette was underneath did he then raise the bus again to relieve the pressure on her? It was a question that had haunted him for months and he wanted an answer. I sat there for a few moments. Bloody hell. What a question. I genuinely didn't know the answer and couldn't recall any of the investigation team having ever mentioned it before. But it was a question that needed answering. I told him that the Coroner Mr Horsley would give him and Tania every opportunity to ask questions of any of the witnesses and that if he had any other questions then the Inquest was the right place to ask them.

After a couple of hours chatting to them I got back into the patrol car and sat there in silence for at least ten minutes mulling over that question.

The atmosphere within the Coroners Court was electric. It was packed out, the difference being that all the witnesses remain within the Court throughout rather than being kept outside until it's their turn to give evidence.

One of the first witnesses was WPC Julia Shaw who was

based at Fareham nick. She had been in the yard at the police station saying goodbye to her husband who was a serving Traffic officer and had just finished his 8-4 shift. He cycled out of the yard and turned right towards Quay Street roundabout to head home.

Only three or four minutes had passed when Julia got into her panda car to go out on a call. As she got to the roundabout she saw the bus stationary in front of her and under the front of it lay a pedal cycle. Her immediate thoughts were obviously that her husband was involved. She quickly drove around the roundabout, parked behind the bus putting the blue lights on to help protect the scene and then ran down the nearside edge of the bus to the front of it where she found Dennis Sharp and another man standing there. She said that Sharp just stood there with his hands in his pockets as if holding a casual chat with the man she assumed had been on the bike, which to her immediate and obvious relief was not her husband.

She asked the man if he was OK? He looked somewhat confused and said he was fine but he wasn't so sure about the girl who'd been on the bike and he indicated towards the offside of the bus. Julia looked around the side of the drivers cab towards the front wheels and was horrified to see Bridgette's head sticking out from under the side of the bus with the rest of her body underneath it.

She ran straight to Bridgette whilst frantically calling up on her police radio and screaming for an ambulance and some back up. She got down on her knees and tried to reassure Bridgette that help was on its way. She tried pulling her out from underneath but she was firmly wedged in place. She tried getting under the bus with her but there just wasn't enough room. She continued talking to her but knew she was slipping away.

Julia broke down in the witness box and sobbed. She

apologised to Mick and Tania saying she couldn't do CPR on Bridgette or heart massage because she couldn't reach any of the relevant areas to conduct any lifesaving first aid. The tears streamed down her face and she wasn't the only one. She went on to say that she stroked Bridgette's cheek and continued talking to her, trying to comfort her but she knew inside that it was too late. There was a deafening silence in that room as Julia stepped down from the witness box and as she walked back towards her sea, Mick stood up and touched her hand and thanked her for staying with Bridgette, it meant a lot to him and Tania.

We then heard from the Pathologist who had conducted the Post Mortem and much of his testimony was medical with all the associated jargon that accompanies it but the bottom line was that Bridgette had been crushed to death and could not have survived even if immediate first aid had been applied.

Dennis Sharp stood in the witness box and on instructions from his solicitor was very brief in the answers he gave to Mr Horsley. He looked straight ahead towards the Coroner and never once turned his head towards the rest of us, almost as if we weren't there. He wasn't as confident this time, his voice faltering occasionally but he continued to give the impression that the crash wasn't his fault. Then Mr Horsley asked him what he had done to assist Bridgette once he'd realised what had happened. Sharp thought he might have called for an ambulance on his mobile but he couldn't remember for sure.

"Yes but what did you physically do to help the victim in this case, did you try to get her out, did you talk to her as the young WPC did, what did you do? Enquired Mr Horsley.

"I waited for the ambulance to arrive" came Sharps reply.

"So you didn't render her any assistance whatsoever? Asked the Coroner.

"I called an ambulance" repeated Sharp.

In other words no he didn't render Bridgette any sort of help, he just stood there, as Julia Shaw had said, with his hands in his pockets at the front of his bus, several feet away from his dying victim. If anybody had any doubt during the trial about this man's indifference towards a fellow human being then this exchange confirmed just how callous and cold hearted an individual he really is. And right now he had the perfect opportunity to turn towards Mick and Tania to say sorry for their loss, as an absolute minimum. Do you think he did? Of course he didn't. He walked right past them, looking straight ahead and left the Court.

Stan Gibbs was called to give evidence. Everyone I've ever met had the very highest regard for Stan and his totally professional approach to his work. He'd been a police officer for over 30 years and then carried on the role as a civilian accident investigator for many years after that. He always delivered his evidence in a manner that was clear and concise so that everyone within the Court understood even the most technical of details. He repeated much of what he'd said during the trial so there wasn't that much that was new until Mick asked him *that* question.

Stan said that upon his arrival at the scene he had examined the bus in situ, it hadn't been touched by anyone else and that the hydraulic system was in the standard position for driving and had not been lowered as far as he could tell. He did test it and it was in good working order and lowered the bus to four inches above the ground rather than the standard eight inches. He was then asked if the system was operated automatically when the handbrake was applied to which the answer was no, it had to be manually operated from a separate switch. Could it have been accidentally operated asked Mr Horsley, obviously now intrigued himself, but Stan said that was highly unlikely.

I'm pretty sure he answered everything as honestly as he could and I think it helped put Mick and Tania's nightmare scenario to bed.

The verdict was never in doubt of course and Mr Horsley recorded it as Accidental Death. After finalising all the official business he declared the Inquest closed and then stepped down from the bench and came over to talk to Mick and Tania. He quite often did this and it put a personal touch to something very formal which was a nice gesture. There was no celebration after the Inquest as there had been after the trial, everyone was somewhat subdued and there was an air of finalisation about it all. It's usually at this stage that I exit the family and leave them to their own devices but Tania asked me if she could meet Julia Shaw for a personal one to one chat. I said I'd ask her and get back to her as soon as I could.

Jeff Reines did yet another full page article on the Inquest and centered on Mick's anger towards Sharp for not saying sorry. The article pulled no punches and left all those who didn't witness it at first hand just how cold hearted Sharp was.

In the end it took a couple of weeks for me to arrange for Tania to meet Julia. I picked her up from Fareham nick and on the way over to Gosport she said she was a bit apprehensive about meeting them on a personal basis but said she was struck by just how nice they had been during the Inquest. The four of us sat in the front room. The cat and I now had an understanding about my leg and he just sat by the window glaring at me.

We all settled down with a cup of tea and both Mick and Tania thanked Julia again for everything she had said at the Inquest. They basically wanted to hear it again but in more personal detail and it wasn't long before the tears started to flow again.

Julia then revealed that following the crash she was signed off sick for nearly six months with a stress related illness, which at first I thought was a bit extreme, until she started talking about her father's accident only a few weeks prior to Bridgette's. He lived in Kent and was knocked off his cycle and run over by a tipper truck. He died instantly. The comparisons between the two are obvious and for her to be the first on the scene of an almost identical accident to her father's only a few weeks later must have really played on her mind.

As a mother Tania sympathised with Julia and obviously understood her pain and the pair of them hugged each other before Tania nipped into the next room and came back with a huge bunch of flowers for Julia. I know I've said it before but Mick and Tania really are two of the very nicest people you could ever wish to meet and there's your proof. After that the mood lightened somewhat as they proudly played a couple of tracks from one of 'Rolling Dogs' CD's that featured Bridgette on bass guitar and vocals. It was a slightly surreal experience but hearing her voice and being able to do that whenever they needed to must bring a small degree of comfort.

After a couple of hours I drove Julia back to Fareham as she clutched that bunch of flowers. She didn't say much and I left her to her own thoughts. I'd said my goodbyes to Mick and Tania at their door and thought that was probably going to be the last time I saw them, which for me personally I found a bit difficult. I'd grown rather fond of them but I knew I had to be professional, and so that was the end of that. Without doubt the death of Bridgette Panormo had been the most challenging of jobs for me personally and I hope that my enforced intrusion into Mick and Tania's lives helped them out in some small way. My only regret is that I never got to meet their daughter; I think I'd have liked her.

Two months went by. My mobile rang, it was Jeff Reines.

"Have you heard the news?" he asked.

"No, what?"

"Dennis Sharp has been given his old job back and he's

driving buses again," he exclaimed.

"Do Mick and Tania know?" I asked.

"Yeah, I've just told them, it's terrible isn't it" and he sounded genuinely upset about it "and the worst part about is he's driving the same routes as before, it's a real kick in the teeth for Mick and Tania".

I had to ring them. Tania answered the phone because Mick was out. She was clearly upset but almost resigned to the fact that he was entitled to his job back but she really didn't like the idea of him driving the same route, especially as it virtually passed the end of their road. She was particularly concerned for Mick who just wasn't coping with things anyway and this was just going to add to his pain.

The next day's edition of The News had Jeff Reines in full flow again lambasting First Bus for allowing Dennis Sharp back behind the wheel of a bus. There were various quotes in the full page article from Mick and myself, followed by an intriguing one from First Bus spokeswoman Patricia Gray who said;

"Both First Bus and our driver have expressed our deep sympathy with the family of Bridgette Panormo and we have no wish to add to the pain they are having to face" she continued "However, there is no reason why our driver should not resume his career and continue to serve the community of which he has been a part for nearly 40 years".

If First Bus as a company ever offered their deep sympathy towards the Panormo family it was never delivered at the time or since and this statement was nothing more than an empty gesture designed to make them feel better about themselves. In truth Mick and Tania had not received anything from the company except a veil of silence. Its been my experience on many occasions in such circumstances that a letter or a bunch of flowers or something is communicated towards the family just to acknowledge their sympathy, without prejudice in accepting liability, but just a simple note to say sorry for your loss. And we all know about Dennis Sharps 'deep sympathy' don't we.

THOMAS CLANCY & MARK DAWSON

Operation NEVADD
Category C
28th February 2004

2004 Hampshire fatalities = 63
2004 Nationally fatalities = 3221

I staggered into the office for 8am feeling really tired. As soon as I stepped over the threshold so Sgt. Paul Diamond pointed his finger at me and said "Ah, just the man" which meant I was either in the shit or he was about to stitch me up with something and from the hive of activity in the office from officers who weren't on early turn

but were actually left over from the previous days late turn and night shift I guessed it was going to be the latter. And I was right. There had been a fatality late last night on the A27 and there had been no night duty FLO on duty and rather than call one out from home he'd taken the decision to bring me on board when I came on day turn.

The victim was 54 year old Thomas William Clancy who was an epileptic and who had apparently suffered a seizure whilst travelling as a passenger in the rear of the Toyota Town Ace people carrier that his partner Lucinda was driving. He'd apparently opened the side sliding door and stepped out of the vehicle at 60 mph and out onto the A27. He suffered massive head injuries and died at 0540 at the QA Hospital.

Apparently the G28 and I.D statement had already been obtained which was a good start. However that meant that I was going into this one second hand which I personally hated. It had always been my experience that if you are there right from the start with the family and you break the news to them or you are there when their loved one dies then you share a bond with them that is difficult to describe. You have shared in something incredibly personal with somebody you have only just met and that allows you to develop a relationship that is just different to anything else I have ever experienced. However if you go in there afterwards, after another officer has broken the news then I always feel like the gooseberry, almost an intruder in the situation and the relationship is slightly different or it can almost be non-existent.

Mr. Clancy and his partner Lucinda lived in Pulborough, West Sussex but Lucinda's mother, Margaret Dawson-Daley lived in Waterlooville and that is where Lucinda would be today. So I had no scene to visit, no wrecked vehicle to examine, no body to I.D, no death message to deliver, no G28 to fill out, in fact none of the usual routine tasks that I usually faced. What could possibly go wrong? At midday I arrived at the neat bungalow in Stakes Hill Road, Waterlooville and parked on the driveway. My heart was pounding as I walked towards the front door, took a deep breath and rang the bell. It was answered quickly by a very smart looking lady whom I guessed was Lucinda's mother Margaret. She showed me into the lounge and there sat on the settee was Lucinda who was busily breast feeding her four month old baby Julian, which was a rather embarrassing introduction for both of us really. The house was bedlam. The baby was crying, two year old Theodora was in the play pen making quite a bit of noise whilst 10 year old Saffron sat at the table doing some colouring. Lucinda's two other daughters Bethia aged 12 and Imogen aged 15 were elsewhere in the house but popped into the room every now and then. Every couple of minutes the phone would ring and Margaret would have to go and explain to a concerned friend or relative what had happened.

I sat there patiently for over an hour until some form of order had been restored. The baby dropped off to sleep, the eldest girl went into another room and even the two year old piped down for a bit as Margaret came in with a tray of tea. There were no spoons with the cups and so I stirred my tea with the end of my pen, an act I'd been doing for years, much to the amusement of both Margaret and Lucie. Nobody called her Lucinda apparently and she insisted that we also refer to Thomas as Billy because that's the name he'd always used. My pen routine had broken the ice it seemed and I no longer felt like an intruder.

Lucie then started to talk about the events of only a few hours earlier. She and Billy had been over to see Margaret for the day and had left Waterlooville about 10pm. She was driving their Toyota people carrier whilst Billy sat in the rear with the three kids. He obviously wasn't able to drive because of his severe epilepsy and so Lucie always drove. She said the first she was aware of anything going wrong was when she heard the sliding side door being opened and when she looked over her shoulder she saw Billy at the door and then he just vanished. She stopped as quickly as she could from 60 mph and ran back along the A27 to find him lying on the hard shoulder. Another couple of cars had stopped to help but it was obvious he was in a bad way. The tears were now streaming down her face.

She went on to describe Billy's unusual type of epilepsy in that his wasn't the usual seizure kind with the archetypal head and body shaking. His condition meant that he would go into a trance like state and then do the most bizarre things. She quoted a couple of examples like when he made himself a cup of coffee but had used Weetabix in the cup instead of coffee. On another occasion he was wall papering the lounge and mid-way through suffered a seizure and papered over the windows and the door with the paper at all sorts of strange angles. I asked her if she thought it might have been suicide but she was adamant that it wasn't and that he had probably had another seizure and that on this occasion the unusual pattern of his behaviour had resulted in him opening the door. She kept looking at their four month old baby and saying how proud Billy had been with their latest arrival.

We then got down to the serious business of the media and between them they quickly decided that they would issue a family statement. However there was a complication in that so far they hadn't been able to contact three close relatives, one in Manchester and two in Ireland and the last thing they wanted was for them to find out via the papers or the radio. I agreed obviously and they said they would do their best to inform them as soon as possible. Lucie said she would do her best to get the family statement written by tomorrow and that she had a photo of Billy holding the new baby and she was particularly keen for this one to be used. After completing one or two other formalities I said my goodbyes and said I'd be back tomorrow to collect the statement and photo, and return some property of Lucie's from the car. Margaret followed me out to the door and it was clear that she was going to be a tower of strength for her daughter at a time when she needed it the most.

I went back to the office to start a new FLO log and to sort out a few other administrative duties. I got my pen out and it was full of tea! That's never happened before.

The next morning I drove back up to Waterlooville. Margaret answered the door and she looked dreadful, she had a hanky pressed against her mouth and there were tears streaming down her face. My initial thoughts were that Billy's death had obviously just hit home. I couldn't have been more wrong.

"I'm so glad you're here Steve, I've had the Police here all night" she blurted out.

" Why?" I asked.

"They found my son Mark dead in his flat down in Southsea last night" and with that she burst into tears and leant into my shoulder.

I put my arm around her and led her into the lounge. Lucie was sat in exactly the same place I'd left her in and she was just staring into space. I sat Margaret down and then paused for a moment. In the space of 24 hours Lucie had lost her partner and her brother whilst Margaret had lost her son and her son in law. Bloody hell.

"I think he was murdered," said Margaret.

"Murdered? What makes you think that?" I asked.

"He was beaten up really badly last week by an evil, evil man who stole lots of his stuff and I think he's died from his injuries," she went on.

Then Lucie chipped in.

"Mark was a heroin addict so no-one will care less about him," and I presumed by that she meant the Police.

"Well that's not true when it comes to murder Lucie," I retorted.

100

Over the next half an hour or so Lucie and Margaret gave me a quick rundown on Marks heroin addiction and how he was desperately trying to stay clean in order to save his marriage. His Turkish wife Asuman had basically thrown Mark out of the family home and into a bed-sit in Southsea as a last resort in the hope that

he would change his ways and get himself off the heroin. As part of his treatment, like many heroin addicts he was prescribed methadone by his GP which is usually taken under strict control whilst at the chemist point of collection; it is rarely if ever allowed to leave the premises.

Just over a week ago Mark was badly assaulted by two men who were trying to rob him of his possessions in order to feed their own drug habit. Mark spent several hours in casualty at the QA and Margaret said he really suffered, particularly with the facial injuries that he had. She said he was terrified of these two men, in particular Michael Bowden and Mark begged his mother to allow him to come back to her house but she refused telling him that he needed to stay in his bed-sit otherwise his marriage would be over.

Now of course she was feeling very, very guilty. Margaret seemed particularly confused about what the police were going to do to investigate this incident and asked me as their FLO if I could find out more on their behalf. I nipped outside and phoned Sgt. Simon Goss and asked him to contact Southsea CID so that we could find out the full facts.

He phoned me back 10 minutes later to say that a Detective Sergeant would contact me later to appraise me of the incident. I went back inside the house and Margaret seemed particularly comforted by the fact that I was now able to help her further. I still couldn't quite believe what was going on, I mean to lose two members of the same family within 24 hours is just unthinkable and the pair of them seemed completely lost and bewildered. Needless to say Lucie had not completed the family statement for the press and frankly that was the last thing that was on my mind at that moment in time and I told her not to worry about it and the press would have to wait. After a couple of hours I left and said that as soon as I had some more information then I'd be back in touch with them.

By 4.15 that afternoon I hadn't heard anything from the DS at Southsea and so I phoned his office to be told that he'd already gone home! Well thanks for that I thought, thank you very much for your concern. However I did speak to a DC who told me that he had done the ID at the mortuary with Margaret that afternoon. I have to say I was pretty angry at this point and felt that the old CID versus Traffic mistrust had reared its ugly head once more. He went on to state that the post mortem was being carried out tomorrow and at this moment in time it was being treated as a suspicious death due to the assault that took place the previous week and he would liaise with me further once he knew the results of the PM.

Although I'd only met Margaret a little over 24 hours before I already knew her well enough to establish that by now she must be completely overwhelmed by what was going on around her and that she probably felt that everything was completely out of her control, so I phoned her just to reassure her that I would do my utmost on her behalf to try and make this as easy as possible. I was right to phone her because she was extremely distraught having just had to identify her son at the mortuary, having to support Lucie, look after three small children, whilst still trying to contact relatives and friends to let them know what had happened. On top of that she now had two separate police officers investigating two separate incidents that were intrinsically linked and despite her best efforts she was becoming very confused about the whole process and who could blame her; I was pretty confused myself. When I put the phone down I sat back in my chair to reflect upon the whole situation and even with the amount of experience I had I couldn't quite comprehend just how awful it must have been for those two women and I was determined to do my very best for the both of them.

By mid-morning the next day I was back at the house to discuss one or two matters with them. Margaret came into the lounge with a tray of tea and they both laughed when I stirred my tea with my pen. It was good to see them smile a bit and before we got down to business we talked about a few personal things. I talked about my own family and children which they were genuinely interested in and I think that helped them knowing that I was also a family man and not some cardboard cut-out that was just going through the motions in order to pacify them.

When we eventually got down to talking about the circumstances of both incidents we agreed that as far as the Press were concerned we would keep both these incidents completely separate otherwise they would have a field day and it wouldn't matter what I did to protect them they would have a queue of journalists a mile long knocking at their door. Lucie still hadn't finished the family statement, in fact in truth I think she had hardly started it but she promised it would be ready by tomorrow. I didn't want to pressurise her as they had enough to contend with but I felt at this stage it may have helped her to write a few things about Billy in order to take her mind off Mark, because it did feel as though Mark's death was now overshadowing Billy's.

I left the house and went straight to the CID office at Southsea where I spoke to the DC I'd spoken to the previous day hoping that he might give me some news on the results of the PM. However the PM had been postponed until later that afternoon but he promised he would keep me updated just as soon as he knew the results.

The following day I received a call from the DS and he stated that Mark Dawson did not die as a result of the assault or from any other injuries and that he was likely to have died from a heroin overdose but we wouldn't know the results for certain for another 14 days until the toxicology tests have been completed. We agreed a policy that I would become the FLO for both incidents and that he would keep me updated on their investigation.

I went straight back up to the house to tell Margaret and Lucie and they were visibly relieved but now even more confused. They were adamant that Mark was off the heroin and that they would be the first people to know if he was still using and they doubted very much that Mark was back on the brown stuff. So if he didn't die from the injuries he sustained in the assault then what did he die of? This was a question I obviously couldn't answer until the toxicology tests had been completed.

Margaret came in with another tray of tea and a spoon this time which she insisted I use and they then told me that they were having severe difficulties in trying to attend to all the formalities like funeral arrangements, issues with the bank and informing relatives that they still needed to do. Because they spent most of their time dealing with three small children, it made it virtually impossible. Was there anything I could do to help in that direction? All they needed was just three hours respite away from the kids so that they could attend to all of the things that needed to be done. I couldn't see a problem with this and felt sure the Victims Support Service would be only too willing to assist. Leave it with me and I'll see what I can do.

They had two other requests; Lucie wanted rid of the car that was currently sitting on the driveway because it was now just a bad memory and every time she looked at it all she could see was Billy. I said I knew somebody who may be able to take it away on her behalf but that once I had put them in contact with each other I would leave the financial arrangements to her because it wasn't something that I thought I should become involved in.

Then Margaret asked if I could possibly trace Mark's father who was last heard of several years previously in Hertfordshire. The good news was that Lucie had finally finished the family statement for the press together with a lovely photo of Billy holding their young baby. The statement read as follows;

'Thomas William Clancy touched all who knew him with his honest, down to earth outlook on life. He was a competent runner, completing the London Marathon twice. His passion for horses remained central and he made a successful career in the racing world where he earned great respect. He worked in Norfolk, Gloucestershire, Somerset, Sussex and France. He leaves behind many true friends and a heartbroken family'.

I left the house again and shot back to the office to sort out the press release before contacting Victim Support to see if they could offer any kind of respite care for the three kids for an hour or two. After speaking to three different people at Victim Support and relaying all the facts to them the simple answer was "no" they couldn't help.

"What do you mean you can't help?"

It didn't fall within their remit was the answer.

"I have two victims who need support; surely this is exactly what you were set up for?"

" Well yes it is," came the response. "But on this occasion we can't help."

"Well who can help me then?"

After a long pause I was told not to bother with social services because they probably couldn't help either and in fact there was nobody that she could think of that would be able to help.

Absolutely bloody useless. I cannot think of a needier situation whereby the very words 'Victim Support' could be more appropriate and yet this charitable organisation had neither the resources, the inclination nor the appropriate knowledge to point me in the right direction. I doubt I will ever phone them again.

I spoke to Sgt. Mick Streeter, one of the FLO coordinators and he said the best person to phone was Hampshire County Council emergency planning unit and within 30 minutes I had received a positive response from them and everything was organised for the following morning.

I went straight back up to the house to give Margaret and Lucie the details and they seemed very relieved, although I didn't tell them how useless Victim Support were. I then spoke to Lucie about her car because I was concerned that if she just got rid of it that would leave her with no transport, at a time when she probably needed it the most. So I came up with the idea of exchanging the Toyota for another car which she thought was a great idea and asked me to organise it on her behalf.

The respite care organised by Hampshire County Council's emergency planning unit went like clockwork the following day and that enabled Lucie and Margaret to organise the funerals and sort out all the other formalities that one has to go through in the event of somebody's death. Apparently the two carers who attended took the kids to the park and they had a thoroughly enjoyable time and the relief on Lucie and Margaret's face was palpable.

Having now completed all these formalities both women were keen for the funerals to take place. Billy's body was released by the Coroner about this time but of course we were still waiting for the toxicology report on Mark and it was unlikely that his body would be released until such time as that investigation was complete. I did warn Margaret on more than one occasion that there could be complications with regards to this and that she may have to be a bit more patient. But there was only one thing on her mind and that was laying her son to rest so I started to badger the CID department at Southsea and on 12th March I received an email stating that Mark's body could now be released to the family. So I phoned Margaret to let her know that she could now carry on with the funeral arrangements.

Four days later whilst on my rest days I received a phone call from Margaret who was in a very distressed state and she stated that the Coroner was refusing to release Marks body but wouldn't say why. Both she and the funeral directors at Barrels had been phoning the Coroner's office all week but they were failing to return their calls and she was now asking for my help once again. However right now I was unable to do so until I returned to work the following day. I found myself cursing other people and other organisations for causing another bereaved family further unnecessary distress at a time when they needed it the least. It did seem to me as an FLO that I spent much of my time apologising to the families I was dealing with because of other people's cock ups.

By 8:30 the next morning I was in the office and on the phone to the Coroner's office where I spoke to Bob Bradley and within 15 minutes he had received official confirmation that Marks body could be released and he had phoned Barrels funeral directors to confirm this and stated that the death certificate would be issued to Margaret within the next couple of days. So I got straight back onto the phone to Margaret and once again she seemed very relieved.

Almost a month passed and I was on my rest days again when I received another phone call from Margaret, again in a very distressed state because she had just discovered that the three rings that Mark always wore were missing. She had assumed that at the time of his death he would have been wearing them and that prior to the funeral they would have been returned to her as part of his property. However the funeral directors stated that at no time had they ever seen Marks rings and that following her own enquiries with the CID office it transpired that on the night he was found he wasn't wearing them.

Margaret went on to state that she had been to Marks flat today for the first time since he died and found that it had been burgled. Much of his personal property like CD's and videos were missing and that there was property there that didn't belong to him including a bicycle and two skateboards. She called the police but they stated it couldn't be recorded as a burglary because Mark was dead!

I couldn't believe what I was hearing; I mean for Christ's sake what utter nonsense and a complete copout by the officer that she had been speaking to. Yet again it seems that other people had conspired to cause me a problem that I now needed to sort out on her behalf and I promised her that I would contact Southsea CID upon my return to work tomorrow.

She went on to state that she had spoken to Mark's neighbours in the block of flats that he lived in and that they had told her on the night he died they saw a very shifty looking man coming out of Marks flat and that he was trying to hide his face. Margaret was convinced that this was the same man who had imprisoned Mark in his own flat prior to the serious assault that took place a few days before his death. The neighbours also confirmed that since Mark had died that they had seen lights going on and off and heard movements from inside his flat. It begs the question just how detailed the police investigation into .Mark Dawson's death had been. Maybe Lucie's initial outburst that nobody will give a shit because Mark was a heroin addict was right. How embarrassing.

The first thing I did the next day when I returned to work was to phone the DS and he stated that the toxicology report was now in and that the cause of death was a massive overdose of methadone and dihydrocodeine. I then explained the problems concerning the rings and the burglary and he stated that he would detail an officer to investigate immediately and so I phoned Margaret to update her on the cause of death and told her that she should receive a visit or a call from another CID officer concerning the burglary and the missing rings. After I put the phone down I sat back and wondered why Marks body had been released for burial more than a week before the toxicology report had been received. It did seem to me at this point that the investigation had been swept under the carpet and that it was probably pure guesswork that Mark had died from an overdose.

Two weeks passed and I hadn't heard from Margaret in all that time and so I phoned her seeking an update on the investigation. I was staggered to learn that no one from CID or anywhere else had made contact with her concerning the burglary or the missing rings. I was so embarrassed; it seemed that every time I made a promise to her the rest of the organisation let her down. I detected a slight change in Margaret's attitude in that she was no longer upset but angry and who could blame her.

I promised her I would phone CID office immediately and start banging on the table for some answers. However I was in a slightly awkward position here in that I was now questioning the professionalism of fellow officers in a department that has traditionally not always seen eye to eye with its Traffic colleagues. Nonetheless if I didn't question them then who the hell would? I stormed into the CID office determined to confront the DS but he was on leave, so I spoke to the DC I'd spoken to a few weeks earlier and he knew nothing of the alleged burglary or the missing rings which basically confirmed my suspicions that nobody gave a shit. I asked the obvious questions about whether anybody had spoken to Mark Dawson's neighbours and he couldn't remember. He also confirmed my suspicions that nobody had spoken to the two males responsible for the assault on Mark and who Margaret suspected as being responsible for stealing Marks property and perhaps dumping other property not belonging to them in Marks flat for safe keeping. I pushed him a little further and in the end he snapped back that Mark Dawson was just another smack head who accidentally overdosed on his methadone and that his family would just have to get used to that fact. I was severely unimpressed with his attitude but didn't feel I could push things any further.

I decided that I would do some investigations of my own and the first thing I did was to locate the scene photos taken on the night Mark Dawson died. When I received the photo album it clearly showed Mark sat on the settee with his head back and his mouth wide open. The flat was a mess with methadone bottles strewn all over the floor. There was just something not right about the position of his body and the bottles. It is pure supposition on my part but it looked like somebody had grabbed his hair from behind forcing his head back and had force-fed him the methadone, and then discarded the bottles across the floor.

I then went down to Southsea to the block of flats and banged on a few neighbours doors. Two of them were adamant that they had heard movements from within Marks flat in the days following his death but unfortunately they didn't call the police at the time. When I spoke to the lady who had seen this shadowy figure that Margaret had told me about it was literally just that, a shadowy figure and she couldn't describe this person in any way shape or form and as witness testimony goes it was a nonstarter. The other witness I wanted to talk to had, sadly, moved on with no forwarding address and as I didn't have a name anyway, I again came up against a brick wall. I was also hampered by the limitations of time as I had recently taken on another FLO commitment following the death of a pedestrian in Portsmouth and this had to take priority. However I had an idea that may force things to take a new direction as Marks inquest was due to take place shortly.

On June 4th Mark Dawson's inquest took place at Portsmouth Coroner's Court. I collected Margaret, Lucie and Asuman and drove them to court. They were all very nervous but I reassured them that I would talk to Mr Horsley, HM Coroner before the case started so that I could appraise him of their concerns and mine. I had also given the girls a list of questions that they needed to ask of the Coroner and any witnesses. Before the inquest commenced I entered Mr Horsley's chambers at the back of the court to speak to him in private. I told him of the family's suspicions surrounding Marks death and how severely unimpressed I was with the police investigation and that perhaps he should ask some far-reaching questions when it came to the police evidence.

He raised an eyebrow on more than one occasion at my intervention on behalf of the family and promised me they wouldn't leave without knowing the full facts. Part of me felt somewhat disloyal about this but at the same time I felt incredibly angry that this case had clearly not been investigated properly.

Mr Horsley opened the inquest into Mark Dawson's death and the first thing he did was to reassure the three ladies sat in front of him that he would do everything in his power to ensure that they got the answers they were looking for and told them that they could ask any questions of him or any witnesses they liked. This seemed to reassure Margaret and Asuman in particular and I was very pleased with Mr Horsley's approach towards them.

The first witness was the Home Office pathologist Dr Basil Purdue who had carried out the post-mortem and after going through the usual routine concerning the time of death he concluded that Mark Dawson had died from a massive overdose of methadone and dihydrocodeine.

When asked by the Coroner how much methadone would be required to kill a 42-year-old male he stated that it would be substantial. It was then the turn of the DS to take the stand and I have to say that the manner in which he delivered his evidence was awful. When he gave his evidence in chief he was reasonably confident, however as soon as Mr Horsley started asking him searching questions with regard to his investigation he started to stutter and became extremely flustered and basically couldn't answer most of his questions.

Margaret and Asuman then asked him a number of questions most of which again he could not answer and it was painful to watch from where I was sitting. They were simple questions concerning the investigation into the assault, the alleged burglary, the missing rings, whether the two suspects had ever been questioned, why witness statements had not been taken from the occupants of the other flats in the building, and whether or not fingerprints had been taken in the flat and in particular on those methadone bottles. The DS was unable to answer any of these questions and it was clear that Mr Horsley was as unimpressed as I was. He then halted the inquest and adjourned it to a date yet to be decided and directed the DS to go away and reinvestigate Mark Dawson's death properly.

Could it be much worse? The DS left the court in a big hurry and didn't even make eye contact with me. Mr Horsley then took time to come down from the bench and sat with Margaret, Lucie and Asuman to ask them if they had any further concerns. They then had a brief chat about a few issues before we left the court and I drove them home. They all seemed quite upbeat that at last we might get to the truth.

On September 7th the inquest was reconvened at Portsmouth Coroner's Court and this time the DS was far better prepared. However it was blatantly obvious from where I was sitting that a whitewash was taking place and at no time had the two suspects ever been spoken to which I found astonishing. The bottom line appeared to be that there was insufficient evidence to question these two men and that was basically the end of that. Mr Horsley, I think remained unconvinced as well and unusually returned an open verdict which basically means that if any further evidence was to be forthcoming then he could reopen the case. I cannot tell you how uncomfortable I felt during this process and Lucie's words will haunt me forever because I fear that she was right.

The following year Michael Bowden was sentenced to life imprisonment after being convicted of the attempted murder of his girlfriend and for arson with intent to endanger life after he set fire to the block of flats that she was living in.

I later attended Portsmouth Coroner's Court for the inquest into the death of Billy Clancy. I collected Margaret from home and we were due to meet Lucie at the court because she had travelled from her home address in Sussex. I hadn't seen her since September last year and she greeted me with a hug. I have to confess that the Coroner's Court in Portsmouth is situated in probably the worst place imaginable in that it is the last court on the right-hand side of the main corridor in the Magistrates Court building where all the scumbags and their friends meet prior to going into court. It really is the most inappropriate place for the bereaved to have to sit and listen to all the foulmouthed and offensive goings-on by those who treat the Magistrates Court as some kind of social club.

The Coroner Mr Horsley obviously recognised Margaret and Lucie from the previous two inquests that they had attended and treated them with the utmost respect. Given the circumstances of Billy's accident today's inquest was going to be little more than a formality and the verdict of accidental death was quickly reached.

As is usually the case the end of the inquest usually means my exit point from dealing with a particular family. Lucie hugged me again and thanked me for everything I had done which, considering the circumstance surrounding her brother's death, was more than I deserved. I then took Margaret home but told her to phone me if she ever came up with new evidence or just wanted a chat. Just like Lucie she thanked me most sincerely and as I watched her enter the house all I could see was a broken woman.

SHIRLEY BARTLEY

Operation STANHOE
Category B
11ᵗʰ June 2004

2004 Hampshire fatalities = 63
2004 Nationally fatalities = 3221

For some reason I seemed to get lumbered with all the probationer constables when on their two week Traffic attachment. I say lumbered but in fact most of the time I actually quite enjoyed destroying some of the preconceptions about the department that so many of them seemed to arrive with. Most thought that all we ever did was issue speeding tickets and they weren't looking forward to their attachment at all. By the time they'd completed their two weeks most of them had changed their opinions completely, plenty of them asked for an extension and several chose our department as their career path for the future. I'm not saying I'm responsible for this on my own, far from it as other officers on other Relief's were tasked with taking out the proby's allocated to them, I'm just saying that as a group it didn't take us long to educate the majority of them that there was a whole lot more to being a Traffic cop than just dishing out tickets.

There were two things I was always uneasy about when taking out a new probationer on their attachment; one was the very real dangers about policing the motorway. It is a hostile environment and a number of trainee officers have lost their lives or been seriously injured over the years because they didn't follow, or perhaps weren't instructed properly about the rules on personal safety when out of the car at motorway incidents and secondly; many of them get to see their very first fatality when on their attachment and for some it can have a profound effect upon them. The trouble is when experienced Traffic Officers attend such incidents they go into automatic pilot, they have a job to do, they need to secure evidence and start the entire investigation process. The last thing on their minds is babysitting a new probationer.

It was a warm and rather pleasant Friday morning in June and we were on early turn. I had a WPC starting her Traffic attachment with me for a few days and so I spent the first hour or so giving her my usual lecture about motorway safety together with a run down on how our motorway system works. I'm sure she thought I was some old bore but frankly I couldn't care less what she thought, I wasn't going to lose a probationer whilst they were out on attachment with me. I think we went to a couple of breakdowns and some debris in the carriageway but nothing too taxing, all very quiet for a weekday morning and we were just heading back to the office for breakfast.

Mike Control to any Mike Charlie units please for an RTA A27 westbound at the Broadmarsh off –slip, car versus pedal cycle.
Mike Charlie 01
Thank you Mike Charlie 01, now getting further reports and its looking serious

We were less than five minutes away and other units were

also traveling towards our location. The A27 is a two lane dual carriageway that basically runs along the south coast from Brighton to Southampton with the M27 taking its place on the section from Portsmouth towards Southampton. This section of the A27 travels past Havant town before heading towards Chichester. The west bound slip road where this RTA had taken place commenced just after a very slight left hand bend and had a large amount of very high foliage and trees partially obscuring the start of the off-slip. We'd had a number of accidents there over the years but never anything too serious until now.

As we passed the scene on the east bound carriageway I quickly looked over the central barrier and could see a body lying in the carriageway with a number of people standing close by with several cars parked on the grass verge. It wasn't a good sign. We shot down the off-slip to the roundabout, turned and headed back up the west bound slip road to the scene. Basically an elderly female was lying on her side about 30 feet along the entrance to the off-slip, so not on the main carriageway, more on the slip road itself. I parked the X5 right behind her to protect her and as I ran towards her I was struck by the number of people just standing there looking at her. It was quite obvious she was in a bad way and I knew an ambulance was en route. I bent down beside her and found a pulse; she was still alive. I immediately called it in as an all services, which without me needing to say anything else meant that every resource available would now be heading in my direction.

I needed to get this lady into a position where I could assess her better because the manner in which she was positioned didn't convince me that she was still alive. I checked her pulse again and couldn't feel anything. I lifted her eye lids and her pupils were very dilated. I moved her onto her back and at the same time I told my probationer to secure witness details and speak to the driver if that was him sitting on the crash barrier crying. I checked the lady's pulse again; nothing. I was joined by a young lad who asked if he could help because he'd done some first aid training.

"Does that include CPR?" I asked

"Yes" he replied.

"Good, then that's exactly what we are going to do" I said

So as I did chest compressions so this young man started doing mouth to mouth and it wasn't long before we seemed to get a response and certainly a pulse. We kept it going for about two minutes (which actually feels a lot longer than that) before the ambulance arrived and as luck would have a passing GP and they took over.

By now the rest of my office had arrived and coned off and closed the whole of the slip road to protect everyone there and to preserve the scene. There were several emergency service vehicles now parked behind my car all with their blue lights in operation so we were well protected. The ambulance crew quickly picked the lady up with the doctor still performing CPR on her and whisked her off to QA. There was a pedal cycle lying on the nearside grass verge and it was quickly ascertained that the lady had been cycling west along the A27 and as she was cycling past the slip road so a car exiting the main carriageway clipped her side and she had fallen off. There was some debate as to whether or not she had then been run over by another vehicle because there was quite a large amount of blood on the carriageway.

I heard one of my colleagues shouting about a car. To my amazement I saw not one but two cars had actually come through the line of cones from the main carriageway so that they could use the slip road. One of them drove straight through the puddle of blood. I was livid; I couldn't believe they could be so bloody stupid. As the cars drove up the slip road I threw my clip board at the last car but it missed. I screamed all sorts of obscenities at them. Then I turned around to be confronted by the front bumper of another car that had also come through the cones and had now stopped behind me. In hindsight I think I was rather calm, all things considered;

"And what do you think you are doing sir?" I asked as I put my head in through the open driver's side window to be confronted by a couple in their 60s.

"Well I need to come off the main road here to go up the slip road" he said rather meekly.

"It may have escaped your notice but you have just driven past a sea of emergency service vehicles, all with their blue lights on, then a couple of 'Road Closed' signs before somehow managing to squeeze your car in through those cones over there and into the middle of a crime scene". I said through gritted teeth.

"Sorry I didn't realise" came his pathetic reply.

"Well what did you think this was all for then?" I asked.

"Well I don't know really"

I then gave him very specific instructions to reverse his car a few feet and then I'd remove a couple of the cones so that when it was safe for him to do so I'd direct him back out onto the main carriageway. Did he understand? Yes, he understood.

So he started to reverse and I rather foolishly then diverted my eyes away from him as I bent down to pick up one of the cones only to hear a hideous metallic crunching noise. He'd reversed straight into the front of my patrol car.

"What the hell are you doing?" I shouted.

"Well you didn't tell me to stop" he said accusingly.

"Would you like me to drive the bloody thing for you as well then?" I shouted back.

Luckily there was no damage to either car and one of my colleagues then took over guiding our blind motorist away from the scene before I throttled him. People like him are why officers like me have to lecture the probationers that come on their Traffic attachments.

The car driver was in a bad way, almost hysterical. He needed medical treatment and so it was decided that I would take him up to QA rather than tie up the services of another ambulance, where I would hand him over to another Traffic officer who was already up there so that he could take his first account statement, whilst I then resumed my role as the FLO and try to ascertain who our lady was. I met the other officer as arranged and he said that at the moment the lady was still alive but very poorly in Room 1.

I entered the room with my probationer and it was a hive of activity. The medical people were still working on her but it didn't look too hopeful and just before 11am the Registrar pronounced her dead. The nursing staff handed me quite a lot of property including a mobile phone (which had several missed calls on it, all from the same number), some cash and an AA route finder printout of the south coast. But there was no handbag, no purse and more importantly no ID. I called up on the radio and asked those at the scene to do a thorough search of the immediate vicinity to see if there was a bag or purse there. Whilst we were waiting for them to get back to us so I was approached by the A&E receptionist to say that she had just taken a phone call from a receptionist at the Portsmouth Sixth Form College to say that they had an elderly gent with them who was a stranger to the area and he was asking if there had been any RTAs this morning involving a female cyclist. It was too big a coincidence so we said we'd be there in 10 minutes.

We got to the college and found the gent sitting in the foyer. He said his wife was taking part in a round Britain charity bike ride on behalf of Child Line and that she had missed their designated rendezvous point and he couldn't raise her on the mobile. I asked him to describe his wife, what she was wearing and her bike. Finally I asked him what his phone number was and it was the same number that I'd found on her phone. He kept asking me if she'd had an accident and did I know anything. I told him the awful truth and he became very distraught. His name was Jim Bartley and his wife was Shirley and they were from Rainham in Essex. They'd been married for almost 50 years.

After five minutes or so he asked if he could go and see her and at the same time said that he needed to get in touch with his son and daughter. I said that once we had established that it was Shirley at the hospital then I would help him all I could to make any arrangements necessary.

We arrived at QA just after midday and I sat Jim in the relative's room whilst I spoke to the medical staff to arrange for Jim to see Shirley. They had placed her in the side room opposite and I popped in there to make sure it was her and not somebody else, made sure the blinds were shut and that there was a chair there for him to sit on if he needed to. I went back across the corridor and asked Jim if he was ready for this. He took a deep breath and nodded. We entered the room and Jim confirmed that it was Shirley. I left them in private and went back to the relative's room to make us a cup of tea.

He was in there for quite a while which is understandable and when he came out said he needed to talk to his son Chris. He phoned him from the relative's room and broke the news to him before breaking down and sobbing. It's often the case that until someone actually starts to tell other people what's happened they remain in relative control but once they start talking to others about it then the flood gates open. I then spoke to Chris to give him directions to the QA and he said he'd get there as soon as he could but that might be over two hours depending on the traffic on the M25.

We sat down and Jim started to talk about Shirley's charity bike ride. At the age of 69 Shirley intended to cycle some 3000 miles starting from Gravesend in Kent, along the south coast to Penzance then up into Wales, up the west coast, then across the top of England from Carlisle to Sunderland before dropping back south along the east coast to home. I couldn't have done that even at my fittest let alone at the age of almost 70. Sadly this was only the sixth day out of a planned schedule of almost 60 days of cycling. Jim's job was to be her back-up man, to drive ahead to various business venues armed with a stack of leaflets to help publicise the event in an effort to raise further funds and to sort out their accommodation at the end of each day. He was immensely proud of her and it transpired this wasn't the first time she had undertaken such a ride. She'd done a similar 4000 mile trek a few years ago.

After a while I introduced my role to him and said there were a few things I needed to go through including the G28 form, ID statement etc. which we did without any fuss. But then we got onto the thorny issue of the press and I outlined the usual options to him. To my complete surprise he said he wanted as much publicity and press interest as possible because that's what Shirley would have wanted. Jim said that they wanted to high light the plight of children who needed to contact Child Line and so any publicity about it, even in death was a positive thing and so he was quite prepared to talk to as many journalists as I could muster. It actually helped perk him up quite a bit and gave him something positive to think about. I said I'd help out all I could.

Chris Bartley arrived just after 3pm and after paying a visit to his mother we sat down and I went through the circumstances again. We sorted out a few logistical issues bearing in mind that they weren't exactly local and then Chris and I drove back to the college to collect Jim's car. By the time we'd sorted all that out it was gone 5.30 pm and I then bid Jim goodbye. He was quite a character.

I got back to the office and phoned Sarah Hill at Child Line, a contact that Jim had given to me. She knew about Shirley's cycle ride and so I had to tell her the tragic news. She was very upset but said she understood Jims request for maximum publicity and said she'd get their media people to contact me. Within five minutes I got a call back from them and they said they would do all they could to help out and would contact Jim tomorrow. I then turned my attention to the Portsmouth News but none of my usual contacts were answering their phones so I spoke to the news desk and gave them everything they could possibly need.

The next day it got a full page article including quotes from Esther Ranson, Child Lines founder and Chairperson and by Tuesday the following week another full page item with a lengthy interview with Jim and lots of information about Child Line itself. My contacts at The News also promised that they would ensure that the local papers in the Rainham area were also briefed.

Because Jim lived so far away all my contact with him thereafter was either by phone or letter. It wasn't the best way of staying in touch and trying to help but he had his family around him and I think that was all he needed really.

In the end the driver pleaded guilty to careless driving and the inquest verdict was accidental death.

JAMES ALABASTER

Operation CHESTNUT
Category B
5th May 2005

2005 Hampshire fatalities = 90
2005 Nationally fatalities = 3200

It was an early summers evening and we were all sat in the office busily catching up on paperwork. My Relief at this time consisted of some of the best officers I had ever worked with in my career, all totally dedicated, thoroughly professional and good friends to boot. We socialised together and there were always wind-ups going on. There was a major piss taking session going on when my mobile

rang. They all knew that if my phone rang it was invariably a family I was currently dealing with and so they instantly shut up and kept quiet. Except it wasn't one of my families ringing, it was my eldest daughter Kelly and she sounded quite distressed.

"Do you know about this accident on the Eastern Road?"

she asked.

"No," I replied, looking down at my radio to make sure it was switched on.

"It's right by the golf course, two motor bikes have collided and I think they are both dead, Dad it looks awful." I could hear the panic in her voice and I said we'd be there as quickly as possible.

The office emptied in seconds as myself and two other patrol cars headed towards the Eastern Road some two miles away. As we did so I updated Charlie-One and within seconds they said they were getting several reports about it including one that stated the bikes were on fire.

The A2030 Eastern Road is one of three arterial routes into and out of Portsmouth and as the name suggests it runs up the eastern side of Portsea Island and joins the A27 and M27. It's a very busy dual carriageway and I'd attended countless fatal and serious RTA's on it over the years.

The crash had occurred on the north bound carriageway between the junctions of Tangier Road and Burrfields Road. As we approached from the north it looked like a scene from one of those disaster movies. On the corner of Burrfields Road is a Texaco petrol station and about 20 yards south of that was a large capacity Yamaha motorcycle laying on its side in a ball of fire, the flames from which were 10 feet high. Another 75 yards further south one of the bikers was laying on his back with blood pouring from a head wound and people doing CPR on him. Another 50 yards further south was the other biker with other people working on him. The second bike, an Aprilia 998 was lying beside the central barrier and a few yards further south two lanes of stationary traffic were now desperately trying to get out of the way of an ambulance that was attending the scene.

I drove past the bike that was on fire and headed south along the north bound carriageway and stopped a short distance away from the first casualty. Amongst the crowd around him was my daughter and she ran over towards me. After ascertaining that she was OK and not physically involved in the crash she said that she had been driving north up the Eastern Road in her yellow Citroen Saxo when a large group of bikes overtook her. She was at pains to point out that they weren't travelling fast or being stupid. The group of bikes and all the traffic behind them then stopped at the red lights at the Tangier Road junction. After the lights went green she moved off and as she came around the slight left hand bend only a few seconds later the crash had already occurred but she didn't see how it happened. I told her to go back to her car and move it just in case it was in the way of any other emergency service vehicles. I told that a fire engine arrived behind us to deal with the motorcycle that was on fire.

As the paramedics got to work on both casualties I have to say it didn't look good and we called it in as an all services incident. And sadly we were right and although the ambulance crews continued working on both men they were both declared dead upon arrival at the QA.

Whilst all this was going on I'd noticed a group of bikers standing on the embankment on the other side of the road. I ran over to them and it transpired that this was the remainder of the group and amongst them was a face I recognised. His name was Del Morton and he was one of Boarhunts recovery truck drivers. Both he and the others were in a state of shock and clearly upset that two of their group were in a serious way. Del then gave me a brief outline about what had happened. He said that they had ridden from the burger van up on Portsdown Hill down into the city and along Southsea seafront and were now making their way back up the Eastern Road towards Portsdown Hill again. When they pulled away from the lights one bike was in the outside lane and a car, which he thinks had just come out of Tangier Road, was going really slowly and the bike behind it swerved to avoid hitting it and instead hit the other bike sending them both crashing into the central barrier. Between them they gave me the biker's names as Jim Alabaster (who'd been in the outside lane) and Ricky Peacock, whom they said was in the Navy and they didn't really know him, he'd just tagged along for the ride.

Within the hour I had been appointed as the FLO for Jim Alabaster and after ascertaining all the usual checks and details I found myself heading towards Malvern Road in Southsea to trace his next of kin. It goes without saying that I got no reply from this address and after doing a few more checks I then travelled to an address in Glenthorne Road in Copnor. Again I got no reply but after knocking on the neighbour's door I was given a mobile phone number for Jim's girlfriend Sarah. I rang the number and Sarah answered the phone. I introduced myself and told her that I needed to come and see her personally but she didn't believe who I was. That's understandable I suppose in this day and age and it took me some while to convince her that I was genuine but only on the understanding that I arrived outside her house in a fully marked police car with the blue lights on. She stated quite clearly that if I didn't she wouldn't answer the door.

Within 10 minutes I was at the address in Paddington Road, North End. As requested I stopped outside the house with the blue lights on and waited for her to make an appearance at the window.

Once she had acknowledged me I parked the car and knocked on the door. I entered the house to be greeted by Sarah and her young daughter and we all sat in the front room. I have to confess that I wasn't happy about breaking the worst news in the world to Sarah with her daughter in the same room but by now I think she'd guessed that my visit wasn't exactly a social call and that perhaps she was relying on her daughter as some sort of security blanket. If she was happy for her to stay then who was I to argue with her.

I broke the news to her and she sat there in silence. She

lit a cigarette and sat back in the chair. Her immediate concern was not for herself but for Jim's family, he had an ex-wife and two children to be told plus his mother and brother. Within 10 minutes Sarah and I were in the patrol car and heading the short distance to Mayfield Road to inform James's ex-wife Cher. This obviously wasn't going to be easy for Sarah or Cher to contend with but it had to be done. Cher answered the door and saw us both standing there and she knew immediately. Thankfully neither her 15-year-old son nor 13-year-old daughter was in the house and it was agreed that breaking the news of their father's death would be left for her to deal with. Both women were starting to ask questions about whether it was really Jim or somebody else that might have been riding his bike and the obvious next stage was to do the ID at the mortuary and so I made various phone calls in order for that to be facilitated as soon as possible. Sarah and Cher agreed that Sarah would do the ID and then phone Cher immediately from the hospital.

By the time Sarah and I got to the mortuary it was 11:30 and I have to say the mortuary staff had done a fantastic job in preparing Jim so quickly. Sarah made a positive ID and despite her own personal feelings was on the phone to Cher within a couple of minutes which was incredibly brave of her. As if that wasn't bad enough we now had to drive 12 miles north to Petersfield to notify Jim's mother. Sarah was understandably very nervous about this especially given the fact that she'd only met Jim's mother twice in the three years that they had been together. En route Sarah started telling me about Jim. He was a very talented artist by all accounts and was also a part time lecturer at Portsmouth University which is where they had met as Sarah also lectured there. He loved his bikes and whenever he got the opportunity he would get out and ride.

We arrived in Borough Road, Petersfield just after

midnight. The house was a bungalow set amongst several other nice looking properties on a small estate. Jim's mother answered the door in her dressing gown, took one look at Sarah with me stood behind her and clasped her hands across her face.

"I'm so sorry Marion," said Sarah with tears now streaming down her face.

"Not that bloody motorbike," said Marion "Is he….is he…."

Sarah just nodded her head as Marion let out the most horrendous scream. As we stood in the doorway she just screamed and screamed and screamed. It was so loud that half the estate must have heard and would have probably called the police had they not seen my patrol car already parked outside the house. I ushered them both inside and shut the door.

We ended up in the lounge where Marion just continued to scream and scream. Sarah tried to calm her down but to no avail, Marion just kept screaming. Sarah looked at me with pleading in her eyes. She barely knew Marion and felt as helpless as I was useless right now. Marion continued her screaming for a full 10 minutes before Sarah finally managed to settle her down in a chair whilst I found the kitchen and put the kettle on.

Once things had calmed down a little Marion wanted her other son Rupert to be here. The trouble was he lived in Croydon and eventually Marion plucked up the courage to phone him. He said he'd be there in just over an hour and Sarah volunteered to stay with Marion until he arrived. In the meantime I took Sarah's daughter, who had been sitting outside in the patrol car during all this, back to their home address in Portsmouth and agreed with Sarah that once Rupert had arrived she would give me a call and I would come and collect her.

It was 3:15 am by the time Sarah called and after having a

brief chat with Rupert about the circumstances of the crash I took her home and after updating my FLO log, booked off duty at 4:30 am.

I was back in the office by 9 am and by lunchtime had met up with Rupert, Marion and Sarah to go through the formalities of the G28 and the press release which Rupert said he would have ready by mid-afternoon. Their biggest concern centred on Jim's mobile phone because many of the people they needed to contact to notify them of his death were contained on that phone. We agreed to meet again in a couple of hours by which time I would have located the phone and they would have completed their family statement.

Upon my return the family gave me a nice photo of Jim together with the family statement which read;

Jim was a charismatic man full of life and fun. His talents were endless, ranging from being the most gifted artist and writer to an accomplished businessman. He made friends easily and many will be saddened by his premature passing. He was the most wonderful father to his two children a son aged 15 and daughter aged 13.

Some families require a lot of help from their FLO, others much less so and it was more than two weeks after going through all the formalities before I heard from Sarah again.

The biking community in Portsmouth wanted to stage a tribute convoy to the two motorcyclists taking in the route they would have ridden on that fateful evening and would I or the police in general be willing to escort a large number of bikes on such a ride? I personally couldn't see a problem with this however in the back of my mind something was telling me that I would need to seek some sort of permission for this to take place and my suspicions were correct in that the police could not officially sanction such a ride under police escort just in case something went wrong. You can imagine the finger-pointing that would be done by certain sections of the media or by ill-informed local politicians who would have a field day. I was told in no uncertain terms that I would not be allowed to escort this convoy but if I happen to be in the area at the time then for safety's sake it might be a good idea if I tagged along at the back!

I agreed to meet Sarah at the Viewpoint car park on top of Portsdown Hill which was the meeting place for many bikers and car enthusiasts alike. This large car park overlooks the whole of Portsmouth city, the Solent and the Isle of Wight and offers unparalleled views both day and night and is a unique vantage point for anybody wishing to just sit and admire the view.

As I entered the car park I was staggered at the sheer number of motorcycles that had gathered there to partake in this convoy, there must have been over 150 bikes and a few more followed in behind me. Despite being a motorcyclist of many years standing myself I have to confess that I was somewhat nervous about the reception that I might receive from some of the bikers gathered there. The relationship between some bikers and the police isn't always favourable and I was acutely aware of this.

As I got out of the car I saw Sarah walking towards me and as I shut the door she gave me a big hug and thanked me so much for coming. I then saw Del Morton who shook me by the hand and who thankfully didn't give me a big hug! I think their greetings towards me reassured many of the other bikers there that maybe I was actually okay. However I needed to lay down some ground rules about this tribute ride and so I climbed upon a two foot high concrete bunker and beckoned them all to gather around me. I felt like Field Marshal Montgomery rallying his troops before entering battle.

Sarah came with me in the patrol car as we followed this huge group of motorcycles slowly down Portsdown Hill into the city and along Southsea seafront before heading north back up the Eastern Road to the scene of the accident some two weeks previously. It was a very impressive sight and Sarah took several photographs of the convoy as it weaved its way slowly through the city. The entire convoy stopped at the crash scene blocking the whole of lane one of the two lane carriageway. It was at this point that I got out of the patrol car and stood behind it waving my arms and directing traffic past the scene whilst Sarah joined the other bikers in holding a two-minute silence. The bikers' behaviour was impeccable and the tribute they paid towards their two friends was a very moving experience and it was my privilege to assist them in doing so.

This was to be my last contact with Sarah and the rest of the family for almost a year. As I said previously some families require very little intervention by their FLO once the initial formalities are over and this was certainly the case concerning the Alabaster family. Little did I know at this time just how difficult things were to become when we arrived at the inquest.

PC Bob Boggs who was the SIO wanted to meet the family to discuss the findings of the police investigation prior to the inquest in a couple of weeks' time. There is nothing worse for a family than to find out certain facts about the case at a public hearing and it is only right that they should be informed of all the facts prior to everybody else knowing them.

I spoke to Sarah and after consulting the rest of the family it was agreed for various reasons that it would be better if Bob Boggs and I visited her and outlined the case and she could then relay that information back to the rest of the family prior to the inquest. The biggest issue and the item most likely to cause upset was the CCTV video evidence which actually showed the collision taking place. This somewhat distant and blurred image would obviously be played to the Coroner at the inquest and much of our concern was geared towards the families that would be attending and we needed to give them the opportunity to watch it first in private with us so that they were fully aware of the impact such video footage might have upon them.

Sarah declined to watch the video and felt certain that the rest of the family wouldn't want to watch it either and I reassured her that come the time that video evidence was to be played at the inquest that both she and the family would be given time to leave the court until the footage was over.

Sarah's biggest concern was the inquest itself and she seemed somewhat worried about the formality of it all and so I reassured her that the Coroner Mr David Horsley was brilliant with the relatives of the deceased. I told her that at the beginning of every inquest he would address the family's personally and tell them that this inquest was for them and that they could ask questions of witnesses and that it was his aim that those families didn't leave his inquest with more questions than answers. This seemed to reassure Sarah and she said she would pass on what I'd said to the rest of the family.

On 27th April 2006 I met Sarah and Rupert outside Portsmouth Guildhall. The Coroners Court is usually held inside Portsmouth Magistrates Court but at this time the courts were being refurbished and so all inquests were currently being held in room 2 inside the Guildhall. I met Mary Hopes the Coroners Officer outside the court and she reassured Sarah and Rupert about the formalities that were to follow. As we waited in the corridor outside so a large number of other people started to arrive including Ricky Peacock's family, various witnesses, the press and some of the bikers. In all there must have been over 50 people there which for any inquest is a large number. I hadn't been into room 2 at the Guildhall before and as we entered I was somewhat shocked at how small it was. It was a typically grand Court like room with large solid oak tables along the two edges of the room with the top table reserved for the Coroner himself. In front of his table were a number of other tables reserved for the press, lawyers and other legal beagle's to reside at. At the far end of the room just by the door was a large video and TV screen set up ready to show that CCTV footage.

Mary showed us to our allocated seats and we were basically sat adjacent to the Coroner and were almost close enough to touch him. There was so little room that I had to find another chair and sit behind Sarah and Rupert with my back firmly planted against the wall. I was somewhat surprised when Ricky Peacock's family were ushered in and sat right next to Rupert with one of the males from the family sat directly behind him. Immediately there was an atmosphere of hostility in the room even though nobody had said anything. By the time the witnesses, the press and all the legal people were seated you could barely move in that room and with the lack of air conditioning or any form of ventilation it quickly made everybody feel very uncomfortable.

The inquest was due to start at 1030. However by 1045 Mr Horsley had not arrived and this only added to the tense atmosphere. I kept looking at Mary and she basically just kept shrugging her shoulders because she had no idea where he was or why he was late. Then five minutes later she asked the court to stand as Mr Horsley resplendent in his black robes entered the room. He beckoned to us to sit and then formally opened the inquest into the deaths of James Alabaster and Richard Peacock. Now I've attended a fair number of inquests in front of Mr Horsley and without exception he has always followed the same routine in that he would ask everybody who they were in relation to the deceased, who the legal representatives were and who they were representing. So I was somewhat surprised when he didn't do this and even more surprised when he didn't distinguish who the two families were and who represented each estate. He did however state in general terms that members of the families could ask questions of witnesses if they so wished although he didn't lay down the usual ground rules to that effect.

And so we started with witnesses to the accident who gave verbal evidence and this was followed shortly thereafter by the showing of the CCTV video. To my horror Mr Horsley instructed Bob Boggs to commence the video footage without first giving the families and other people present the opportunity to leave the room. In fact it was Mary who intervened and suggested to Mr Horsley that there may well be people in the room who might not want to watch the video. He seemed somewhat irritated by this but agreed to allow those people who wished to leave the room to do so. Several people including Sarah then left the room and Mr Horsley then instructed Bob Boggs to play the video not once but several times. The footage was taken from a CCTV camera some 200 yards from the crash scene and it basically just showed a blur that was the two bikes colliding with the central barrier, a huge cloud of dust followed by the two bikes sliding down the road before one of them burst into flames. It wouldn't have mattered if you'd watched it 100 times or more you still wouldn't have been able to decipher exactly how this accident happened because the images were too blurred. After those present were satisfied that they'd seen enough Mr Horsley asked the others to return to the room and we continued with the evidence of the crash investigation unit and the officer in the case.

Mr Horsley then read out a couple of witness statements one of which was from one of the motorcyclists from the group that James Alabaster had been riding with. Rupert then lent forward and politely asked Mr Horsley why that witness had not been brought to the inquest to give his evidence in person, which, given the evidence that was in the statement seemed to be a perfectly reasonable request. Neither Rupert or I or anybody else in that court room expected the response that we then received.

Mr Horsley exploded and shouted at Rupert "How dare you interrupt me, who do you think you are, you aren't here to ask me questions, who are you anyway?"

"I'm James Alabaster's brother" replied Rupert.

"You do not question me, it is for me to decide who I call to give evidence, not you" snarled Mr Horsley.

I couldn't believe what I'd just heard and neither could anybody else in the court room. In my 28 years as a police officer I had never heard a Coroner speak to anybody let alone a family member of the deceased in that manner and I was appalled. And it was just so unnecessary. For a start if Mr Horsley had done his usual at the beginning of the inquest he would have known that Rupert was Jim's brother. Mr Horsley then decided that now was a good time to adjourn for lunch and he stormed out of the room.

I ushered Sarah and Rupert out into the corridor where I met Mary and Bob who were as astonished by Mr Horsley's outburst as I was. I apologised to Sarah because all of the reassurances I had given her prior to the inquest had just been completely blown out of the water and I was somewhat embarrassed because of it. Rupert was incredibly angry and who could blame him. He wasn't a stupid man and was an astute businessman who worked in London and he certainly wasn't expecting the reaction he got from the Coroner for asking a simple question. Mary went back to the office whilst the rest of us went for lunch.

After we reconvened it was time for Mr Horsley to sum up the evidence and reach his verdict. However during his summing up Mr Horsley misrepresented a key fact in the evidence in that he stated that Ricky Peacock was an experienced motorcyclist in the same vein that Jim Alabaster was. This was clearly not the case as Ricky Peacock had been a provisional licence holder for only four months prior to the crash and had leapt from a learner motorcycle onto a 1000cc Yamaha. The crash was clearly his fault because he had pulled out from behind a slow-moving car directly into Jim's bike causing them both to collide with the central crash barrier. Sarah and Rupert were clearly upset by Mr Horsley's inaccurate portrayal of the facts but were simply too frightened to question him at this point. The verdict was always going to be accidental death but in denying the Alabaster family the opportunity to ask the questions they wanted to ask, Mr Horsley broke his own golden rule in that they left his inquest with more questions than answers.

In the days that followed I had a number of conversations with Sarah and Rupert and they were clearly very upset by the whole inquest procedure. They sought my advice on making an official complaint about Mr Horsley and I said that I would support them in any way I could.

I spoke to Mary Hopes on a number of occasions about this inquest and she was as upset about it as the rest of us and stated that she would assist us as best she could in finding out the correct procedures to enable us to make a formal complaint. I've never made a complaint against a Coroner before and could not recall anybody else having to do so either, so it was difficult trying to find out what the procedure was and who to get the best advice from. It transpired that the complaint had to be made to the Home Office in the form of statements from Sarah, Rupert and myself, together with written transcripts taken from the tape recordings of the court proceedings.

In particular we wanted copies of the recordings that are always made in court because it wasn't so much what he said but more the aggressive manner in which he said it. This proved to be very difficult in fact nigh on impossible because the recordings were made on a double speed tape machine so you can't just copy it onto another tape. It therefore needed to be sent away to London to be transcribed at a cost per word and at a rough guess would cost approximately £50 per hour of actual talking in court, so a good £150 - £200.

I got back to Sarah and she wasn't keen to spend that sort of money when all it was going to do was state what words were used and as we all kept saying it wasn't quite so much what he said but the unacceptable manner in which he said it. So for the time being she would write a formal letter of complaint and enclose a similar letter from Rupert direct to Mr Horsley first and see what result that brings.

A few weeks later I was back at Portsmouth Coroners Court for the inquest of Billy Clancy. As we were leaving Mr Horsley asked me to come and join him in his chambers at the back of the court. He shut the door behind him and what followed was the most bizarre meeting I think I have ever had with anybody during my time as a police officer.

He started asking me questions about the debacle that was the inquest into James Alabaster and Ricky Peacock and that he hoped one of *his* police officers, i.e. me, would not be supporting any formal complaint about the manner in which he had conducted his inquest. He went on to suggest that he had been badly let down by his Coroners Officer who had shown a remarkable degree of disrespect towards him.

I couldn't believe what I was hearing. Here was one of the most powerful men in the country telling me in no uncertain terms not to assist a family that I had been looking after for some considerable time in making a formal complaint against him. In his opinion the complaint was completely unjustified and he warned me that if I became involved then there could be consequences for me in my career. This was a direct threat towards me and was beneath contempt. I said very little during all this, partly because I was completely dumbfounded, but mainly because I didn't want to become embroiled in a heated argument with him especially as I had my suspicions that the conversation may have been tape-recorded. However I couldn't just stand there and say nothing;

"Mr Horsley I have to say that I'm more than a little surprised that we are even having this conversation but as we are I have to remind you of a couple of things. Firstly I am not one of *your* police officers. I answer only to the Chief Constable and secondly my focus will always be on the family that I am assisting and if that means helping them lodge a complaint about you or anybody else then that is my duty and I will fulfil it to the best of my ability. I will be making a full pocket book entry of this meeting".

I couldn't get out of that room quick enough and virtually ran back out through the court and into the corridor where I met Margaret and Lucie. I went back to the office fuming. I wrote several pages in my pocket note book detailing my meeting with Mr Horsley. I then had a long talk with Chief Inspector Howard Marrs who did his best to calm me down a bit.

A few days later I hit the roof again when I found out that Mr Horsley had sacked Mary Hopes! Why? What the hell did she do wrong? It transpired he got wind of the fact that she was helping me obtain the correct procedure for making that complaint. All the poor woman was doing was answering the questions I put to her on the phone but he saw that as a direct threat to his authority. He also blamed her for the atmosphere at the Alabaster/Peacock inquest. In truth he couldn't actually sack her because she was a serving WPC and not one of his officers as he had so arrogantly labelled me as. He apparently phoned the Chief Superintendent demanding she be sacked but he was no fool and sent the HR Director straight down to the Coroner's Office where Mary was promptly removed from her post and reassigned to a new position, thus not giving Mr Horsley the satisfaction of actually chucking her out of his office.

Sarah and Rupert submitted their letter of complaint to the Home Office and received acknowledgement that it was being investigated but they didn't hear anything further after that, which is just not acceptable.

JENNIFER NETTLETON

Operation **BELLEFONTE**
Category **C**
20th June 2005

2005 Hampshire fatalities = 90
2005 Nationally fatalities = 3200

Early turn invariably knocks me for six. I've never been a morning person and by the time I've completed three or four earlies I'm like a bear with a sore head, or two sore heads if I've had a disturbed night. Being an FLO meant that I was placed on the call-out rota which meant that for an entire week I  could expect to be the first call-out for any fatal anywhere in Hampshire and for the following two weeks I would be second and third call out respectively. That meant keeping my mobile switched on beside the bed all night and more importantly no alcohol during call out weeks! For the privilege of being kept on a short leash the FLO receives no monetary or time off in lieu compensation, it's all done for the love of the job. To be fair I didn't get as many call outs as some other FLO's seemed to for which I was very grateful, but even so when that phone goes off in the early hours.......oh god its painful.

I'd just completed my fourth early turn and I was shattered. I went to bed just after the news had finished and was asleep before my head had even touched the pillow. My ability to do this has always annoyed my wife especially if I start snoring, which of course I have always denied.

It was just after 2am when the phone rang. I had to get the control room operator to repeat what she'd said at least three times before I could comprehend it all. But basically I needed to get the 3am car ferry to the Isle of Wight because there had been a fatal on the south side of the island and they needed an FLO. I fumbled around in the dark looking for my uniform, had the briefest of shaves and ran downstairs as quick as I dare. By the time I got to the nick it was already 2.30 and as I gathered my kit together, grabbed a radio and a set of car keys my mobile rang again. It was the control room stating that I would be met the other side of the water by a local unit who would guide me to the scene, which was on a fairly narrow road above the cliffs between Ventnor and Whitwell; in fact the car had left the road and was perched in a tree over hanging the cliff. I found the spare travel warrant that we kept in our office for just such an occasion and then drove to the ferry port to catch the 3am ferry. I just made it.

The ferry was full of postal vans and goods lorry drivers all making their way across to the island as I suspect they do every morning. As I sat there drinking my first cup of tea I tuned into the local island channel on the radio to listen to the updates on the crash. It was remarkably quiet, but then I suppose in comparison with the mainland area where many of the roads are arterial routes the location of this one meant that it wasn't going to affect too many people at that time of night.

The ferry docked at Fishbourne at 3.45 and, sure enough, there was a local section car waiting for me to follow him down towards Ventnor. He took the pretty route down through all the country lanes bedecked with their high hedgerows and uneven road surface. Suddenly he swerved to the left and then the right. The road was awash with rabbits, bloody dozens of the things. They scattered like cock roaches in all directions, but some of them didn't make it and both the section car and me ran over quite a few of them. I felt terrible.

We arrived at the scene about 20 minutes later. It was a medium sized country road that ran parallel with the sea on the south side of the island. On one side of the road was a high hedge and on the other a sort of grass verge area about twenty feet wide that met an area of woodland that formed the upper slopes of the cliffs, so not actually a sheer drop but not one you'd choose to walk that close to. I met the local Traffic crew who led me across the grass to the only car involved, a bright yellow Jordan Honda Civic that had collided head-on with one the trees. The young lady driver had been pronounced dead at the scene and was still in the car. I got into the car with her to check and log personal items like jewellery and other possessions so that when the time came for them to be returned to the family I could be certain that everything was there. It was a bit precarious getting in and out of the car because I wasn't entirely sure that it was completely secure, given its final resting place and I'm sure the health and safety police would have given me a right dressing down if they'd ever found out.

It appeared at this stage to be a single vehicle RTA, there was no evidence to suggest otherwise. There was a single tyre mark on the road but little evidence at this stage to prove that it was left by the victim's car either. There had been some confusion over the location of the crash because the lady who first called 999 had done so after she got home a few miles away having seen the cars tail lights in the undergrowth as she past by. However the first police unit dispatched to the area couldn't locate the scene and so eventually the lady was collected from home by the police and after some considerable time the Honda was located.

The local Sergeant said he knew her family very well and that her name was Jennifer Nettleton aged 18, making her just a year younger than my eldest daughter. A shudder went down my spine. He said he'd take me to their house as soon as I was ready.

We drove another five minutes along the road to the village of St. Lawrence where the Nettleton's ran the local post office, which was adjacent to their house. We parked in a lane at the side of the building and he showed me to a side pedestrian access gate that led to the door of the house via the garden.

"I'll leave you to it then Steve, rather you than me mate" he said, shutting the gate behind me, sort of trapping me inside the garden.

"Are you not coming in then? I thought you might as you know the family" I asked, hinting that it might help me a bit.

"You must be joking," he whispered back. "I've never liked delivering death messages, I leave that sort of thing to experts like you."With that he beat a hasty retreat back towards his car.

It was just getting light as I made my way across the dew laden lawn. Except for the dawn chorus of a manic Blackbird you could hear a pin drop it was so quiet. As I made my way across the garden towards the house the long short walk had never felt so lonely. I knocked on the door and then took a few steps backwards so that if anyone looked out of the upstairs windows they would be able to see me. I heard a dog barking and within seconds a man looked out from one of the windows. I beckoned him to open the door and within a few seconds the interior lights came on and Mr. Nettleton answered the door. He invited me in and I asked him if his wife was here because I needed to speak to both of them. He disappeared back upstairs and I stood at the lounge window taking in a quite magnificent view of The Channel with a couple of big oil tankers cruising by on the horizon. The tranquillity of the place wasn't lost on me nor the fact that I was about to shatter it.

Mr. and Mrs. Nettleton came downstairs. He sat on the settee with the dog at his feet whilst Mrs Nettleton stood in the doorway. I broke the terrible news to them. Mrs Nettleton shot upstairs whilst Mr Nettleton sat there in complete silence for about five minutes. Mrs Nettleton then returned to the lounge, bleary eyed and sat next to her husband. There were no questions, no tears, nothing. Then Mr. Nettleton stood up.

"Well I suppose I'd better go and open up the shop then" he blurted out.

"What?" said his wife.

"Its nearly 6 o'clock love, they'll all be in for their morning papers in a minute, you know what they're like," he replied.

"For God's sake Doug, this policeman has just told you that our daughter is dead," snapped Janet. "We can't open at all today, they can all get stuffed".

"Yes but you know what they are like, they won't understand or care, all they'll want is their papers"

Doug felt he needed to do something constructive to take his mind off the dreadful news and so it was decided that he would go into the shop to cancel the paper and milk delivery for the day. I told them that the shop and the post office would have to remain closed for at least today and that if necessary the locals could come and talk to me about it and that I'd quite happily tell them where to stick their morning paper.

As Doug went into the shop so Janet and I sat and chatted for a bit about the Island as I had lived there for a few years as a youngster. Doug returned a while later and said that he had spoken to both the delivery men who had shaken him by the hand and expressed their sorrow. But he couldn't continue to do that with everyone who came to the shop because we had things that needed doing and so having ascertained they had a computer and printer, I typed out a note that stated the post office would be shut until further notice and taped one to the door and another to the sandwich board outside. I then parked the patrol car right next to it as some kind of hint that something out of the ordinary might have occurred.

As I got out of the car I saw one of the locals, an elderly male with a walking stick rattling the door of the post office. I told him it was shut until further notice and then explained that he would have to get his paper elsewhere. He looked completely bewildered, I do mean completely. Here I was standing between two human beings; one had just been told his daughter was dead and the other that he wouldn't be getting his copy of the Daily Mail this morning. It was difficult to determine quite who was the more bereft.

I went back into the house to tell Janet and Doug what my role as their FLO was going to be and how I would help them as best I could to get them through the next few days and months.

Once we had gone through some other formalities Janet suddenly became concerned about their two other daughters Sandra and Helen. It transpired that Helen only got married on Saturday up in Coventry and obviously the entire family was at the wedding with Jenny acting as one of the bridesmaids. As if that wasn't bad enough Helen and her new husband, George, had jetted off to Canada on Monday afternoon less than 24 hours ago and she obviously needed telling about her sister's death. However Helen made it quite clear to her family and friends at the wedding that apart from actually going to Canada she had little idea of what they were doing when they got there. This included not knowing which hotel they were going to be staying in and what their travel arrangements were for their big tour of Canada. It was all to remain a big secret, partly because Helen and her husband did not want to receive any phone calls from work, friends or family asking them how they were getting on. It was all a bit of a joke really and they were determined to keep their privacy but on this occasion it had backfired badly. Doug said he'd make some phone calls to his son-in-law's family to see if they had any idea where the couple might be staying. They also needed to go and see Sandra to tell her and to make other phone calls to friends and other relatives and at this point I decided to leave them to it and said that as soon as the mortuary at St Mary's Hospital were ready to do the ID then I'd come back and collect them and drive to Newport.

It was now just after 7am as I drove to Shanklin police station where I grabbed a cup of tea and started my latest FLO log. I was rather impressed with the speed at which the mortuary staff at St Mary's prepared Jenny for viewing because by 10 o'clock I was back at the house picking up Janet and Doug to drive them the 15 miles or so to the hospital.

As we drove towards St Mary's Janet had made up her mind that she did not want to see Jenny, so Doug and I entered the room where he made a positive ID of his daughter which is something no parent should ever have to do. We came out of the room and Doug just looked at Janet and nodded his head and they hugged each other.

When we got back to the house Janet made us all a cup of tea. She then said that she needed to phone their boss at the Post Office to inform him that they would be closing the sub-post office for the day. Apparently you can't just close it; you have to obtain permission first. Thankfully that was granted which meant that I didn't have to intervene on their behalf.

It was now time to fill in the G28 for the Coroner, update them on the police investigation and talk about the press policy. These are never easy things to go through especially the G28 which I always found so intrusive. It was only 11am and less than five hours since I'd delivered that dreadful news and here I was asking them personal questions about their daughter's life like where she was born, what her occupation was, her GP details, her marital status and several other formal questions.

But as sometimes happens you tend to get side tracked and it wasn't long before Doug and Janet started to tell me about Jenny in a more relaxed and informal way. She was, by all accounts the class joker with a wicked sense of humour whom everybody loved. She was on the brink of going to Liverpool University to study drama and was a talented student. One of her biggest loves though was cars; fast cars, hence the limited edition Jordan Racing Honda Civic she had purchased. Like any parents Janet and Doug were rather concerned about her love for speed, especially when she joined the local car group Isle of Wight EVO Cars whose passionate members all loved fast and exotic motors.

We were busy talking when there was a knock at the door. It was the local vicar who had just heard on Isle of Wight radio about the crash. Jenny's details had been released to the media, which meant that the entire population of the Isle of Wight now knew about Jenny's death before Janet and Doug had even had the chance to notify other members of the family and their closest friends. This meant that her death had been announced even before Doug had made a positive ID at the hospital. How could this possibly have happened? I mean I hadn't even finished filling out the G28, the family hadn't given me any kind of family statement to pass onto the press and we certainly hadn't given the press the authority to release her details, so who in the hell had done that?

I went outside and phoned Media Services at

headquarters in Winchester and really let rip at them. They were adamant that the story and the details had not come from them and that the only other source of information was the police control room on the island. But then I remembered this was the Isle of Wight where everybody's business belonged to everybody else no matter what. Having lived on the island myself for a few years I fully understood how quickly the gossipmongers started beating their jungle drums but on this occasion they had truly excelled themselves. Somebody somewhere had made a big mistake and I was livid.

Thankfully the vicar didn't stay very long and we quickly got to grips with finishing all the paperwork. Sandra arrived with her husband Steve and by now Doug was asking questions about the crash itself like where, when and how and I suggested to him that visiting the scene may help him understand a little better.

After ascertaining that the scene was completely clear I drove Doug and his son in law Steve up to Whitwell Road where we stood on that grass embankment looking at the group of trees that his daughter had driven into. There was nothing else to look at really, with only that single tyre mark and the tyre tracks in the grass that led to the trees being the only clues that might help him visualise why his daughter's car had left the road.

We went back to the house and Janet was now concerned about trying to contact Helen, she had to be told even though she was on her honeymoon. The family felt it was important that Helen be told so that she could then make the decision whether to return home or not. The only details they could give me were that she took a flight from Gatwick to Calgary yesterday evening with Continental Airlines and that was that. It wasn't a lot to go on and it was made doubly complicated by the fact that they suspected she had booked the flights in her maiden name and not her married name although they couldn't be 100% sure about that. So off I went back to

Shanklin nick where I sat in the traffic office to start the hunt for Helen.

My obvious starting point was the airline itself and yes they did confirm that Helen and George were on the flight to Calgary but after that they had absolutely no idea where they went. They did however tell me that the flight was booked through Holiday Hypermarket in Coventry and that maybe they would be able to help. I phoned them and they in turn put me onto a company called Globespan who then put me onto another company called Chapman Freeborne who put me onto another company called Airtransat who in turn sent me back to Globespan before finally, after two hours and some 50 phone calls later I tracked Helen and George down to the Hawthorne Hotel in Calgary. I phoned the hotel to be told that yes they did stay there overnight but that there was a possibility they had already left although there was some confusion over this and there was also the possibility they may be staying a second night but at the moment there was no reply from their room but that they would leave a message for them.

That just wasn't good enough for me, I couldn't leave it up in the air like that and because I wouldn't tell the hotel receptionist exactly what the problem was for obvious reasons, I wasn't entirely convinced that they would get the message. I therefore phoned Calgary City Police and requested that they send an officer to the hotel to physically track George and Helen down and request they phone Helen's parents immediately. It might then also give the hotel staff themselves a better understanding of the urgency involved if a local police officer was also seeking their whereabouts.

It worked and within a couple of hours Helen had phoned her parents and they had the awful task of having to tell their eldest daughter on her honeymoon that her little sister was dead. I cannot begin to imagine just how difficult that must have been for all concerned but in particular for Helen and her new husband.

Before I left them for the day I gave them my card with my contact details on and said they could phone me at any time they liked day or night if they had any questions or concerns. Doug then said that my name might cause a bit of confusion because their son in law was called Steve and they knew three or four other Steve's so would it be alright if they called me PC Steve? We all laughed for the first time. Doug was an extremely affable chap and in part this was his way of dealing with the situation he and his family now found themselves in. I agreed to the name of course although it felt a bit odd when I called them and announced "Hello its PC Steve here".

The next morning I was on the ferry crossing The Solent back towards the island again. When I got to the house I was amazed to find that the Post Office and the shop were open with Janet behind the counter and Doug busily lumping some stock in from the back room. There was a note on the door telling their customers about Jenny and politely asking them not to mention it whilst in the shop. I'm not sure I could have done that, in fact I can't think of many people who would have carried on as normal on the outside whilst probably screaming on the inside. But it was their way of coping, to do something familiar. There are no rules remember.

I returned certain items of personal property from the car to Janet and Doug. They then told me that Helen and George had decided to stay in Canada to continue their honeymoon but would return in time for Jenny's funeral. There seemed little point in them coming home early as there was nothing they could do to assist. They did ask me if I could contact the mortuary again and request that the jewelry that Jenny was wearing on the night she died including a necklace that she had received as a thank you gift for being a bridesmaid be left on her body and not removed.

Janet then handed me the family statement that they had put together which read as follows;

Jenny was a bright and vivacious young lady who was hoping to go to Liverpool University to study film and media studies. She was a talented drama student, as an actress and in directing. She had recently started working part-time as a barmaid at the Mill Bay Pub in Ventnor and was a member of the car group IW – Evo cars. She had a great love of cars in particular Japanese cars. She recently returned from the wedding of her eldest sister in Coventry at the weekend where she had a wonderful time as a bridesmaid'.

She gave me a photo of Jenny to accompany the statement and I could see why they called her the class joker. I said I'd e mail the photo and statement to Media Services at Winchester and return the photo as soon as I could. I stayed for a couple of hours drinking their tea and chatting about Jenny and the rest of the family and her friends, many of whom had set up a shrine at the scene last night and sat there playing music and reminiscing about her.

It seemed that Janet and Doug were very practical sort of people and I suspected that they wouldn't need too much assistance from me. They had supportive family around them and for the time being this would probably be my last visit to them unless they had any particular issues that needed dealing with. They had my number and could phone it anytime as I would them from time to time just to check on them.

A week went by and I hadn't heard anything from them so PC Steve decided to give them a ring. Doug answered the phone and he was his usual jovial self until he mentioned the item about Jenny in the local paper. The Isle of Wight County Press is only printed once a week on Friday and of course Jenny's crash, her photo and all the details were front page news. It's hard enough for any family to deal with but of course Janet and Doug ran the local shop that distributed the

County Press and so they had to sell copies of the paper that contained all the gory details about their daughter's death. How bloody awful for them and I felt terrible because I hadn't given that aspect of things any thought whatsoever.

Jenny's funeral was held a few weeks later with the funeral cortège led by a number of the Isle of Wight EVO Cars group. Jenny had been dressed in her bridesmaids dress. Everyone was asked to wear bright clothing as it was to be a celebration of her short life with pop music played, including her favourite track 'Enola Gay' by Orchestral Manouvres in the Dark. Doug, Helen and Sandra all read items they had written about Jenny but as Janet started reading her piece she broke down because the emotion of it all was just too much and the vicar had to read it out on her behalf.

The inquest was held at Newport Coroners Court on 24th January 2006 and the Coroner Mr. John Matthews recorded a verdict of accidental death. Very little new information came out of the hearing. The Pathologists report clearly stated that Jenny had died instantly which must have brought some solace to her family. However the Police Crash Investigator could find no actual cause for the crash. There were no drugs or alcohol found in Jenny's system, there were no defects with the car and the road was subject to the national speed limit. There was only one skid mark which couldn't be positively linked to Jenny's car and there were no striation marks left on the road surface (NB; these are marks left by a cars tyres as the car starts to slide sideways) and so it wasn't possible to say for certain how and why she had left the road and collided with the trees. Was she travelling too fast and lost control on the bend? Did she swerve to avoid an animal? Did she fall asleep at the wheel? As an inexperienced driver was that Honda Civic just too powerful for her? We'll never know.

After the inquest we went to the café in the Court building for a cup of tea and a chat. Doug was very concerned for the welfare of other young drivers on the island which had seen more than its fair share of fatal and serious RTA's in recent years. Most of the roads are little more than country tracks although there are a number of faster 'A' roads but with some rather tight bends on them. He wanted to see if some further training could be given to the islands younger drivers, perhaps on a skid pan. I thought it was a brilliant idea because as an Advanced Police driver I've been privileged in using skid pan training facilities several times over the years and have always advocated that you learn more in half an hour on a skid pan about car control than you do in a life time of driving on the road. And once that skill is installed within your memory banks then come the time something goes wrong your brain can react accordingly. I wished him luck with the idea but learned later that he had come up against a brick wall when trying to promote his idea with the Islands authorities. How very short sighted of them.

However he wasn't put off completely and received help from the head of the islands Fire and Rescue Service whose daughter was a friend of Jenny's. They produced a DVD called 'Head On' that portrayed a young lad showing off to his girlfriend in the car. He crashed into a tree and she died. The DVD then shows the fire service cutting her out and the hospital staff telling her parents. It was a hard hitting film that hopefully got the message across to those who saw it no matter what their age.

Janet also told me that at the crash site they had installed a carved wooden flower as a permanent memorial because Jenny's handle with Isle of Wight EVO Cars was Jenniflower. And they also had a bright pink metal seat made by a local fabricator and had it mounted on the grass verge close to the bend where Jenny's car had left the road. A few years later another car lost control, mounted the grass verge and collided with the seat, writing off the car and the seat but possibly saving the lady drivers life. Her name was Jennifer!

GEMMA LITCHFIELD

Operation McNEAL
Category C
19th October 2005

2005 Hampshire fatalities = 90
2005 Nationally fatalities = 3200

In 2004 Hampshire's Traffic Department (now renamed the Roads Policing Unit or RPU which I personally hated) had received a rather prestigious award from the government as the best unit in the country. In all honesty we barely raised an eye brow over it, despite the swanky framed certificate that now adorned every Traffic office wall in the county. It was something for our senior managers to pat each other on the back about and to quote at meetings or in letters to others, but you know how coppers can be and we rather churlishly dismissed it as a bit of a gimmick.

However, the award caught the eye of the BBC who had recently aired a new series called 'Traffic Cops' which featured the work of South Yorkshire Police Traffic Department and they were looking for another force to feature in the next series. Who better than the newly elected 'best in breed' winners? And so for two months a number of us were 'specially selected' (that's a police term for stitched up) to be shadowed by a cameraman who would be given access to just about every aspect of our work. I'd done a fair bit of TV work the previous year with Sgt. John Geden for the Southern Crime Stoppers series so I was quite used to wearing a butterfly mic and staring down the front end of a lens talking to camera (as TV people call it) and quite often cocking up my unrehearsed lines completely!

There were two cameramen, Chris and Kevin, their Producer Simon Meehan and the Director Bruce Lipold. All four were consummate professionals and we all got on very well. They weren't too obtrusive at the scene of anything because they would stand several yards away; in fact quite often on the other side of the road and use the zoom lens to pan in on the action, so you never felt like they were breathing down your neck, in fact a lot of the time you forgot they were even there.

It was a damp but humid morning in mid-October and there had been heavy overnight rain which had only just stopped as we got to work. We were on early turn sipping our first cup of tea at a little after 6am. Mick Anderson was winding Mike Batten up about something as only Mick Anderson could. He really was the king of wind-up merchants and even if it wasn't him undertaking some mischief he invariably got the blame which he found even more amusing. We had a new boy on the department by the name of Ian Houghton and he was to be my crew mate for a while. Chris was our BBC camera man for the day and he joined in with the banter. Starting work at 6am on our department is essential because the motorway rush hour is already in full swing by then and we averaged three to four RTA's on our section of motorway by 9am most week days. I'd barely rubbed the sleepy dust from my eyes when the radio blurted out our first call of the day.

Mike Control for any Mike Charlie unit for the M275 J carriageway please, RTA car into central barrier
Mike Charlie 07 on the way

The two Michaels were out the door in 30 seconds flat whilst I tried gathering all my stuff together as Chris followed me around the office trying to stuff a battery pack into my pocket and wire the butterfly mic onto my jacket. Within a couple of minutes the three of us were clambering aboard the X5 and heading towards the motorway.

Mike Control to Mike Charlie 07 and 01 we've had a further update on this RTA, it would appear that the original vehicle has been hit for a second time by a van and the female driver of the car is trapped. Hampshire Fire and Rescue are now en route

It obviously sounded serious and as 07 arrived they immediately called for the motorway to be closed and for further units to attend. As we passed the scene on the southbound carriageway I got a very quick glimpse of the crash and saw that all the traffic behind it had already stopped which is never a good sign. As we got to our turning point at Rudmore roundabout it was already choked with stationary traffic, most of it trucks and caravans emerging from the ferry port as the early morning ferry from France had just disgorged its cargo. I fought my way north up the J carriageway, weaving in between three lanes of stationary traffic and trying to keep my cool when somebody either couldn't or wouldn't get out of my way.

We arrived at a chaotic scene with two vehicles apparently involved. The main activity seemed to be centred on a Fiat Punto that was facing the wrong way on the hard shoulder with massive frontal damage. The second vehicle was a green Mercedes Vito van which was in lane 2 some 75 metres away having also sustained major front end damage. Hampshire Fire and Rescue were all gathered around the Fiat and as I walked towards it so the first ambulance arrived behind me. I saw Mike crouched down by the driver's door of the Fiat and he was supporting the head of the young woman driver. She seemed to be unconscious and by the all too familiar look on Mikes face it was serious.

"Call it all services Steve" he said.

I did just that which meant the full RPU investigation system would start right now. Local city units were called to close the entrance to the M275 from Rudmore roundabout and the entrance prior to that at Mile End.

The paramedics took over from Mike and he came back to where Mick and I were standing on the hard shoulder talking to the main witness Robert Wake. He said that the Fiat was ahead of him in lane 3 and just before the brow of a crest in the road it went through a large amount of surface water. It was an area where we often get an almost river like stream of water about 20 feet across that travels from the central reservation across the whole motorway and onto the hard shoulder.

The Fiat lost control, spun sideways and the front end collided heavily with the central barrier which then spun it another 90 degrees where it stopped in lane 3 facing the wrong direction, but with no lights on because they'd been smashed. Mr Wake stopped on the hard shoulder and ran back towards the Fiat whilst dialling 999 on his mobile. He couldn't get from the hard shoulder across to the car because the traffic was quite heavy, most of it HGVs from the cross channel ferry which had just docked. He was shouting at the girl to get out of the car but she didn't appear to be fully conscious or she just couldn't hear him. At the same time he was trying to give the Police control room details of where the crash had occurred when to his horror the Mercedes van hit the front of the Fiat at 70 mph and catapulted it 75 metres up the motorway and across to the hard shoulder where it came to rest.

"The poor girl didn't stand a chance" he said as he sat down on the barrier.

He was quite shaken up and I said we'd get one of the ambulance crews to check him over once another one arrived. The Fire Service Crash Tender arrived and set to in cutting the girl out of the Fiat. The driver of the Mercedes van then approached us to state he was worried about the gas cylinders he had in the back of the van because of the impact. Mick shot off to liaise with the Fire Service because that was their remit but the last thing we needed them doing was setting up some kind of 200 metre exclusion zone until they'd made them safe. That didn't even bear thinking about. The BASICS Doctor arrived to help the ambulance paramedics.

We'd been at the scene for less than 10 minutes and everything that needed to be in place to get the driver out of the car was here. An action plan was put into operation to try and get the traffic diversions set up throughout the city as the morning rush hour was now in full swing and we were already getting reports of drivers doing U turns behind us and driving the wrong way down the hard shoulder even as other emergency service vehicles were still arriving. We called upon the services of the Air Support Unit to assist with the traffic flow and to take aerial photographs of the scene.

Closing any motorway costs the country more than £1m an hour in lost revenue so the pressure is on right from the start to keep any closure time to a minimum. That doesn't include time trying to assist casualties obviously but during the subsequent investigation by the Crash Investigation Unit you'd be amazed at how much pressure they are put under to get the motorway open again. Mind you most of the CIU guys I know are so thick skinned that they'd put two fingers up to any such request!

Mike and I stood and watched the fire fighters, paramedics and the BASICS Doctor all doing their best to get the girl out of the car. By now the roof was off and the medical guys were inside the car with her as the delicate operation to separate her lower limbs from the tangled wreckage began. The control room came back to us with the name of the registered keeper of the Fiat as Gemma Litchfield from Kingston Road in Portsmouth, a five minute drive from the scene. That information matched the details we'd obtained from the bank cards we'd found in her hand bag and so we asked for a local unit to go and call on the address to see if there were any relatives there and to get them up to the QA as soon as possible.

After almost an hour the girl was cut free and I escorted the ambulance from the scene up to the QA Hospital some 3 miles away. She was taken straight into Room 1 where a team of surgeons were ready and waiting for us to arrive. The local unit had also just arrived with the girls partner Barry Cooley. He confirmed her details as 27 year old Gemma Litchfield, a trainee nurse who'd been on her way to work at St. Richards Hospital in Chichester. We sat in the relative's room waiting for Gemma's parents to arrive. He'd called them as soon as the Police had knocked on his door.

It wasn't long before they arrived and I briefed them about the circumstances and as best I could about Gemma's injuries. I said I'd get one of the medical team to see them just as soon as they were free to do so and in the meantime I made us all a cup of tea. A couple of nurses popped in to reassure them all that everything that could be done was being done and that as soon as they had any further news one of the doctors would come and talk to them. It must be agony for any parent or close relative to have to just sit there, feeling helpless whilst your loved one fights for their life at the other end of the corridor.

Just before midday a young doctor and a nurse entered the room to talk to Bob, Jayne and Barry. Gemma had sustained serious head and facial injuries, both her lungs had collapsed and she had broken both her legs. Jayne clasped both her hands over her face. Her injuries were life threatening and she is currently in surgery. At this stage there was nothing else I could do so I left my card with them and wished them luck.

I drove the short distance back to our office where the rest of the guys had just got back having only just reopened the motorway. I updated them on the severity of the girl's injuries and it was decided to keep it on as a potential fatal at this stage until we heard otherwise. We spent the remainder of our shift sorting out all the paperwork, bagging property and evidence, sorting out witness details and talking to Media Services who were being bombarded by the press, not for an update on the driver's condition but moaning about the traffic gridlock in and around the city that morning. Tell them to sod off was the collective reply from our office!

That evening's edition of the Portsmouth News dedicated the front page, two full pages and the editorial comment to the crash but concentrated almost entirely on quotes from people who'd been caught up in the total gridlock within the city. And didn't they moan. I couldn't get to work, my kids had to walk to school, I didn't move for over two hours, it was chaos, nobody told us what was going on, just what were the Police doing about it?

Get real people. Portsmouth is an island with only three routes into and out of the city. If one of them is blocked by a crash then it stands to reason that the other two aren't going to cope. Oh and by the way whilst you were all doing your best Victor Meldrew impressions a young woman was fighting for her life.

I phoned ITU at the QA for the next two mornings but the situation remained the same; critical but stable. We had a new Sgt. on our Section and Adrienne Jerram called us into her office, she'd just been given a recording of the 999 call that Robert Wake had made on the day. You can clearly hear him running up the hard shoulder as the traffic rushes by. He's telling the operator what he's witnessed and trying to give the location. He then says he's standing opposite the crashed car, there's real panic in his voice and you can hear him shouting at Gemma "Get out, get out" and then telling the operator that he can see her head moving but she might be unconscious, he isn't sure. He was desperate to get out to her but the traffic was just too heavy. He shouts out again "Get out of the car, get out". Then there's an almighty bang, almost like a bomb going off followed by a two second pause. "Oh my God, she's just been hit by a van, oh no" he screams and repeats again what's just happened as you hear him running back down the hard shoulder towards where the Fiat eventually landed. It was a chilling piece of evidence and we sat there staring at the tape machine for ages.

A couple more days went past and we found ourselves dealing with yet another very serious incident and I took up my usual position at the QA before meeting the parents of the latest crash victim upstairs in ITU. In all I was there for a couple of hours before leaving.

As I came out of the door I bumped into Jayne Litchfield and her youngest daughter. They had been visiting Gemma next door in the other ITU. They were both smiling having just been told that she was making good progress and they hoped to take her off the ventilator this afternoon. I was so pleased for them and asked them to keep me updated on her progress. I went back to the office and told them the news which pleased everyone. It was a good end to a particularly challenging week and we were all looking forward to having three days off.

We returned to work on early turn and were sifting through countless new e mails and other correspondence when we got dragged out to the first RTA of the day, a four vehicle shunt on the M27 between junctions 12 and 11. While we were there a second one came in on the A3M some ten miles away and it took a couple of hours or so to get it all sorted, by which time it was breakfast and one by one we drifted back to the office like homing pigeons.

We all had our little routines when it came to breakfast; Mick would just eat a couple of rounds of toast, Mike would do the same but just *had* to have his pain au chocolate pastries or he was like a bear with a sore head, whilst I would always eat nine Weetabix having already had three before I left the house at 5.30 am. I don't know why but I was always really hungry on early turn.

We were busily stuffing our faces and making a lot of noise because Mick had locked Mike's computer terminal again just to wind him up and he was having a really good rant about it which somehow made it all the funnier, when the phone rang. I picked it up and the Staff Nurse on the other end asked for me. I put my hand up towards the others as a sign to shut up, which they always did. Gemma Litchfield died earlier this morning. As I obtained a few more details so the others cottoned on that it was the hospital staff I was talking to. I put the phone down and told them. There was a stunned silence in the room. We really thought she was going to pull through; it had been almost ten days since the crash.

Mike sat on the edge of the table, he looked genuinely upset. It was him after all who'd spent some considerable time holding her head together, talking to her and trying to reassure her that things were going to be OK. There was a connection there, albeit a brief one. Coppers can be cynical bastards at times, especially Traffic officers, but it's nothing more than a coping mechanism for dealing with some of the things we have to deal with. But there was no cynicism here, we were all really upset that this young lady had lost her fight.

I obviously needed to contact the family again but it was too early right now as they were probably still at the QA or on their way home maybe, so I decided to leave it until around midday. We had a number of other things to attend to as this was now a confirmed fatality which was going to keep us busy for a while. But by midday I had no choice but to make that phone call. I found this rather difficult and felt like I was really intruding this time. I mean you could say we intrude into people's lives in such circumstances all the time and it's true, we do, but there are times when it just feels worse and this was one of them.

Bob answered the phone and after offering my sincere condolences I asked if it would be OK for me to pop over to the house to go through all the formalities.

An hour or so later and I arrived at their immaculate house in Denvilles. Bob and Jayne looked absolutely shattered. We sat in their front room as they told me about Gemma's final moments. It was heart breaking for them and Jayne said that even though she worked at The Rowans Hospice and dealt with death almost daily, nothing could have prepared her for that of her own daughter. We went through all the usual formalities of the G28 for the Coroner, press policy and information about the vehicle examination and Gemma's insurance company. I updated them on the Police investigation to date and said that I would get back to them once that had been finalised but at this point it looked like a genuine accident, which is a rare thing, there is nearly always someone to blame for it. They opted to produce a family statement for the press but didn't really want Gemma's photo put in the paper, which was fine.

After an hour I left them in peace and as I got back to my car I couldn't help but wonder why it always seemed to be the really decent families that these tragedies seemed to befall. Whilst I wouldn't wish a road death on even the scummiest of families it did seem to me that all the families I'd ever dealt with were at the opposite end of the scale. It just seemed particularly unfair.

Before the press got hold of news of Gemma's death we needed to make contact with two other people first, the van driver and the witness. A colleague was dispatched to talk to the van driver Paul Alwyn whilst I volunteered to see Mr Wake.

I called at his address but got no reply and then found out from a neighbour that he was working in London and probably wouldn't be home until 10pm tonight. I asked the control room to pass me his mobile number and rang him.

Like the rest of us he was really shocked and upset by the news.

We were on lates the following day and I drove over to Denvilles to collect the family statement but it wasn't ready yet. Bob apologised and said that things were really tough at the moment and they just couldn't sit down and find the words. I told him not to worry, there was no pressure from me at all and the press would have to wait. I got the impression that Bob was a very astute man and there was no waffling with him and I doubted he was going to require my services for too long.

He rang me later that evening to say that they had now written a brief statement and a letter to the van driver telling him that they felt compelled to reassure him that in no way did they blame him for their loss. I told you they were thoroughly decent; less than 24 hours after their daughter had died they were thinking about other people's feelings. He said that I could come over and collect both items which I did prior to going off duty. The statement read;

Gemma was just three months short of qualifying as a registered mental health nurse. Sadly she died in a road traffic accident, but to our great relief didn't suffer. Gemma was a pupil of Bosmere Middle School and Oaklands R.C School.

She was a vibrant, loving and vivacious daughter who was caring of others. We all loved her dearly and she will be sadly missed, always and forever.

A couple of days later I went to meet Gemma's partner Barry at their flat in Portsmouth to take a statement from him. He had been the last person to see her before she left for work that morning. He was very quiet and obviously still in a state of shock.

The Portsmouth News did a follow-up piece on the crash but it was an assassination job on the 'slow response of the

Police and the other emergency services' who apparently waited for more than 15 minutes following the first impact and had they arrived earlier they might have been able to prevent the second collision and thus a tragic death and, more importantly (to them), it wouldn't have led to the traffic gridlock for the rest of the day.

Almost exactly a year before Gemma's accident there had been another fatality on the M275 during the evening rush hour which again grid locked the city. The council had no plan in place then and rightly faced a lot of criticism but since then had gone to great lengths to do their bit to ensure that it wouldn't happen again. Although it was still bad, it was no-where near as bad as the previous experience. But this reporter had clearly decided that the magic wand that he assumes we are all issued with wasn't working on this particular day and that gave him carte blanche to rubbish those of us who were there. How dare he lie, for that's what it was, about the length of time it took us to get there and on what basis did he write that item? My concern here was for Gemma's family and friends who might have read this garbage and concluded that whilst we sat around on our backsides in the office drinking tea their daughter was trapped and all alone in the wreckage of her car until we deemed it important enough for us to attend.

A couple of days later I was back at the house to hand deliver a sympathy card from the witness Robert Wake and then went to great lengths to reassure Bob that the article in the paper simply wasn't true in anyway shape or form. I felt compelled to give him chapter and verse about just how quickly we had got there and what we did to comfort Gemma until the fire service and paramedics had got her out. He needed to know, just in case there was any doubt in his mind, that we did everything humanly possible to get her out and keep her alive. He said he was more than satisfied with what we'd all done for Gemma and asked me to pass on his families thanks to everyone.

Two days later my wife pointed out an item in the obituary column in the Portsmouth News under Gemma's name. It read;

The family would like to say a big thank you to everyone for their kind words and support during this sad time. Also we would like to express our heartfelt thanks to all the staff at the Critical Care Unit at QA, the Road Traffic Police Accident Unit and the Fire Service, who have helped and cared for us and Gemma with such dignity and kindness.

A couple of weeks went by and Adrienne called me into her office. She'd recently had a couple of phone calls from Robert Wake who she said was really suffering and had been since the crash, he couldn't get out of his mind the fact that he'd done nothing to help Gemma and should have got her out after the first crash. She said she was no expert at dealing with such things and could I go and see him and perhaps "work my magic" on him. I'm not Harry bloody Potter you know and anyway my magic wand is in for a service.

But she was right to be concerned about him, he really was a mess, racked with guilt, he kept going over the scene time after time, trying to find that gap in the traffic so that he could run out there and pull Gemma free. I told him that he'd done everything he could under the circumstances and that there were two important things he probably hadn't taken into consideration; one, that Gemma was probably unconscious from the first impact and already trapped in the wreckage and two, if he had gone out there and was trying to get her out he would have been killed instantly when the van hit, of that there is no doubt. His family would then have to deal with his death just as Gemma's family had to do today.

I'm not a counsellor; I've not had any professional training in such things, just training in life, as all coppers learn through experience and all I could do was tell him how I saw it. We sat there for two hours, he cried as he drank his coffee but eventually conceded that I was right, his instincts were telling him when he was on that hard shoulder that his life would be in serious danger if he ran out into the carriageway, so deep down he knew. But it didn't stop him from feeling guilty. I told him to make an appointment with his GP as soon as he could and to ask for some proper counselling. He promised he would and I told him to phone me direct if he wanted to talk further. I didn't hear from him again.

It was early February 2006 before I contacted the Litchfield family again and as suspected they'd had no need to contact me. I asked to speak to Bob alone and so we sat in his front room with the door closed. This was quite possibly one of the hardest conversations I was ever likely to have with any bereaved family I'd dealt with. I told him that the BBC had filmed the aftermath of Gemma's crash including her lengthy extraction and had interviewed a number of us during and after the investigation and that through me, they were now seeking his family's permission to air that footage during a future episode of Traffic Cops.

Bobs eye brows raised slightly and he asked me a number of significant questions about it. I reassured him that the film crews had been very professional and hadn't got in anyone's way at the scene and certainly hadn't hindered Gemma's rescue at all and that the programme's intention was to show the public how difficult such things are to deal with. It would be shown in a very sympathetic light but it was entirely his call, there would be no pressure from me or the BBC, if he and his family didn't want it shown then I wouldn't ever mention it again and the BBC would not be permitted to contact them. He said he needed to consult Jayne and the rest of the family first and would get back to me. I sat back in the car and breathed a huge sigh and thought of all the obscure things I'd been tasked with since becoming an FLO, none of which had ever been covered on my course.

Bob phoned me a couple of days later giving his family's permission for the BBC to show the film of Gemma's accident. It was a very brave decision and I said I'd phone him nearer the time when it was going to be aired so that he could warn everyone.

It was mid-May when that episode was shown. I sat at home watching it with my family. They showed the very earliest footage of me arriving at the scene shortly after the two Michaels and then focussed on the physical rescue plus me explaining to Mike how the crash had occurred. It was going quite well until they switched to a second story with the opening line "meanwhile on the other side of Portsmouth PC Pete Haywood and his probationer have been sent to another accident" making it sound like he was just swanning around town whilst the rest of us were dealing with a potential fatal.

Well for starters that simply wasn't true, Pete wasn't even on duty that day and the crash he got sent to happened a couple of weeks later. But more important than that was the manner in which they portrayed Pete dealing with it. He made a bit of an arse of himself because he couldn't quite understand how the accident happened and then threatened to arrest the innocent party involved because he swore at him. The BBC had added in some sort of Laurel and Hardy type music along with some rather sarcastic commentary from the narrator Jamie Theakston which turned the whole feature into a bit of a comedy routine. Then they switched back to Gemma's crash. I cringed, it was awful and they'd chosen the wrong mix of stories. It was wrong of them and the more I watched it the angrier I got.

The next morning I e-mailed Bruce Lippold the Director of the series and berated him for the manner in which the programme had been edited especially as it had fallen upon me to seek the family's permission to use the footage and I'd promised them that the BBC would be very sensitive about it and that I was more than angry that they had then turned it into a comedy about Pete Haywood. He was acutely embarrassed and apologised and said I was right, they'd got it wrong. He said he'd write to the family offering his apologies.

The inquest into Gemma's death was heard on 26th July and was recorded as accidental death. It was a short hearing and there was nothing contentious about it and so the number of witnesses was kept to a minimum with only the Pathologist and the Crash Investigator being called.

The van driver read about it in the paper the following day and he was rather upset that he hadn't been notified because he wanted to meet Gemma's family in person to offer his condolences. Instead he had to write them another note.

Her death proved to me that other people outside of the immediate family and friends can be badly affected by such incidents. As I said during the TV programme, Gemma's crash was one of those rare occasions where it could actually be classified as a tragic accident. There was no-one to blame or hold to account but nonetheless the two main parties involved, the van driver Paul Alwyn and the witness Robert Wake felt incredibly guilty and the events of that day will live with them forever.

CAROLE MILLER

Operation **PAPAYA**
Category **B**
30th October 2005

2005 Hampshire fatalities = 90
2005 Nationally fatalities = 3200

I made a tactical error and opened my mouth when clearly I should have kept it firmly shut.

In 2004 the Isle of Wight had, for reasons I will never understand, fallen under the jurisdiction of Cosham RPU. During internal changes within the Hampshire Constabulary it meant that the islands Traffic Police were now incorporated into Coshams resources and figures. Most importantly for us on the ground though it meant that if they were short of man power on the island due to sickness or annual leave then one or two of us would be dispatched across the Solent with a bucket and spade. Strangely though it wasn't a two way street and we never got back up from the island when we were short! My mistake was to inform a certain Sgt. that I used to live on the island and that I knew it rather well. I was therefore deemed to be the perfect candidate for the occasional deportation.

On 30th October, 2005 there was to be a large custom car rally in Ryde and the islands RPU section only had an acting Sgt. available. It clearly wasn't sufficient so PC Pete Haywood, his probationer and I took two cars onto the ferry and headed across to Fishbourne. Our new found friends at the BBC decided that this was too good an opportunity to miss and so Kevin the cameraman came with us.

I'd been trialling a hybrid Lexus RX400h as a new patrol car for a few weeks and testing it out on the islands awful roads seemed like a good idea. It was late afternoon as we arrived in Fishbourne and then drove south to Shanklin nick where we got briefed on the evening's entertainment. They were expecting several hundred custom cars to attend and at similar events in other parts of the country there had been some disorder. In Essex two bystanders had been killed when a car doing doughnuts to amuse the crowd lost control and ploughed into them. So a visible police presence was required.

Briefing over it was time to feed our faces and so we found a nearby chip shop and took our grub back to the nick. As we entered the canteen we heard radio traffic from the mainland about a serious RTA in Cartwright Drive, Fareham. Within minutes it was being called in as an 'all services' and being the nosey sods that we were we turned the radio up to listen in whilst quietly chuckling to ourselves that tonight, for once, being on the island was the best place to be. But we weren't chuckling for long because they also required an FLO and it transpired that the only two FLO's on duty in Hampshire tonight were Pete and me. Trouble is Pete was due to fly out to Hong Kong in the morning to start his annual leave and so that left moi.

Wayne Voller was the Sgt. in charge at the scene and I had a quick chat with him on my mobile and although it wasn't a confirmed fatal the ladies injuries were apparently so bad that it was likely to be. He went on to explain briefly that the scene was horrendous and that a local gypsy had been arrested after doing a runner.

I gulped down the last few handfuls of luke warm chips before climbing aboard the silent running electric patrol car and headed back towards the ferry port. The car bounced and ricocheted around the narrow, twisty and ludicrously uneven island roads as I floored the throttle in an effort to make the 7 pm ferry. I arrived with seconds to spare and stopped at the entrance to the port and quickly explained why I needed to be on *that* ferry. He radioed down to the guys loading the boat to tell them to remove the last two cars from the stern of the ferry and let me on. He then waved me through and as I reached the bottom of the loading area I could see them reversing two cars back down the loading ramp which meant they'd have to wait another hour for the next one. I was somewhat embarrassed by this so if it was you and you're reading this……sorry.

I made my way up to the lounge area, grabbed myself a cup of tea and then listened in on the frantic radio traffic from the scene. Mike Batten seemed to be orchestrating everything from getting a second dog unit to the scene and demanding that control room get air support in from either Surrey or Dorset because our aircraft had been grounded. Mike was concerned that we had another body lying in the dense woodland because the driver had murmured the words 'Christian' a number of times and because the hood was smashed to pieces on the car it was feared that Christian may have been ejected from the vehicle or had wandered off in a daze through the woods. There was also the possibility of a second offender hiding in the area and that the Air Support unit's thermal imaging equipment was vital to the search. Wayne also required Scenes of Crime to attend and it appeared that this was looking like a potential Section 1.

Within 45 minutes the ferry was docking in Portsmouth and as soon as I got off, on went the blue lights as I hot footed it west along the silky smooth M27 towards Fareham.

Mainland roads always feel so much nicer after you've spent time on the Isle of Wight.

It took me just over ten minutes to get to the scene and as I approached it I worked out that from the time I left Shanklin nick to my arrival in Fareham, including the ferry trip, had taken me an hour and a half, which was pretty good going I thought. I parked the patrol car just outside the taped off cordon and walked towards some poor probationer stood there with a clip board signing people in and out of the scene. As he lifted the tape to let me through I could see Chris the camera man up ahead panning his camera towards me, so it meant that I'd been filmed getting my instructions to leave the island and then had my arrival at the scene captured which I suppose would make for perfectly synchronized telly, almost as if we'd staged the whole thing!

Wayne came across and as we walked towards the scene so he explained what had happened. Basically a small green Mazda MX5 sports car being driven by a 50 something lady had been rear ended by a BMW X5 at a speed roughly estimated to be close to 100 mph. This had resulted in the Mazda being catapulted off the road and into the nearby woods where it had decapitated a decent sized tree before coming to rest some 40 feet from the road. The car was now little more than the size of a kitchen table and I'd not seen such significant damage to a car for a long time. The impact with the tree was via the driver's door which had bent the car into a U shape and the ingress from the tree was now touching the gear lever. That meant that the driver stood in the way of the tree as it made its way through the car hence her life threatening injuries.

I stood next to the crushed and battered remains of what used to resemble a Mazda MX5 as Mike Batten joined me and we both agreed that it was a miracle that anyone had survived the initial impact and he went on to say that the BASICS Dr., who had attended, rated her chances of survival at just 10%.

Those are not good odds. He also told me that the driver of the BMW X5 had run off after the crash but had been located a couple of hundred yards away by the first dog unit on the scene and that the big hairy German Shepherd had had a little nibble. Good boy.

Every now and then you attend an incident where everyone who attends is appalled by the circumstances or feels particularly sorry for the victim. So it was tonight that all of us present were absolutely determined to bring the person responsible for this horrific crash to justice and bring some solace to the victim, 56 year old Carole Miller. In comparison to the investigators job, mine was relatively easy, so I set off towards the QA again, ready to face another shattered family.

On this occasion though I didn't have to deliver the news because that had already been done for me and the family was already sat in the relative's room at A&E. Sitting at the far end was Carole Millers 26 year old son Christian, to my left was her 22 year old daughter Verity and her fiancée Jon. Sitting opposite them was Mr. Miller. I was introduced to them by the young PC who had broken the news to them and brought them up to the hospital. No sooner had he done the introductions when he did a runner. I gave the family a brief update on the investigation so far but got interrupted by Mr. Miller.

"Is it right that the other driver was a pikey and he did a runner?" he asked in a rather understandably aggressive manner.

"You're very well informed," I said.

"Yeah, well I've got a couple of good mates who are firemen and they phoned me from the scene to let me know. They also told me that he was pissed" he replied somewhat smugly as he folded his arms.

"Oh did they," I said "Well in my experience it pays to listen only to those involved in the actual investigation and not to rumour and speculation.'

There was a definite atmosphere in the room, even before our little exchange and it was interesting to watch the family dynamics at work. Neither Christian nor Verity spoke to him and he didn't speak to them. Christian just stared at the floor; he looked like he was in complete shock, whilst Verity and Jon tended to whisper to each other. I left the room to go and see if I could get an update on Carole's condition. It took me a while but eventually I found the duty Doctor, who looked exhausted. He said that Carole's injuries were massive; in fact he thought that just about every bone in her body was broken, except for her skull which appeared to be intact. She had just been taken upstairs for emergency surgery but he doubted she would survive because the trauma of her injuries was just too severe. He said he'd pop along and talk to the family as soon as he could.

I went outside and found my usual spot by the wall to phone Wayne Voller and update him that we could call off the search for Christian because he was with me. I then phoned the Bio-Chem Lab on the fifth floor at QA to secure the pre-transfusion blood samples that would have been taken from Carole. These were vital evidence in the police investigation and have to be secured at a very early stage before they are disposed of or contaminated. The police need to have these blood samples analysed for alcohol and illicit drugs. It's obviously not always possible or appropriate to obtain blood samples in the usual manner in such circumstances and so this is the only way.

I then went back into the relative's room to discuss a few things with them. I found Verity and Jon talking about their wedding which was due to take place in just two weeks' time.

"I'm not getting married without my mum there" said Verity "Even if we have to postpone it for a few weeks, I don't care just so long as she's there".

Jon sensibly agreed just as the Doctor and a nurse entered the room. He was as gentle as he could be but left them in no doubt just how serious her condition was. They all sat there, heads bowed in total silence. Mr. Miller got up and said he needed to make a phone call and left the room.

"Why is he is even here?" Christian asked Verity through gritted teeth.

"He had a right to know," she replied.

"I don't think mum would want him here do you," he snapped back.

It wasn't my place to ask but it was clear that Mr. and Mrs. Miller were no longer Mr. and Mrs.

I decided to appoint the two Miller siblings as the next of kin at this stage, given what I'd just heard and whilst Mr. Miller was out of the room I gave them my mobile number and contact details and said I'd be in touch with them tomorrow.

It was always different in cases such as this where the victim was still alive, I mean there was no formal ID or mortuary visit to do, no press policy, no family statement, no anything really other than exchanging contact details and keeping your fingers crossed that she pulled through. I reassured them that their mother was in the best place possible, not to give up hope and that the staff here did some quite incredible things. They all smiled for the first time.

I returned to the scene to find that the Crash Investigation Unit led by Steve Hoynes was in the middle of arranging a mechanical fit with the two vehicles, which had always fascinated me. The Mazda had been removed from the woods and placed at the point it had left the road. The BMW was suspended from a Hiab crane on the back of a Boarhunt recovery truck and slowly it was maneuvered into position until the damage at the front of it matched the damage to the rear of the Mazda. It was just like finding two pieces from a jigsaw puzzle that locked into place. It was a perfect fit. It clearly showed that the front nearside area of the BMW had collided with the rear offside of the Mazda. The impact damage was huge and clearly showed that the speed of the BMW was far greater than that of the Mazda. Including the recovery team, firemen, policemen and camera man there must have been about 20 of us standing around the two cars and I think a shudder went down the spines of all of us as we stood there in silence for a minute or two and contemplated what Carole Miller must have thought and felt as her car was projected from the road like a missile into the woods.

News filtered back to us that the BMW driver had provided two positive breath samples at Fareham nick. Wayne handed me Carole's hand bag and I returned to the QA to hand it over to Verity. They hadn't heard anything else and were determined to stay the night. I nipped into the staff room on the other side of the corridor and made us all a cup of tea. I nicked a few cheese sandwiches from the staff fridge whilst I was there to make sure they had something to eat but I don't think they were that interested in them frankly. It was gone half midnight by the time I left them and way past 2 am by the time I'd filled out the latest FLO log and updated a few other things. I drove home very slowly mulling over the evenings events. I wonder if Pete enjoyed the car show?

I was back on late turn the following day and as I hadn't heard anything I phoned ITU at QA for an update. At first the nurse refused to speak to me because there was no password so I had to get her to phone me back via the control room. Once she was satisfied that I was legit she told me that Carole was on a ventilator with life threatening injuries. It wasn't much to go on but at least she was still with us. We agreed on a pass word and I said I'd phone back later.

My phone rang and it was Jeff Reines from The News. He was his usual inquisitive self and asked me so many questions that I wasn't able to answer, not because I was being awkward it was just that I didn't know the answers. I was actually quite pleased that he would be the reporter on this case because I knew he would keep it in the headlines once he had got his teeth into it.

The following evening I agreed to meet Verity at the intensive care unit at QA in order to hand over some of her mum's property from the car. She and Christian were stood at Carole's bedside. She was a pitiful sight with all manner of tubes connected to various electrical apparatus that beeped and buzzed, but importantly were keeping her alive. We went into the small side room where I handed over the envelope containing her watch and a necklace and the pair of them just stood there looking at it, their lips pursed, unable to speak and comprehend what was happening to their mum. I gave them what little information I could about the investigation and told them that we would do everything we could to ensure that the man responsible for this would be brought to justice.

I phoned every day for over a week and slowly but surely Carole started to show small signs of improvement to the extent that she was taken off the ventilator and moved to a high dependency ward. Although she was off the critical list she had a long way to go yet. Her back was broken, she had multiple breaks of both legs and arms, including compound fractures to her legs, all her ribs were broken and she had all the trimmings to match. Of course she couldn't talk much but what she did say shocked her family and me beyond belief.

As she lay trapped in the wreckage of her car, unable to move with injuries too horrific to contemplate she became aware that a group of men and women had surrounded her vehicle. They were shouting at her and threatening to kill her and her family for causing the crash, telling her it was her fault and not to tell the police anything. They ran off when they heard the first sirens approaching. The word callous just isn't strong enough, in fact I've actually tried finding a word in the dictionary that is but without success. How could any human being stoop so low as to threaten to kill a lady who is currently trapped in the wreckage of her car with horrific injuries? Just imagine for a moment that was you. Your car has just been violently hit from behind with an impact so severe that it becomes airborne. It travels through the air towards the woods where it hits a decent sized tree about three feet up, cuts it in half but in doing so causes huge damage to both you and your car. It eventually comes to rest and you are trapped with compound fractures to both your legs and you are bleeding badly. You know you are in serious trouble, its dark and you are all alone drifting in and out of consciousness. But then you hear voices. Thank God for that I'm going to be rescued. But no, instead you are surrounded by a pack of baying, snarling Hyenas who want to inflict further damage on you. How terrifying and surely beyond the comprehension of most of us.

I went back to the office to let Wayne know and it made him all the more determined to nail the man responsible. He was confident that DNA samples taken from the air bag inside the BMW would reveal that the man detained near to the scene was the driver. We would have to rely heavily on such evidence because on the night of the crash some of the investigation team went to the Traveller encampment some 500 yards from the scene to enquire about the ownership of the vehicle. As is usual when dealing with Traveller types, nobody knew anything including who owned the BMW. The car was registered to a person up north who didn't exist, wasn't insured or taxed and was one of those ghost vehicles that always causes the police huge amount of problems in trying to tie down exactly who owned it.

By the end of November the hospital were telling Carole and her family that there was a good chance that she could be home by mid-December and at the latest by Christmas, although she still had a number of serious operations including one on her back to go through. I obviously wasn't going to bother her between now and then because her recovery was far more important than me pestering her for further evidence. Thankfully she did spend Christmas at home and during the first week in January 2006 I visited her at her house in Titchfield. It was now almost 3 months since the crash and the first time I had seen Carole since she was in ITU and I was shocked at the state of her even now. Both her legs were still in plaster as was her right arm. She still looked battered and bruised and was clearly still upset about the state that she was in. Her 26-year-old son Christian had resigned from his job in order to become his mum's full-time carer. Although they were receiving nursing care at home on a daily basis, this was only two or three times a day whereas Carole required 24-hour care and Christian was there to attend to all her needs which must have been incredibly difficult for both of them.

I sat next to her bed as Christian brought us in a cup of tea. As we talked about the crash itself and her injuries Carole got very tearful and apologised for being so silly. It took a while but eventually we managed to put pen to paper and she gave me her account of the crash itself. In truth there wasn't much that she could say other than she was on her way home from a friend's house, when she looked in her rear view mirror to see the front of the BMW approaching the rear of her car at very high speed. She recalled the impact then nothing until her car was surrounded by the group of people that were threatening to kill her. The tears flowed down her face once more as she described how terrifying that particular moment was. I felt incredibly angry on her behalf and a shudder went down my spine. Once she had composed herself it was time to get all this down on paper;

'My name is Carole Miller and I reside at the address overleaf. I'm normally fit and well, I'm the manager of the lingerie shop at Whiteley near Fareham. I owned a green Mazda MX5 sports car registration number P253RHX which I had only owned for a few days.

On Sunday 30th October 2005 I decided to drive from my home address to Soberton to visit a friend. I arrived about 3 PM and left there at about 5 PM or shortly after. My intention was to drive directly home and my route would have taken me down Cartwright Drive past the Holiday Inn and then onto the Warsash Road. At this time it was dusk. It wasn't raining and was fairly warm. I didn't have the hood down and I would describe the visibility that I obtained through the rearview window as quite good, certainly better than the Mitsubishi I had before the Mazda.

The last thing I really remember is driving through Wickham to Segensworth and then turning left onto Cartwright Drive.

At some time whilst driving along Cartwright Drive I remember looking in my rear view mirror and seeing a registration plate, possibly with a letter N or M on it. I have to confess here that although I'm pretty sure I saw it in my mirror it might have been from the side or even the front, but as I will explain later in the statement I have had some major problems since.

Seeing that registration plate is the last thing I actually remember until regaining consciousness in hospital some 2 ½ weeks later. I was on the intensive care unit at QA Hospital and for several days after I came around I suffered horrendous hallucinations due to the morphine drip that I was on. I thought everybody was trying to kill me and that the nursing staff was the Devil's disciples. I thought that the hospital was a ship and it was sinking. It was truly terrifying and it didn't stop until the hospital staff realised just how bad the morphine was affecting me. They then changed my medication and from then on I can recollect more.

The physical injuries sustained included the following; an unstable fracture of the third thoracic vertebrae, which now has three titanium rods held with screws which will be a permanent fixture in my back. A fracture of the mid shaft of the right femur which meant that my right knee was shattered and needed rebuilding. My right leg now has several metal pins and rods in it to hold it altogether. Again these will be a permanent fixture. I have also had to have a skin graft on my right ankle and have terrible scars on my leg. My left leg suffered multiple fractures and to date (11th of January 2006) my leg is still in full plaster

182

from my thigh to my foot. I do not know what the long term prognosis is for this leg.

I had four major operations in all, including a bone graft from left hip onto my back. I had many lacerations on my head and six fractured ribs. My right hand sustained massive bruising and swelling and I had severe bruising of the chest and stomach. I was in hospital for seven weeks but am now at home trying to recover.

My life and that of my family has been turned upside down. My son Christian has become my virtual full-time carer at home. I'm completely dependent on him for everyday needs from food and drink, to bathroom needs. I'm completely bed bound and my short-term prognosis is another six months before I can even think about a normal life again. I have just started to use a wheelchair and went outside for the first time this week.

My daughter Verity was due to get married on 19th November 2005. Due to my accident she had to postpone the wedding and you can imagine how upsetting that was for her and for me when I found out. It is now due to take place on 11th February and I'm determined to be there. There was also a financial penalty because she had to cancel various pre-booked items.

On my financial front this has had a profound effect. I was earning a decent wage from my job, which I loved, prior to the accident and now I am on statutory sick pay of just £344 a month. My house was up for sale prior to the accident and Christian had to remove it from the market and get my mortgage frozen, which was no easy task for him.

This incident has completely shattered my life. I know I'm alive and I'm grateful for that but every morning I wake up and think I must be in some kind of bad dream. But then I realise it's not a dream, it's real and I fear for my future. I didn't ask for any of this, I don't deserve the injuries I sustained and my family have suffered as a consequence.'

A week or so later Simon Meehan from the BBC asked me if Carole might be up to being interviewed for the Traffic Cops program, so they could continue the story from the footage that they had obtained on the night of the crash. I really wasn't sure that she was mentally ready for this, but said I'd ask her and the family and get back to him.

I was probably a bit cheeky in the manner in which I approached this because I knew deep down that it would make good TV. My reason for thinking this was quite simple. The crash itself was hugely spectacular and the viewing public would become engrossed in this human story and would probably hate the person responsible as much as the rest of us. However the victim in this needed to have a face, a face that the public could identify and sympathise with and I had no doubt that Carole would come across in just the right way. I suppose I could be accused of using Carole in this context but I genuinely felt that it might help her in the short term and long term and that it might help everybody that knew her to fully understand just what she had gone through.

I got a favourable response from Carole and a couple of days later I was back at the house with Bruce Lippold the program Director together with Kevin the cameraman and the three of us crowded into Carole's bedroom. They filmed for about half an hour and Bruce asked all manner of questions which she answered as best she could and even cried in all the right places! Both Bruce and Kev were as shocked by her injuries as I was and were extremely grateful for her contribution and promised her that the public would have every sympathy with her and her plight.

The results of the DNA analysis taken from the air bag inside the BMW came back as negative, with no trace of any DNA found at all. This was a real setback and was something that none of the investigation team could comprehend given the fact that when an airbag goes off it usually hits you full in the face and traces of saliva are usually found.

However some excellent CCTV footage was found that showed the silver BMW X5 leaving the nearby Travellers site although it wasn't clear enough to see whether there were one or two people in it. A couple of minutes later it showed a large group of people running on foot out through the gate and towards the crash scene. These were probably the pack of feral creatures who threatened Carole whilst she was trapped in the wreckage. It wasn't conclusive but it was a nice piece of the jig-saw.

The following month Carole was just about fit enough to attend Verity and Jon's wedding, albeit in a wheelchair. As Verity had said on the night of the crash there was no way that she was getting married without her mother being there and so they were forced to postpone it until February. I was so pleased for all of them and was particularly chuffed that Jeff Reines had managed to get the whole of the front page dedicated to the wedding, plus most of page three with some fantastic photos and plenty of text. It was something for the family to smile about at last.

The file was sent to CPS for their consideration and we were all relieved when it was agreed that the driver of the BMW X5, Drury John Lee should be charged with dangerous driving whilst under the influence of alcohol and with grievous bodily harm. This was a highly unusual charge to put before somebody involved in a car crash but the circumstances were so unusual and the speed involved so high that it was felt that a GBH charge was proportionate.

By mid-June CPS were asking me to obtain victim impact statements from Carole and Christian. The names of these statements had recently been changed to victim personal statements but nonetheless they still had to have an impact and so I went back to the house armed with a load of witness statement forms. I knew these statements would be read out in public at Crown Court within the next few weeks so I knew I had to get them right. Although Carole was now able to stand she could only do so with the aid of two walking sticks or a Zimmer frame and could barely walk for more than two minutes at a time. Her statement read as follows;

Further to my statement of 11 January 2006 I wish to inform the Court of my current medical condition first. Since January I have had the cast on my legs removed. It transpired that the cast had reacted badly with my skin and I had several nasty ulcers on my legs that required a large amount of treatment. This has resulted in further scarring which will be there for life. The damage sustained to my left knee was not really going to be determined until after the cast have been removed and I could play some weight on it. My worst fears came true when it was revealed to I now need yet another operation on that knee to repair the cruciate ligament. This will mean my leg going back into plaster and me walking on crutches again for several weeks. The operation is due in August and I really am dreading going back into hospital. I also need an operation on my right knee to remove the pin which is currently protruding out the side of my leg will stop I'm hoping that they do this at the same time as my left knee otherwise it will mean yet another hospital stay.

It is now mid June 2006, some 8 ½ months since the crash. Apart from my legs I also still have big problems with my neck. The four titania rods they placed inside restrict my movement a great deal and I cannot then fall to do the simplest of tasks like washing up or ironing. Even reading a book causes me pain, I have constant headaches and need osteopathy and acupuncture.

I get very tired very quickly and I don't mean a quick yawn, I mean total exhaustion. Some days are worse than others and I simply cannot move. I still cry a lot, but lost all my self-confidence and I worry about the future. I was never like this before the crash. I ran a successful business and was a very confident person. Part of that confidence dilemma centres around the fact that my legs are permanently disfigured and scarred. Prior to the crash they were my best feature and now I will have to wear long skirts or trousers otherwise I'll just feel that everyone will be looking at me in the wrong way.

I have lost so much in my family has suffered when they shouldn't have done. Without their help I shudder to think what might have happened to me. My life has been completely ruined, not just in the short term but probably forever. I cannot partake in any sports used to enjoy like running, aerobics and badminton. I can't do any decorating or gardening, I can't even kneel down any more.

So no matter what sentences imposed upon the man responsible for this it will never be as painful was long-term as the sentence I'm having to endure because of his actions.'

When reading Carole's statement you can't help but feel for her but Christian's statement was even more powerful and heart rendering;

'The 30th October 2005 was the worst night of my life. When the police arrived at my door to tell me that my mother had been seriously injured in a car crash my life changed in an instant. As my family and I gathered together in that room at the QA Hospital I feared the worst. I was numb, that's the only way I can describe how I physically felt. When they eventually allowed us into the room where my mum was being treated I was horrified at the extent of her injuries. Although the hospital staff had warned us in advance nothing can prepare you for what I saw. There was so much spilt blood, so many tubes, all attached to machines. It was surreal. This sort of thing happens to other people or on TV, not to ordinary people like us. But this was only the beginning, she was in hospital for five weeks, more than two weeks of that on intensive care, during which time we really did wonder whether or not she would survive at all.

When she eventually left hospital and came home her injuries were so bad that she would need constant care and as I still lived at home it was my duty to undertake that care. I had to do everything for her, feed her, change her clothes, bedding, wash her and help her with her toilet needs. I'm 26 years old and you can imagine how difficult that aspect alone was for me and for her.

By early 2006 I had to give up work for two months, I couldn't look after mum and work at the same time, it was impossible. I became depressed and was prescribed antidepressants by my GP. I'm still on them now. Financially this incident has all but crippled us. We have frozen the mortgage for a year and I've had to sell possessions just to make ends meet. I've had to use the benefits system for the first time in my life and found the system both slow and archaic; we have barely enough to live on at times. I don't drive and have had to rely on lifts from friends or taxis to and from the hospital which have cost us a fortune.

This all makes me sound like I'm whingeing, but I'm not. My mother is still alive for which I'm truly grateful, I really am. But the man responsible for all this has to understand just what he has done to her and her family. The physical and emotional pain she has endured over the last eight months now has been immense. Yes eight months. Just you think for a minute what you have all done in the last eight months and then try and imagine if you can being laid up on your bed with your body completely smashed and having the indignity of somebody else having to do everything for you. And it's far from over yet. She has a long way to go, perhaps another two years before she is completely fit.

I'm not a vindictive person and any sentence passed on the man responsible for my mother's injuries will never compensate, but I sincerely hope he has time to reflect on the incredible damage he has done.'

Whenever I got the chance I would pop across to the house to visit Carole and Christian just for a cup of tea and a chat in the hope that it might keep their spirits up. We had a laugh and a joke about many things and it was good to see her progress, albeit very slowly. A Crown Court trial date was set for 7th November 2006 and was likely to take a week. Before it went to court the CPS wanted me to obtain an updated victim personal statement from Carole;

'Further to my statement of 19th June 2006 I wish to add the following. It is now October 16th, almost a year since the accident and although I am making a recovery I am still receiving intensive medical care.

On 19th September 2006 I was admitted to Haslar Hospital for an operation on the cruciate ligament on my left knee. The cruciate was completely smashed in the accident and has been replaced with ligament from another part of my leg. I left hospital on 21st September and to date my leg is still heavily bandaged to give it support.

I now face yet another operation on my right knee and right foot to remove a couple of screws that are now protruding through the side of my knee and causing me considerable pain. On the mental front I'm really struggling at the moment. My GP has now put me onto anti depressants, which I'm not too happy about. This has come about because in the last few weeks I have started to have several panic attacks. These have been brought on by some of the most bizarre situations like the car versus motorcycle crash advert on the TV asking you to think twice about bikes. The sight and sound of the advert causes me terrible problems.

I have also tried looking in at work but within minutes I had to leave as I really couldn't cope. I still have months of physio to contend with and my GP has recently advised me that it is unlikely that I will be able to return to work in my current employ as I'm required to be on my feet all day and I certainly can't do that at present.

As for day-to-day activity I can now walk a bit. I am being encouraged by my physio to try and walk unaided around the house. However if I go out, which is rare, I have to use my stick for support and I cannot walk for more than about 400 yards or stand for too long. Anything more than that and I have to use my wheelchair still.

So a year on I am making progress, but it is painfully slow and physically and emotionally still very painful.'

Preparing people for court in such circumstances is never easy. Too many times during my career I thought we had a bombproof case only to see the defendant walk because of some legal technicality, because an i didn't have the right sized dot above it or a T wasn't crossed in the proper manner, you know the sort of thing. The last thing I wanted to do was to build up the Miller family's hopes that the man responsible for all of their pain was definitely going to receive a custodial sentence. As I was privy to much of the evidence against him I knew very well that we might struggle to even get a conviction.

Carole and Christian were determined to attend every day of the trial even though both of them were concerned that it might have an exhausting effect upon Carole who was still confined to a wheelchair at this time. I picked them up every day and drove them to Portsmouth Crown Court where the Victim Support Service looked after them very well.

The court was told that Drury Lee was more than three times the drink drive limit and that he had collided with the back of Carole's car at a speed of around 100 mph. Lee denied being the driver and stated that he was the front seat passenger and that another man whom he did not know or would not name was the driver and that he ran off after the crash. The court was told that after the collision the BMW overturned several times before coming to rest on its wheels with the driver's door pressed up hard against a six-foot high wire fence, which meant that the driver's door could not be opened and that the only means of exit was from the passenger door. The most compelling piece of physical evidence that proved beyond doubt that he was the driver at the time of the crash came from a photograph taken at the custody centre at Fareham police station shortly after he arrived there, which clearly showed a friction burn caused by a seatbelt, which ran from his right shoulder, diagonally across his chest to the left side of his stomach. The most ironic aspect of this evidence, as any police officer will tell you, is that Traveller types rarely if ever wear a seatbelt, so this evidence was not only damning but almost unique.

Over the years there have been countless stories relayed about things that have been said or done during court cases, most of them of a humorous nature, in fact somebody should write a book one day detailing them because it would be a bestseller. During our court case we had just such an occurrence and it came whilst the defence barrister was questioning one of the prosecution witnesses who had been in his car, waiting to turn right from Cartwright Drive into the Holiday Inn when the two cars involved were heading towards him and he saw the collision take place, with both cars then leaving the road. He immediately turned right into the hotel car park, got out of his car, jumped over a small hedge and ran almost 100 yards to the BMW X5 and as he got to the car so he saw the passenger door open and Drury Lee fall out of the car and run off. The defence barristers questioning went something like this;

"So let me get this right, you see the accident take place in front of you and you immediately turn right into the hotel car park, where you stop your car, get out, jump over a small hedge and then run almost 100 yards to the scene, is that right?"

Witness "Yes that's right"

Barrister "And you said just now that you covered that distance in about 10 seconds, is that right?"

Witness "Yes that's right"

Barrister "You ran a distance of 100 yards in 10 seconds?"

Witness "Yes that's right"

Barrister "And you're how old?"

Witness "64"

Barrister "Do you seriously expect this court to believe that a 64-year-old man can run 100 yards in what amounts to an almost world record time?"

Witness "Well yes"

Barrister "Would you describe yourself as a fit 64-year-old?"

Witness "Yes I would"

Barrister "How do you qualify that then? Just how fit are you?"

Witness "Well two years ago I rowed the Atlantic single-handed, does that count?"

The court erupted into laughter as this 64-year-old man; small in stature had managed to completely silence the man who was trying to belittle him. It transpired that the Judge was a former sub-mariner and he and the witness then spent the next ten minutes talking about various aspects of their life at sea as if the rest of us weren't even in the room. The Judge then turned to the defence barrister and asked;

"I take it you have no further questions for this witness?"

"Er, no Your Honour, thank you" he replied.

"I didn't think you would" smirked the Judge.

It was a priceless light-hearted moment and I think I knew at that point that Lee would be convicted but it certainly wasn't a foregone conclusion. Lee refused to give evidence and it was left to his barrister to try and convince the jury of his client's innocence. In my experience this is never a good idea, if you aren't prepared to tell the jury your version of events in an effort to persuade them that you are innocent then it is highly unlikely that anybody is going to believe you. It was another plus point as far as I was concerned and made me even more optimistic about the end result but I wasn't going to tell Carole that just in case. After more than a week of evidence the jury retired to consider their verdict.

It took them less than two hours to return. As the Court Usher beckoned us all to return to our seats my stomach felt like a washing machine. It's always a tense moment but today it felt more important than usual. I helped Christian wheel Carole into the court and we were joined by Verity. We parked Carole and her wheelchair on the end of the row of seats with Christian sat beside her. The place was packed and I could only find a seat behind them both.

The court was hushed as first the Judge entered and took his seat before the jury returned and took their respective places. I always find the body language of returning jurors fascinating. If they are looking at the floor then it's invariably a guilty verdict because they can't quite bring themselves to look towards the dock but if their heads are up and they look at the defendant then it's usually 'not guilty'. All of them were looking at the floor.

The foreman of the jury rose to his feet. My stomach was now on its final spin cycle. Guilty on both indictments. I grabbed Carole's and Christian's shoulders from behind and gave them both an almighty jubilant shake before remembering that Carole was still as fragile as a porcelain tea cup. I think they both mouthed the words "thank you" towards the jury as I saw a number of them smile back towards us.

The Judge then asked the prosecuting barrister to read out the victim personal statements and you could hear a pin drop as he delivered them in a manner that left nobody in any doubt as to the huge price that Carole and her family had paid and would continue to endure for a long time to come. Then it was the turn of Lee's barrister to offer some mitigation but what could he say really? His client had always denied being the driver but offered no reasonable explanation as to who was and he had not shown the slightest element of regret or remorse. The Judge then ordered Lee to stand and sentenced him to four years and four months imprisonment and then disqualified him from driving for six years. As Lee was taken down he showed absolutely no emotion. Unlike the rest of us who were over the moon.

We left the court room with smiles as wide as The Solent. There seemed to be dozens of people wanting to congratulate Carole, to shake her hand, kiss her on the cheek and to wish her a speedy recovery. I saw Wayne Voller and shook him firmly by the hand, he'd done a truly fantastic job leading the investigation team, which consisted of some 25 officers and staff over many months and it goes without saying that he was delighted at the sentence.

The next day's Portsmouth News carried a full front page with photos of Lee and the wrecked cars. The following week saw the BBC Traffic Cops program dedicate the entire one hour program to the crash and subsequent investigation. I have to say it was done very well and made gripping TV and hopefully made the public a little more aware just how life changing these events can be for those involved.

In the weeks that followed I received cards and letters of thanks from Carole, Verity and Christian and despite the fact that Carole still had a number of operations to undergo I was so pleased for her and her lovely family that she was now on the road to recovery.

DAVID NUNN

Operation **NORWOOD**
Category **A**
9th November 2005

2005 Hampshire fatalities = 90
2005 Nationally fatalities = 3200

Without doubt 2005 had been a busy year for our office. It seemed like everything we got sent to was cither a confirmed fatality or a potential fatal. Our Section had been depleted of experienced personnel recently and we were babysitting two newish recruits who were proving to be somewhat problematic for both me and the two Michaels. One of them was an experienced Traffic officer who had transferred from another station but was nursing his ex-wife through terminal cancer, which meant he was never at work and the other one had arrived under a bit of a cloud with a reputation for laziness and an incredible ability to bend the truth. None of us trusted him and I'd been given the dubious task of looking after him with a view to kicking his backside if necessary. He'd been given the nickname of 'The Weasel' and it seemed to suit him rather well. Our Sgt. had already made it her mission to either make him or break him but in the meantime it meant that the Michaels and I were basically left to fend for ourselves.

Our current work commitments were already on overload, to the point that the previous Sunday evening had seen us being deployed to yet another serious RTA on St. Mary's Road, Portsmouth, where a drunken 13 year old female pedestrian had lost a game of chicken with a car whilst deliberately running out in front of the traffic with her equally drunk friends. She had massive head injuries and as I crouched down in the middle of the road trying to hold her bloodied, smashed skull together so I looked at the paramedic kneeling on the ground on the other side of this shattered little body and he just shook his head. As he did so I could feel myself welling up, my eyes filled with tears. I looked up at Mike Batten and shook my head towards him. The look upon his face was one of utter despair. Not another one, surely? I couldn't remember a worse summer frankly and I didn't think the three of us could take much more.

By some miracle the young girl survived and within a few days had been discharged from hospital with the biggest alcohol induced headache she is ever likely to have! It was early evening and the three of us were sat in the office busily writing reports and desperately trying to play catch up. I was on the phone to the QA getting an update on Carole Miller.

Mike Control to any Mike Charlie units available for Rudmore roundabout please, serious RTI between a truck and a pedal cycle.

The two Michaels grabbed their gear and made a dash for the back yard as I tried to hurry up my phone call. It took me a couple of minutes to sort out before the weasel and I jumped aboard the unmarked Skoda Octavia and headed south down the M275 towards Rudmore roundabout. It was a typical autumn evening; dark and a little bit damp and the airwave traffic was rife with panic laden transmissions from those who had already arrived at the scene. It was a confirmed fatal. My heart sank.

Rudmore roundabout is the second to last exit from the M275 as it enters the city. It is one of the busiest arterial routes in the area and is positioned right outside the continental ferry port. Closing it to all traffic during the rush hour was not only going to paralyse the city and the surrounding area but was going to need considerable police resources to help sort it all out. But that was someone else's problem right now because our job was to undertake the investigation.

We arrived to a scene of utter chaos. Amongst a sea of blue lights was a 30 ton tipper truck broadside across two of the three lanes circumnavigating the roundabout, having apparently come off the slip road from the M275. A short distance behind the truck was a pedal cycle and lying under the rear axle of the truck was the body of a young man. The fire and rescue service were busily erecting a tarpaulin screen around the back of the truck as two ambulance crews and a paramedic were doing their best to resuscitate the lad. The two Michaels already had things under control, they were so good at coordinating everything that needed to be done in the early stages and they seemed to do it without actually communicating with each other. But we'd had a lot of practice lately.

I had a quick look under the truck and caught the eye of one of the paramedics who shook his head in that all too familiar way. I went back out and liaised with the Michaels. The weasel joined us and it was quickly decided that I would be the FLO and that the weasel would be the PIO, as it would give him some good experience. He seemed quite keen on the prospect and so I left him in the capable hands of the other two and headed towards one of the ambulances that I'd been told contained a friend of the deceased.

I stepped inside the ambulance and shut the door behind me. It instantly reduced the noise outside to a subdued hush, which was a bit of a relief. But that relief was very short lived. Sat on the bench seat was a young man completely traumatised by the events outside. He had just witnessed the death at very close hand of his best mate. He sat there, just staring ahead, as pale a human being as I'd ever seen. He was in total shock, not just shocked at what he had seen but medically in a very bad way. The ambulance crew was busily taking his blood pressure and were genuinely concerned for his welfare. I've seen plenty of people shocked by something they have either witnessed or been involved in but never have I seen anyone so completely anguished. I sat beside him and after some gentle coaxing managed to get his name out of him. Karl then looked at me through tear soaked eyes and asked the question.

"Is he dead?"

"Yes mate I'm afraid he is" I replied.

I let him take that in for a few moments before asking him the obvious question.

"Can you tell me who he is?"

"Dave Nunn, he was my best mate" he replied as the tears now streamed down his face.

"Do you know where he lives?" I asked.

He pointed out of the ambulance window towards the huge block of flats that overlooks Mile End Road and

Rudmore roundabout.

"He lives up there with his girlfriend, Fleur" he said.

I quickly wrote down a few details and then asked him if he had seen what had happened. Very slowly he said that both he and David were industrial painters and had been working on Rudmore flyover all week painting the concrete and steel under structure. The area immediately beneath the flyover was large enough to place a workmen's hut, a ships container to store all their equipment in and have it surrounded by a security fence. The pair of them had finished work for the day and David was about to set off for home on his bike. He put both the lights on his bike because it was dark and Karl had taken the piss out of him because of it. They had an exchange of friendly banter as David then rode away from the kerb. He'd only ridden a matter of a few feet and as he crossed the exit lane from the slip road so the tipper truck had arrived at the junctions give-way lines. Except the truck didn't give-way or stop and ran straight over David, killing him instantly. Karl took a deep breath.

"I can't believe he's gone, I mean I was talking to him only a few seconds before, how can that happen?"

The ambulance crew was still very concerned about him and said they would take him to QA for a check-up. I got out of the ambulance to see the truck driver in hand cuffs being placed into the back of a patrol car and driven away. Sgt. Jerram arrived as did the Crash Investigation Unit, Photographic and Scenes of Crime, together with the Crash Tender that would now act as the hub for the investigation. We all gathered inside the office section of the Crash Tender as the incident logs and policy logs were quickly updated with what had taken place so far and what direction the investigation would now take. From the outset this was declared as a Category A incident and I was officially appointed as the FLO.

Within minutes I left the scene and drove the short

distance down Mile End Road and left into Estella Road to locate David's next of kin. I'd driven past Mile Ends huge block of flats on countless occasions but had never actually been inside one of them. They looked pretty depressing from the outside I have to say and I often wondered quite what first time foreign visitors thought of them as they disembarked from the cross channel ferry to be greeted by the site of a structure more reminiscent of the Berlin Wall than a place to house human beings.

I climbed the stairs to the second floor and could feel my heart pounding, although I wondered whether it was because of my usual anxiety about delivering this latest death message or because I was just so bloody unfit. As I looked out over the balcony to my right I could just about see the scene of the crash and the haze of blue lights beneath the flyover. It struck me as being particularly cruel that this young man had died within sight of his home. I took a deep breath and knocked on the door.

It was answered fairly quickly by a young woman in her late twenties. As soon as she saw me standing there in my yellow jacket and white hat she knew. Her hand immediately clamped across her mouth. She nodded quickly when I asked if she was Fleur and I asked if I could come in. She didn't say anything but beckoned me in. Unusually the stairs from the front door went down and not up and I followed her downstairs into the lounge. She was obviously in the middle of doing the ironing and moved the ironing board away from the front of the settee and then beckoned me to sit down. She then shut the lounge door and sat on the same settee next to me. She looked incredibly nervous and it had a knock-on effect towards me as I could now feel myself starting to shake. And as I started to speak I could hear my voice quivering. I told her the awful news and she buried her head in her hands. We sat there in silence for a couple of minutes before she asked how, where and why. I gave her the briefest of circumstances before she got to her feet and said she needed to tell the rest of the family. She then left the room and I heard her talking quietly to someone else. She returned a short while later and said she'd just told her 12 year old daughter Melissa.

Within a few minutes the three of us were getting into my car to head towards David's brothers house at Hilsea. Fleur couldn't remember the actual address but could guide me there and within five minutes we had arrived outside. We agreed that she would stay in the car whilst I knocked on the door. I took another deep breath, rang the bell and waited. No reply. I rang again, no reply. I went back to the car and spoke to Fleur who suggested we drive up to Drayton to see David's sister Alyson.

Within ten minutes we had arrived outside and this time all three of us went to the door. Alyson opened it and within seconds Fleur had told her about the crash. Alyson cried out and ran into the downstairs loo where she threw up. Both Fleur and Melissa were now in tears. Alyson returned and started asking all the usual questions but within a couple of minutes said she needed to phone her parents to tell them. I asked her if she was able to do that or would she prefer it if I did it. She explained that they were quite elderly and lived on the Isle of Wight so although it was a bit impersonal to tell them on the phone that was the only practical way they could do it. She went into the next room and I heard her telling her parents that their youngest son had died.

Within minutes other family members and friends started to arrive but the focus was on how to get the parents over from the island as neither of them could drive. I told them that was something I could assist with quite easily as I could get a patrol car to pick them up from home and deliver them to the ferry at Ryde and that I would then go down to the terminal this side, collect them and bring them up to the house. It saved them having to think about it and gave me the opportunity to take a breather from the intense emotion taking place. I made all the necessary phone calls and then made my way towards the ferry terminal in the Skoda.

Less than an hour later I found myself standing on the pontoon. The very last couple to disembark was Pauline and David Nunn (senior) complete with a rather old looking white Yorkie type dog. I said I'd drive them up to Alyson's house and they thanked me as only elderly people can. The walk from the ferry pontoon to the car takes you along a rather long railway platform at the Portsmouth Harbour station and as I followed slowly behind them I became fixated by the Yorkies legs because they were stained yellow. Then I noticed that it seemed to be incontinent and was leaving a trail of doggy pee on the platform. I prayed it would empty its bladder before we got to the car.

Thankfully Mrs. Nunn put the dog on the floor in the rear of the car and as quickly as I dare I drove the five miles or so back up to Alyson's house. As we arrived it seemed that there were now so many people in the house that there wasn't enough room for everyone and there were several standing outside in the front garden. This included Daryl who was David's older brother and whose house I'd been to earlier. He and his wife Ali had been out fetching their two young daughters when I called and now of course he wanted to know everything. I got the distinct impression that Daryl was the unofficial head of the family and that he would probably become their spokesman.

However within minutes of our arrival I started to hear some murmurings about the dog. It became obvious that because of its well-known propensity to leak everywhere it wasn't exactly welcome inside the house. Before I knew it a full blown row had erupted in the garden and Daryl had to act as peace maker. It went on for several minutes and in the end a young lad volunteered to go and buy some disposable nappies for it and to speed up the process I drove him down to the shops! Before I did so I phoned the mortuary at the QA to arrange an urgent viewing to get the ID done.

No sooner had I returned to the house it was time to undertake that most abhorrent of tasks, the formal identification. Daryl and his father volunteered and to my surprise so did Fleur. It was now close to 11 pm as we entered the mortuary. The mortuary attendant explained the rules and I asked Daryl to confirm to me formally if it was David. They all held hands as we entered the viewing room and Daryl nodded towards me that it was David. I left the room to allow them some private time together.

I drove them back to Alyson's house and we sat in the front room whilst I briefed them on my role, the press policy and the need to do an ID statement and the G28 which Darryl volunteered to sign in his name. They agreed that a family press statement was the best option and that they would try and get it ready for tomorrow. By the time I left it was gone midnight and I drove slowly back to the office which was a hive of activity with the two Michaels doing most of the work whilst the weasel made the tea. I wrote a number of pages in my latest FLO log and got home sometime after 2am.

I was back on late turn the following afternoon and phoned Darryl to see how things were. The answer was not too good obviously and when I mentioned popping up to see them to return some of David's property he declined stating that everyone was still too upset to talk and as yet they hadn't managed to put a family statement together. He said he couldn't sleep and found himself standing at Rudmore roundabout staring at the scene at 2.30 that morning just so that he could put things straight in his mind. He asked me to phone him back tomorrow morning.

The two Michaels came into the office and shut the door. They were fuming about something and said they'd just come from a meeting with Adrienne because the weasel had spoken to her earlier and asked to be removed from the PIO role because he didn't think he was experienced enough to handle such a case.

"He's a spineless little twat" spat Mike Batten "how's he ever going to gain the experience if he doesn't actually do the job?".

"Trouble is Michael we can't afford for him to cock it up and lose the job in court in 12 months' time can we, so it's going to be down to us three to ensure its done right" said Mick Anderson, being the wise old owl that he was!

"Yeah but don't you think us three have got enough on our plates right now, we asked for help because of our work load and look what we get, more grief than we had before, its ludicrous, we haven't got time to baby sit him" continued Michael.

"Mike, I have to agree with the old bloke in the corner mate, our priority has to be getting the job done to the very highest standards we can" I said "and if that means us taking on even more than we have already then I'm sure that between us we can get a result. Now stop ya whinging and ya whining and go and make the coffee".

"I'll get the weasel to make it, I think that's about the limit of his capabilities" fumed Michael and he slammed the door on the way out.

"He is right though Mick, it's ridiculous that we've had this one dumped on us as well" I said.

"Yes I know but I've got a feeling this one is a possible Section 1 and it needs to be done properly" replied Mick.

Mike returned with the coffee and we had a general discussion about last night's incident and Mick said there were certain things he'd found inside the cab of the tipper truck that might lead towards this one not being a Section 3 but a Section 1, but he was waiting for an interim report from the CIU and the Vehicle Examiner before he would comment any further. We agreed that until such time as we knew he wouldn't tell me anything and that for the time being we would be treating it as an upper level Section 3 careless driving. He said the truck driver Alan Bromley went 'no comment' during his initial interview last night before being released on bail. He was apparently rather disinterested and arrogant about the whole situation. Oh God no, not another one I thought.

We spent the rest of the shift sorting out property, contacting witnesses and arranging interviews with them, batting off the press, writing up policy logs, bagging and sealing some physical evidence and hoping above all else that we didn't get dragged out to another one. It was thankfully a quiet day on the roads.

The next morning whilst off duty I took a call from Darryl. Could he arrange a meeting with me and the rest of the family tonight so that I could tell everyone the same thing at the same time, rather than him having to pass messages and perhaps getting things wrong, which might cause problems for everyone, me included. I thought it was an excellent idea although I wasn't quite sure how many people I'd be talking to.

I soon found out though and learned very quickly that David Nunn's family did everything together and rather than me being the FLO for one person or sometimes two, on this occasion it was going to be about a dozen!

We met at Karen's house in West Leigh at 5.30 that evening. Although I'd seen her on the night at Alyson's house I didn't realise that she was another sister. So there was Karen and her husband, Darryl and his wife Ali, parents Pauline and David, Alyson and her husband, Fleur of course and a couple of family friends. We all filed into the front room and a chair was placed in front of the fireplace facing out towards them. It felt a bit like a job interview and in some respects I suppose it was, they wanted to know the 'ins and outs' of everything.

They wanted me to be completely honest with them and not to leave anything out. This was a difficult one and I had to explain fully that my role was not an investigative one and that for security reasons the investigation team might not tell me everything either. This was not done to cover anything up but to protect the integrity of the investigation and to prevent certain key facts from being leaked to the press and perhaps jeopardising any future trial of the man responsible for killing David. I told them that although they might not agree with this point they had to understand that everything we did from the moment we arrived at the scene to the time we eventually get to court, which will take a year or more was done in the best interests of David and his family with the simple aim of obtaining justice for all of them.

I think that satisfied them and we then moved onto the family statement and issues surrounding the Press. There were mutterings about not wanting them involved obviously and I told them that we would be using the Press in appeals for witnesses etc. and not to be too surprised to see quite a bit of footage in the local paper and on the radio. They agreed between them that they would formulate a family statement by tomorrow and then we would be able to release David's details to the press. It was also agreed that to assist me they wouldn't all be phoning me every five minutes and that my point of contact and theirs would be Darryl and Ali. If however they wanted another family meeting with me or the SIO in the future then all they had to do was ask.

It was a really useful meeting for them and for me and after a couple of hours it was time for me to leave but not before I'd returned a few of David's personal effects to Fleur. She looked completely shattered and in complete shock. Ali put her arm around her and led her into another room away from everyone else.

The next afternoon Adrienne called me into her office to explain that following the receipt of certain information from the Vehicle Examination Unit Operation Norwood was now being upgraded from a Cat C to a Cat B enquiry. Mick's hunch was right. Accordingly David's body had been transferred overnight to the RCH in Winchester so that the PM could be conducted by a Home Office Forensic Pathologist. This will inevitably delay the release of the body back to the family and of course there is always the possibility that Bromley might exercise his right to having a second independent PM. All the signs were pointing towards this becoming a long drawn out enquiry.

Darryl phoned me at home the next morning and said that the family statement would be ready to collect at 4.30 that afternoon. I was there bang on time and then had to sit him down to explain the Home Office PM procedures, the possibility that Bromley had the right to demand a second PM and the fact that the police had upgraded the incident following certain evidence that had been discovered on the lorry. It was a lot to take in and bit by bit we went over it again. He obviously wasn't happy about the PM possibly being delayed because of a lack of Home Office Pathologists and like many people was incredulous that the offending driver had a right to a second independent PM. He was obviously intrigued by the new evidence but as I'd told everyone at that meeting there are certain things we couldn't tell them at this stage. He said he'd pass on the information as agreed to the rest of the family.

I actually collected two statements, one from the family and a second one from Fleur plus a photo of David and Fleur together on holiday in Mexico and e-mailed it all up to Media Services in Winchester.

The family statement read as follows;

Dave, also known as Little David and Nobi was the most genuine and lovable man that we have ever known. He was popular and was very much loved by all his friends and family. He was fun loving and had a way of making you smile as soon as he walked in the room. Dave was a big kid at heart and liked having all the latest gadgets. He had lots of energy and loved his sports, especially his beloved Pompey.

He was a devoted family man who worked hard so that they could enjoy the wonderful holidays that they shared together. Even though Dave had recently changed jobs, his old work colleagues were given the day off work, with which they paid their respects to him in a way he would have liked – down the pub!

Dave will be sadly missed by everyone who knew and loved him. He will never be forgotten and will always be in our memories and in our hearts.

Fleur's statement read;

Dave was a wonderful partner who I spent seven loving years with. He was also a great step-dad to our daughter and when we met I couldn't have asked for anyone as special as him to share our lives with. Dave was very loving and cared so much for his family. He was fantastic and always had a smile for us. Dave will always be in my heart and my memories. He will never be forgotten by us, his family and his many friends.

I'd been off sick for a week with a serious dose of man flu when Darryl phoned me to ask if I'd heard anything about the PM or getting the body released. I hadn't heard anything but said that as soon as I had any news I'd let him know. I returned to work on the 1st December and as luck would have it received an e mail that morning from HM Coroner stating that Bromley and his solicitor had just declined having a second PM and that David's body could now be released. That was the good news.

The not-so-good news was that during the official PM certain tissue samples had been taken from the body for analysis and following revelations in another part of the country where these samples had not been returned to the body prior to burial we now had to give the family the opportunity to say whether or not they wanted these samples returned inside the body, in a separate container with the body or could be disposed of by the mortuary staff. And the person tasked with asking the question? Yep, the FLO.

I really wasn't happy about it and the prospect of even raising the issue filled me with dread. On a recent FLO conference we'd been given some input into how these samples are used, retained and eventually returned to the next of kin. Basically the samples consist of slithers of brain tissue not much bigger than your thumb nail and these are placed on glass slides (like those you'd use under a microscope) and retained inside a small plastic box called a 'block' which was slightly smaller than a matchbox. My job was to ascertain in writing how the family wanted to proceed and to sign a pro-forma statement called the Next of Kin Statement and return it to HM Coroner.

Armed with a 'block' to show the family I arrived at Darryl and Ali's house in Hilsea. They had two young girls and after Ali had managed to pack them off to bed she showed me a drawing that one of them had done. It showed Uncle David lying on the ground with a big black lorry next to him. It was a dark and sinister picture and was clearly her way of expressing her grief. It was a shocking thing to have been drawn by one so young. I said I had a couple of really good booklets produced by the charity BRAKE specifically designed to help parents with issues surrounding their kids in the event of a road death and said I'd drop them in tomorrow.

I gave them the good news first concerning the second PM and told them that they should receive notification early next week about releasing David's body so they could arrange his funeral. It had taken more than three weeks to get to this stage and although it hadn't taken quite as long as one or two previous situations I'd dealt with it's still too long a process geared towards appeasing the defendant which is just plain wrong.

I took a very deep breath and then raised the subject of

the tissue samples. It goes without saying that it was something that neither of them had given any thought to and I have to say they dealt with it very well indeed. They said they would need to consult the rest of the family obviously and could they get back to me after the weekend?

Darryl phoned me the following Tuesday concerning the Next of Kin statement and said that the family had opted to have the samples placed back with the body. I thanked him for sorting this very delicate issue out on behalf of the family and myself, it couldn't have been easy for him. I faxed Karen Hyde at the Coroner's office to update her and waited for a response.

Karen phoned me the following morning. Was I aware that opting to have the samples placed back inside the body was very likely to delay having David released for between two to four weeks? Was I aware? No I fucking wasn't and why the hell did no one from the Coroner's office brief me fully before sending me off to do their dirty work? I was furious and really let rip at Karen. It wasn't her fault personally but it was going to fall back on my shoulders to have to go and tell Darryl and I'm not sure I can do that. Once I'd calmed down a bit I told her to get back to the mortuary at the RCH and to tell them from me that if necessary I'll come up there and do it myself. They had no excuse in delaying things like this and I will take it up with the Coroner himself if necessary. I slammed the phone down and marched around the office kicking chairs whilst cursing and swearing about how pissed off I was that as an FLO I always ended up having to clean up other peoples mess.

Less than hour later Karen phoned me back. She said that the samples should be returned from the laboratory in London to the RCH by next Monday 12th December so it shouldn't delay things for too much longer. That's still another five days away plus then someone will have to replace the samples back into the body before it can be released so that's probably going to take another couple of days at least. What a crap system. Karen agreed, although I feel sure she was just trying to pacify me. Meanwhile she said she'd contact the funeral directors to update them.

I sat there for ages trying to pluck up the courage to phone Darryl. Christ I wish I still smoked. When I eventually found the courage to pick up the phone I got no reply from the home number or Darryl's mobile so I left him a message but by the time I went home at 3pm he still hadn't returned my calls.

I was at home having just finished my dinner around 8pm when my mobile rang. It was Darryl and he was really angry. He'd just been talking to the funeral directors who had told him that the body couldn't be released until next Monday at the earliest because the Police had only sent the necessary paperwork to the Coroner's office today which will delay things considerably. Some of what he said obviously compared with what I'd been told whilst other facts that had apparently emerged from the funeral directors just didn't ring true. But whatever the case it appeared that the Coroner's office in Portsmouth had dropped a massive bollock on this one or there had been a catastrophic break down in communications between us all. Darryl went onto to say that they had arranged for David's funeral to take place next Wednesday and that they had arranged for viewings to take place from Friday onwards. He wasn't angry at me, in fact the exact opposite and I said I'd investigate fully tomorrow morning and phone him just as soon as I could get a straight answer out of someone. After three quarters of an hour on the phone I think I left him in a slightly better frame of mind than when he dialled my number.

At bang on 9am the next morning I was on the phone to

Karen at the Coroner's office and gave her chapter and verse concerning Darryl's call. She had been going to call me first thing anyway because following my rant at her yesterday she had decided to get to the bottom of a procedure that was still in its infancy and had managed to obtain a definitive answer direct from the Coroner and it went something like this; the body had to stay at the RCH until Monday 12th December until the tissue samples had been returned. This cannot be speeded up any further. However if the family wanted the body returned earlier for those pre-arranged viewings, but without those samples then it could be released and collected today. They can then either have the body returned back to the RCH on Monday for the samples to be placed into the body or alternatively the samples can be brought down to the funeral directors and just placed inside the coffin. She kindly offered to speak to Darryl but I politely declined and said I'd deal with it myself.

I phoned Darryl and updated him on his options. He made an immediate unilateral decision to have the body released today and to have the samples placed in the coffin in time for the funeral. He was still angry at a crap system that had caused a huge amount of unnecessary grief at a time when they could really do without it. I couldn't agree more. I phoned Karen back to update her on the decision and asked her to contact the funeral directors to make the necessary arrangements.

I didn't hear anything further from Darryl so assumed that the funeral went smoothly. I didn't contact them at all during that week or during the subsequent Christmas period to give them the space to mourn without any further distractions.

I had no contact with the family for another four months when Ali phoned me out of the blue for an update on the investigation. I did apologise to her for not being in touch but

I had been snowed under with other FLO commitments recently. I knew Bromley was due to answer his bail on the 15th April and we were still waiting on a decision from the CPS regarding possible charges. In the end he had his bail extended to the 28th April because the CPS wanted further clarification on certain defects found on the truck and until they had those answers they weren't prepared to make a decision. I phoned Ali to update her and spent some considerable time explaining the legal differences between Section 1 and Section 3 offences with particular reference to defects on vehicles being classified as dangerous and could mean the difference between a charge of careless driving and dangerous driving. I now knew what those defects were but I couldn't tell her at this stage, they just had to trust us that we were doing all we could to secure a conviction.

The day after Bromley was supposed to return on bail I received a call from a very tearful Ali whilst I was at home. She said that the family just wasn't coping and in part that was due to not having anything concrete to cling onto. I had to tell her that the CPS had still not reached a decision but having spoken to Mick Anderson last night he said that all the indications coming from them were leaning towards it being a Section 3 careless driving.

Ali became very distressed about this and couldn't understand why it couldn't be dangerous driving, if the truck had failed to stop at the give-way lines at the bottom of the motorway slip road, how could it be anything else? I then had to explain the differences between the two offences again and then balance the evidence we had against the likelihood or otherwise of a successful conviction in court. I told her that although the family might be upset right now if he is charged with the lesser offence, their upset would be compounded to a massive degree if Bromley walked free from court because we didn't have enough evidence to secure a conviction for dangerous driving. She said she understood but that the family still wanted to press ahead with a Section 1 because they felt a Section 3 would be an insult to David's memory. She then asked if it would be possible for them to meet up with the CPS and the SIO prior to any decision being reached?

I was on late turn the next afternoon and spent two hours going over the case with Mick. We'd known each other for years; in fact we were both stationed at Southsea together in the late 1970s and early 80s before he moved onto the Traffic Division. Although he'd had no desire to climb the promotion ladder he did study the law books and kept up to date on new legislation to such a high degree that the rest of us used him as the font of all knowledge, even our sergeants and above would seek his advice!

He and Mike had been involved in a serious accident themselves a couple of years previously whilst stationary on the hard shoulder of the M275 one night their patrol car got rear ended at very high speed by a drunk driver. Mick suffered injuries to his hip and leg which would basically keep him office bound for the rest of his service. Having discussed this case at length with him and after removing all the emotion from it, the bottom line was we didn't have a strong enough case to ensure having a realistic chance of a conviction at court on a Section 1. I raised the idea that we have a meeting with the family as soon as possible so that we can then give them all the facts and explain the whole process which Mick was happy to accommodate. He did tell me that the latest information he had from the CPS was that summonses would be issued next week and would include all the offences including Section 1 and 3 but that didn't necessarily mean that come court time that Bromley would actually be prosecuted for Section 1. A glimmer of hope then.

But that glimmer of hope was snuffed out a few days later when Mick learned from the CPS that they had issued summonses for Section 3 and some tachograph offences only with no prior consultation with the SIO at all. Apparently they had also written to the family, although they couldn't actually say who, to inform them of the decision. Bloody marvelous, thank you CPS. That's going to set the cat amongst the pigeons then, especially as the meeting planned with the family is the day after tomorrow.

On Sunday morning at 10.30 Mick and I hosted the meeting in our office with Darryl and Ali, Fleur, Alyson, and Karen and her husband. The first thing Mick did was reveal the defects found on the truck. There were two significant items although one of them couldn't be considered as a defect but could have had a significant bearing on Bromley's view from the driver's seat. The defect consisted of the driver's quarter light window being badly cracked. In fact it was a spider's web of cracks that you just couldn't see through. The other item was a large electric fan, the sort you'd have in an office or at home, was positioned on the far right hand side of the dash facing the drivers face, in effect obscuring his forward and right hand vision. A separate issue concerned the fact that there was no tachograph chart fitted in the truck but following extensive enquiries into the number of hours Bromley had driven prior to the crash it was deemed not to have been a factor in the crash itself but he needed prosecuting for it.

Mick then explained in very great detail why the CPS had opted for the Section 3 offence and that to a large extent he agreed with them and the reason he agreed was that he wouldn't be able to look the family in the eye if Bromley were to walk free from court which was highly likely if we couldn't prove a very weak dangerous driving charge.

One by one they fired questions at us and Mick answered each and every one of them in a clear, concise manner. They weren't always happy with what they heard, which was understandable but in the end most of them said they understood the position better now.

We then went on to discuss a whole load of other

concerns about court appearances, the inquest, private prosecutions, civil claims, meeting the CPS and Victim Impact statements. They were particularly keen to meet someone from CPS. They said we'd been open and honest with them and they expected the CPS to be the same. We had a long discussion about the impact statements and it seemed that all of them wanted some kind of input into it. I suggested that the best thing would be for those that wanted to, to write their own individual statements then hand them to me and I would merge them all into one single statement, taking the most salient points from each and place the whole thing in Fleur's name. They liked the idea and said they would get them to me as soon as possible. After two hours the meeting was concluded and although they were a bit deflated we left them smiling.

I then e-mailed Kate Brown the senior CPS lawyer in charge of the case requesting that she or one of her staff meet with the family.

Two days later she phoned me and gave me two dates of the 8th and 12th June which I passed onto Darryl. He phoned me back a few minutes later to clarify the dates because Bromley was due in court on the 7th June so what was the point in having a meeting after his court appearance? I hadn't realised I have to confess and so I e-mailed Kate Brown back to discuss further. She phoned me the next afternoon and rather glibly said that she couldn't possibly meet the family before 7th June because her diary was full! This was like a red rag to a bull with me and I told her that she had a duty to meet with them, they were nothing to be afraid of, this wasn't some chav family we were dealing with here and if it made her feel any easier then I'd be more than happy to sit in on the meeting and referee it. But she stood her ground and insisted that she was just too busy to meet them before the 7th but was happy to do so on the dates she had already quoted.

I phoned Ali and told her to write to Kate Brown immediately to complain and demand an earlier meeting. It transpired that Fleur had been the recipient of that other CPS letter and so it was decided that she would reply to that and request a meeting. I was later given a copy of Fleur's letter and it was excellent and then lo and behold a few days after that I received a call from Kate Brown stating that owing to a cancellation in her diary she would now be free on the 6th June at 4.30pm but insisted that she would only meet with two members of the family.

Come the 6th June I met Darryl, Ali, Fleur and David senior outside the CPS office. They all wanted to be at the meeting but Kate Brown insisted that she would only meet with two of them and that Inspector Howard Marrs would also be present. I did know in advance that Howard would be there and told him that the family were thoroughly decent people and to treat them accordingly. In the end Ali and Fleur were elected as the family representatives and the rest of us waited outside for the best part of two hours.

When they emerged both of them had been crying and they were very emotional. Again they hadn't liked what they'd heard but now seemed resigned to the fact thatt was the way it was going to be. They didn't like Kate Brown's rather aloof attitude towards them and said that Howard was rather patronising.

Three days later I got a call from Ali. Could I come and see them? I was at another RTA at the time and didn't get there until quite late. There was only Ali and Fleur at the house and both of them had been crying again, they really weren't coping at all. They went over the meeting with Kate Brown again saying that she was rude and just hadn't listened to them. We talked at length about how things work at court and I relayed a few stories to them, both good and bad experiences, some of which made them laugh out loud but I left them in no doubt that even though Bromley was facing the lesser charge there was still no guarantee of a conviction. In truth I think they just needed further reassurance from me about things, especially as they'd had their confidence knocked by the meeting with CPS. I left them smiling at the end.

A date for the inquest was set for 24th October. There had been weeks of inter departmental squabbling about this because the Coroner David Horsley had said it was ridiculous that the inquest was held first because that would severely limit the questions Bromley might answer so as not to incriminate himself prior to his trial, the date for which hadn't yet been set. The family requested another meeting with Mick and I prior to the inquest and so on the 18th October no fewer than 13 members of the family arrived at Cosham nick for a two and a half hour question and answer session. The main concerns were the differences between the two court procedures and the rights that Bromley might have not to answer certain questions at the inquest. The more I met the extended Nunn family the more I liked them. They were a solid and united unit with one aim; justice for David. They were all such nice people and I couldn't help but draw comparisons between them and the Panormo family.

The inquest day arrived and the tension was obvious. Outside in the hallway there was a lot of shuffling of feet and nervous coughing as one by one the family arrived. The press was there as always and then Alan Bromley appeared at the far end of the hall with his solicitor. He was a big bloke in his mid-50s, rather unkempt looking even in his suit. At 1030 we were called into court and it was a tight fit cramming everyone in, so much so that I ended up having to stand against the back wall. One by one a number of witnesses were called, including the Home Office Pathologist and the Crash

Investigator PC Mick Gumby. There were no real revelations and Mr Horsley seemed to whip through the whole procedure in double quick time. But then it came to Bromley taking the stand. The place went completely silent and you could cut the atmosphere with a knife. This was the first time the Nunn family had seen the man responsible for killing David and it must be incredibly difficult to keep your emotions in check when in such close proximity to him. He looked even bigger stood in the witness box and his solicitor immediately informed the Coroner that his client had been advised by her that there were certain questions that he just would not be able to answer. Mr Horsley basically told the solicitor that this was his inquest and that he wouldn't be dictated to by her or anybody else about the manner in which he conducted it. That said he didn't actually put Bromley under any pressure and I think there was only one question he wouldn't answer. He left immediately afterwards having not expressed any condolences towards the family, which in my experience is not a good thing. By lunchtime the inquest was over and the Coroner recorded it as Accidental Death. Outside in the hallway there was a collective sigh of relief that we had at last got over that hurdle.

A few weeks later and we got a date for Bromleys pre-trial review to be held on 4th January. This is basically a formal hearing held in the Magistrates Court whereby the prosecution and the defence outline certain aspects of their case and the Magistrates decide whether or not they can hear the case or whether it should be sent to the Crown Court. It isn't necessary for the defendant to appear in person unless they intend pleading guilty there and then, in which case the Magistrates can deal with it straight away. Mick and I discussed this and both of us concluded that Bromley was the sort of man that might just do that in the hope that neither the family nor the press would be present. I phoned Ali to appraise her and she was very grateful for the information and said the whole family would be there on the 4th January. It was only a couple of days before Christmas and this would be the second Christmas since the crash and she said that this time of year was always going to be difficult. I wished her and the family all the best and hoped that we could get some closure for them in 2007.

The 4th January arrived and the whole family was there in force but Bromley failed to turn up and the case was adjourned to the 15th January. So two weeks later we all reconvened and at least this time he was there and I think he was somewhat taken aback by the sheer number of people who had turned up. He entered a 'not guilty' plea and a trial date of the 12th April was set, proving once again that the cogs of the judicial process turn far too slowly.

The trial was conducted by District Judge Anne Arnold rather than a bench of Magistrates. I suspect that the CPS had some input into this as it was rather unusual. The last time I could recall such a move was for the trial of Dennis Sharp in the Bridgette Panormo case and without doubt a request had been submitted asking for a Judge to preside over the case as it was rather complex. We had about 20 family members and friends attending in Court 1 and Darryl looked at me as he took his seat and said "Is this really going to happen today Steve?"

I smiled at him and nodded my head but knew that there was always the possibility of something going wrong and it being adjourned. Mick and I stood there ensuring that everyone had got a seat before we took ours. Bromley arrived and stood in the dock, staring straight ahead, not looking to his right at the family.

After Judge Arnold had taken her seat so the trial began with the prosecutor outlining the case before calling a number of eye witnesses to the crash itself, all of whom had been on Rudmore roundabout and all of whom had seen David on his bike with its lights on. Other statements were read out to the court and the tears flowed as one of the first Paramedics on the scene described what he saw. But perhaps the most compelling evidence came from PC Mick Gumby from the Forensic Crash Investigation Unit. He told the court about the damage to the window and the fact that you couldn't see out of it in day light and certainly not during darkness as it had been on the night of the crash. Photographs showing the lack of view to the right from the elevated driver's seat, both at the scene itself and in more detail during a number of tests proved that Bromley had a very limited view to his right. Now add in that fan wedged onto the right hand side of the dash, which further obscured his forward vision to the right corner of the windscreen together with the fact that eye witnesses said that the truck had failed to stop at the give way lines, although it had slowed to around 5mph, it merely compounded an already bad situation into one with tragic consequences. His evidence was delivered in a very professional but easy to understand manner and the various photos provided a vivid image about the almost total lack of vision from the driver's seat.

Mick Anderson took the stand to read out the formal interview he'd had with Bromley following the completion of the Police investigation. He was quite reasonable throughout when being questioned about the truck itself and stated that he'd just collected the truck from Adams Morey, a local HGV service centre some three miles away. They hadn't been able to fix the quarter light glass as they didn't have one in stock so he was going to change it later and he was fully compliant about why he didn't have a chart in the tachograph head. He was on his way to the ferry port on the other side of Rudmore roundabout to buy cheap diesel before returning home to Wiltshire. However when it came to answering questions about the crash itself he went 'no comment' which is always frustrating.

Bromley took the stand and after answering a few questions from his solicitor the prosecutor rose to his feet and started to grill him on the crash itself. He said he thought he'd stopped at the junction and that he'd exercised as much care as he could but didn't see David at all. Asked if the damage to the window had obscured his vision he said not because he had the main window open and was looking through that. Well surely if you'd gone to those lengths, ie stopped and wound your window down then how on earth didn't you see a cyclist with its lights on just feet from where you were sitting he was asked? Bromley couldn't answer him and just said he didn't know.

"The truth Mr Bromley is that you couldn't see out of that broken window, you didn't wind your other window down and you failed to stop at the junction and as a consequence David Nunn ended up underneath your truck because you drove carelessly, isn't that right?" asked the prosecutor in a somewhat raised voice.

"No I don't think that is right" replied Bromley in a not very convincing manner.

It was now late afternoon and Judge Arnold retired to consider her verdict. We all filed outside for a breather whilst Mick and a couple of the others went outside for a fag. They kept asking me how I thought it had gone? I really didn't want to raise their hopes and remained fairly non-committal but overall I think it went very well and Bromley didn't come across as being sorry or say anything that may have helped his case. Less than an hour went by and we were called back in. Once everyone was settled Judge Arnold returned. My stomach was churning over and over, my fingers crossed for the right result.

Bromley was told to stand as Judge Arnold addressed him and found him guilty of careless driving and the tacho offence. Bromley showed no emotion whatsoever which is more than I can say for the Nunn family, who remained very dignified throughout but who were understandably overjoyed. Mick and I glanced towards each other and smiled. The prosecutor then asked me to take the stand in order that I could read out the combined Victim Impact statement, which was something I'd written and re-written about 50 times over the last few months in an effort to get it right for the family.

It was written in Fleur's name on behalf of the entire family.

David Jason Frederick Nunn is the victim here. He cannot speak today and we are here to represent him.

We are the family of the victim, our little David, our Dave. We are his parents, his older brother and sisters, his nephews and nieces, his wife to be, his daughter and the child he never got to have but wanted with me so badly, we to are victims. To condense the magnitude of our feelings and the impact this has had on all our lives into two or three pages has been practically impossible and one of the hardest things we've ever had to put into writing together.

First you need to know about Dave and the person he was to both his family and his friends. He didn't have an enemy in the world, you simply couldn't dislike him; he didn't have a bad bone in his body. He was hard working, gentle, considerate, extremely thoughtful, funny and loving. He loved children and animals, even insects! And they in turn loved him. He always had or made time for everyone and could make you laugh with his funny impressions. Above all Dave valued his family and his friends, always working at sorting family get togethers and always there if he thought you needed him.

I am Dave's widow, Fluer. We had our whole lives ahead of us, everything was just starting to fall into place for Dave, Melissa my daughter and I. Dave had asked me to marry him and we had begun house hunting as Dave wanted a better life for his young family. I couldn't have asked for anyone more loving, caring, considerate and loyal than Dave as a partner and a friend. Dave loved being a dad to our daughter but he wanted another child. Just four weeks earlier we had decided to have a baby "I'm going to be a daddy" was all Dave could say with the biggest smile you ever saw; he'd even picked out the names he would like. Dave had just changed jobs; he didn't want to work away or too far from home anymore. He started work on Rudmore roundabout just two minutes from our home. I will never forget that night, those unforgettable words when I was told. My world collapsed in that split second. Every day I walk outside my house I have a view of where my Dave was killed and it hurts like hell. People have asked why don't I move because of this but I'm so torn. My memories with my Dave are here at our home, a mixture of comfort and pain. I need to feel these around me but living where he was killed is a constant torture so either way I lose. No-one could ever know how empty and lonely I felt then and still do. The guilt for not being there, knowing that my Dave was dead at the end of our road. The dreams and future we planned are all gone. Instead I have to carry on without him. I never realized how long one day and one night could be and that's how I live, day to day. I don't see the future, I cling to the past, wishing every morning I'd wake up from this nightmare that is now my life. I've had to return to work, I have no choice. I am emotionally and financially ruined but I have to do day to day things I really don't want to because I am now a single parent and have to go on for my daughter Melissa. My life has changed forever and so have I; I'm angry, my heart is broken and so am I as person. Our daughter Melissa has become extremely introverted and clingy, trying to hide her emotions for fear of upsetting me, trying hard to reassure me when it should be the other way around. Instead of us spending our free time doing and planning things, as you all do, I plan everything around my visiting Dave at the cemetery, it's the only way I can be with him but I'll never feel his touch, hear his voice or see him, only in my memories. Our future was stolen from us so unnecessarily, so cruelly. We feel so alone now its just the two of us, the future a black cloud we can't see through. I want what I can never have; I just want my Dave back.

On the day of the accident David's parents Pauline and David had their whole world turned upside down. They feel their life and dreams of retirement on the island are no longer of any interest, indeed they dread each time the phone rings, as that is how they received the news that their baby had been killed. They also feel a deep need and an obvious urge to be near their other children, they are lost and completely distraught with grief and loss. You do not expect to outlive your children, especially your youngest child, your baby. This is every parents nightmare. They have found it extremely difficult to cope since November 9th and have found the words for this statement virtually impossible to come up with. Just how do you express in words the realization that you will never see your son again, you can't. instead they have to try and comfort themselves with holding onto their precious possessions from throughout his young life. Some clothes, even baby clothes, music CDs and DVDs, his old toys and his many gadgets. Their prized bed, on which as a toddler David had scrawled on the head board 'mum, dad and little David' in the middle (where he would have climbed into bed with them). They have photographs of him of course, however they are no substitute. But above all they have been denied the chance to see David and I as parents to any grandchildren we may have brought to them. In their opinion not only was Dave's future wiped out but so were their hopes and dreams.

Dave's older brother and sisters all feel unimaginable hurt, disbelief, grief, guilt and frustration that they can't change what's happened or bring their baby brother back. Everyday they wake up hurting with the knowledge of what's happened and instantly the overwhelming feelings well-up inside. Karen cries constantly and feels the pain of her two sons Stephen and Daniel who weren't just Daves nephews but work colleagues and more importantly his mates. They are both expecting their first child whom Dave will never know. Alyson cries constantly, reliving the nightmare of that night on the 9th November 2005 when the police turned up with me and Melissa and the news which she then had to break to her parents about their youngest son, news she knew would shatter their lives forever. She then had to explain through her own grief the same nightmare news to her three young children Lorin 11, Katie 10 and Maigan 8. they adored and loved their Uncle David, though sadly they would see him no more, something so hard when only the day before they had been laughing and joking with him. Then there is Kate and her young sons whom Dave lived with when he first left home. He was her rock as a single parent, he was always there for them in every possible way, helping Kate guide the boys through life and helping wherever he could, acting like a big brother and father figure to Luke 16, Jordan 12 and Jack 11. Kate feels so hurt and angry that her youngest son Billy 3, will forget those precious memories with Dave only remembering what she has told him, they had so little time together, it's so unfair.

Then there's Darryl, Dave's big brother and best friend; they were inseparable. Our two families were like one, socializing, holidaying, planning future dreams of setting up a business together and maybe moving abroad with our families to improve the quality of our family's lives. That will now never be. Dave and I were even in Darryl and Ali's will to bring up their daughters if anything ever happened to either of them. They have two daughters, a 14 year old and a 5 year old. They were so close to Dave and the effect on them is heart wrenching. Charley has become clingy, quiet and has made a hidden shrine of photos and memorable items to him and goes quiet and cries randomly. Brooke goes to bed only to wake in the early hours crying inconsolably and asking us to bring him back, or she says her uncle Donzey visits her and has some of her juice. She's drawn pictures with two lorries, one white, one black and calls the black one the bad lorry. PC Woodward has witnessed this himself. She has a new board game she refuses to play with anyone but uncle Donzey. Darryl feels guilty. He was his big brother and feels he should have protected him, looked after him, he doesn't know what to do. He see's his parents and sisters all hurting and in pieces and can't change anything. He sees me and Melissa and the pain is excruciating, he feels like a big brother to me and is extremely protective towards me and Melissa. He tries to be strong for everyone but inside he is so churned up. He's lost his baby brother and his best friend, the best you could ever have. Dave was/IS special; he made Darryl laugh, reassured him when he was low; they shared life. There's an emptiness that's obvious with his every waking moment. He has distanced himself from his friends, he

226

avoids talking about Dave because then he has to face the harsh reality of the truth which he tries to hide from, he's not here and he can't cope with that. Darryl constantly thinks of the "if onlys" and the "if onlys" make his head want to explode. The 9th November 2005 was the worst day of his entire life and a part of him died that day to. He is a broken man and our family is consumed with grief and loss; we all loved him so much.

We have been informed that the most acknowledgement we could hope for is a ban and a fine, which is bad enough, however we have also been informed that Mr Bromley and his team could plead this would affect his livelihood. What about Dave's livelihood, our daughters and mine? Dave's father has suffered continued ill health due to the strain of these court appearances as has Darryl, who was rushed into hospital the day before the last court hearing with what we all thought was a suspected heart attack. I myself have had to seek medical advice due to the stress and depression this has all caused, it could have been so much easier to just give up, however this is a choice I didn't really have because of our daughter Melissa, I have to keep going. Indeed every one of us has suffered both physically and mentally, putting additional strains on individual relationships.

None of you will understand or realize the difficulties, tears and frustration it has taken in writing this statement. Whether the full impact and implications of this tragedy could possibly be put across to your good selves is doubtful. We are writing this for Dave and the fear of it being wrong and letting him down is the only thing we can do for him because today is soul destroying.

Alan Bromley. You did this, you changed all our lives forever, you caused this unimaginable pain we all feel. Unimaginable pain which you heightened by ensuring we could not lay our Dave to rest for several weeks whilst you took your time to decide whether or not you had a second post mortem carried out, something you eventually declined but took your time in doing so.

227

(It was at this stage that I felt myself welling up. I had tears in my eyes and could hardly see what I was supposed to be reading and I could hear my voice starting to shake).

You even decided after taking Dave's life away when we, as his loved ones, could put him to rest. An accident we're told. Dave was only 26 with a life ahead of him. He did not die of natural causes, he was killed. You Mr Bromley were in control, as owner of this company and as the driver there were three factors in this accident that you had the control over to change and you could have avoided this happening. Firstly, in peak time traffic at a notoriously busy roundabout whilst in control of a 32 ton vehicle you failed to stop at the give-way lines, even with the knowledge that your window was broken thus reducing your visibility. Your tachograph was not in use. Had you been driving too long and thus you were tired? We will probably never really know. It's your business, your responsibility. When you hit our Dave and eventually stopped were you in shock? NO. Did you get out and check on our Dave? NO. Did you immediately phone an ambulance? NO. Thinking only of you and the consequences to yourself and your business you sat in your cab and started filling out documentation to falsify your tachograph records. You were cold, calculated, callous and inhumane. Dave isn't just anyone, he is our son, brother, uncle, nephew, cousin and friend to many. He was robbed of marrying the woman he loved, of being a great dad to Melissa and having a child of his own he so longed for. You did this and have shown no remorse whatsoever, you've destroyed all our lives, you took Dave's.

You Mr Bromley will never really be held accountable for your actions. You have shown what an arrogant, spineless, selfish and self absorbed man you truly are by having the audacity to try and blame Dave, the innocent man you killed, knowing that he cannot speak for himself. The system seems to be on your side and not that of the victim whose life you took or those of us left behind in total devastation. We have felt powerless and have been totally frustrated by a system that seems to be geared towards looking after your needs and not that of the victim.

228

You know that all you face are fines and a possible ban if we're lucky. Is this justice – NO. You never acknowledged Dave's death at the time and the system still doesn't now but neither Dave nor we have a choice. We love you Dave and always will. We tried xx.

I looked up and across the other side of the court towards the family. Every single one of them was crying. I looked down at Bromley's solicitor and she was crying, I looked at the Judge whose head was bowed, the two journalists were sobbing and when I looked at Mick he was slowly shaking his head. I looked at Alan Bromley. Nothing, no emotion, he just sat there staring straight ahead. Well as an impact statement it seemed to have had the desired affect and I couldn't believe it had got to me the way it did. I must have read it 100 times in preparation for this day but maybe the emotion of it all affected me more than I thought possible. At least I'd managed to hold it all together; it would have been really embarrassing had I not. I took my seat back with the family as Bromley's solicitor mitigated on his behalf about not fining him too heavily or banning him at all because of his livelihood, just as Fleur had predicted. Thankfully she didn't waffle on too much and after five minutes or so sat down.

Bromley was ordered to stand as Judge Arnold addressed him.

For the offence of careless driving, fined £2000.
For the tachograph offences, fined £2000.
Disqualified from driving for 12 months.
You will pay £2000 towards the court costs.

I looked at Mick and we both mouthed the same thing at the same time. I'll leave it to your imagination as to what that might have been! But two grand for careless driving is unheard of and even the most serious of tacho offences rarely commands that level of fine and another £2000 towards court costs? Wow, just wow, £6000 in fines was more than I'd ever thought possible. And for the first time Bromley looked visibly moved, so it must have hurt him.

We poured out of court like kids being released from school for the summer holidays! The whole family was happy with the result and in particular the fact that Bromley had been banned for a year. When Mick and I started to explain the level of fines it made them even happier. One by one they shook us by the hand, hugged us, kissed us and thanked us for everything that we had done. It was frankly my absolute pleasure; they were an amazing family and they'd done Little Dave proud. PUP.

One by one they left as Mick and I walked back towards our car.

"You bastard" said Mick with his trade mark fag hanging out the corner of his mouth.

"What?" I exclaimed

"You nearly got me in there, I thought I was going to burst into tears" he said.

"You mean you didn't?"

"No, not quite"

"You heartless bastard"

"Come on, I'll buy you a coffee, I think we deserve one"

ALFRED MORRISON
(names changed to protect the family)

Operation BURWELL
Category C
17ᵗʰ February 2006

2006 Hampshire fatalities = 72
2006 Nationally fatalities = 3047

Even with over 28 years' service I still get shocked from time to time by the animal that is the human being. Our capacity to inflict pain upon our fellow man, whether it is physical or mental knows no bounds, especially if there is the smell of money involved.

Charlie One to any Mike Charlie units please for a serious RTA Wych Lane, Gosport, believed to involve a car and a mobility scooter MC-07 and 08 attending

Both units arrived within a couple of minutes and immediately called it in as an all-services. I knew I was the only FLO on in the county today so I started to make my way across before I got called. Even if a FLO isn't required I can at least help out in other ways. Being an FLO kept me busier than I'd ever been during my entire career and it was nice sometimes to have the opportunity to do something else. But within a matter of minutes of arriving at the scene it was obvious that I would be undertaking the FLO role and nothing else.

It appeared that an elderly gent riding one of those mobility pavement scooters had ridden out from between two parked cars and into the path of a Toyota which had hit him broadside. He had sustained serious head injuries and as I arrived so the ambulance crew was placing him into the ambulance and I was directed to escort them from the scene to the QA. Escorting ambulances is quite rare and only done in the most urgent cases to facilitate a quicker and smoother route for the ambulance by using the patrol car to clear the traffic as the ambulance follows on behind. Getting anywhere along the busy A32 road out of Gosport was a nightmare at the best of times and the escort was an obvious solution. Within 15 minutes we had arrived at the hospital and the 89 year old man was wheeled straight into room one where the hospital staff did their best to save him.

As they did, so I started to sift through his personal property in an effort to find out who he was but he didn't appear to have any identifying documents on him. However he did have a mobile phone which for a person of his age was somewhat unusual. There weren't that many numbers on there but one of them gave the name of Jenny. I phoned the number and spoke to Jenny who appeared to be quite elderly herself and somewhat confused by my call. She said that it was possible that the phone may belong to one of her neighbours Alf Morrison and that she would cross the road and knock on his door to see if he was in. She would let me know as soon as possible. 10 minutes later she phoned me back to state that there was no reply from his door. I said that I would get another police officer to come and talk to her and see if he could get a reply from the house. Within half an hour I had received a phone call from that officer who stated that it was very possible that the victim was indeed Alf Morrison and that his next-door neighbours Dennis and Jean Brown would come up to the QA straight away in order to identify him.

The doctors were still doing their best in room one as Mr and Mrs Brown arrived at the hospital. Given what they said about Mr Morrison using a mobility scooter as his means of transport and from the description I gave them of him and his clothing it certainly appeared that we had the right name. Dennis Brown went on to tell me that he and his wife looked after Mr Morrison on a daily basis and had done for more than two years. They fed him, did his washing and ironing and just about everything else for him because he had nobody else. Mr Brown was a Yorkshire man and as is often the case with Yorkshire men was somewhat forthright and blunt when he spoke.

"He promised me his car you know" said Mr Brown.

"Well I don't think we need to worry about that right now" I replied somewhat taken aback by the fact that Mr Morrison was still with us.

One of the doctors then came out of room one and I knew before he even said anything. We went into a side room where he told me that despite their best efforts Alfred Morrison had died from his injuries. As usual the A&E department looked like a war zone and it wasn't long before they brought Mr Morrison out of room one and placed him in the side room. Dennis and Jean Brown asked if they could sit with him for a while because they didn't feel that he should be left alone. Although they weren't close relatives this at least allowed me the opportunity to get a positive identification, albeit not an official one.

Whilst all this was going on I received information that Mr Morrison had a daughter called Anne who also lived in Gosport and that arrangements had been made to collect her and bring her up to the QA. She arrived half an hour later and appeared none too pleased that Mr and Mrs Brown were currently sitting with her father. She refused to talk to any of the hospital staff and insisted on seeing her father first which I could understand.

However a staff nurse came with us and as we entered the small side room we found Alf Morrison on a hospital trolley immediately inside the door with Mr and Mrs Brown sat over in the right-hand corner. As Anne stood beside the trolley so Dennis Brown greeted her with the words;

"Huh, what are you doing here?"

"I've come to see my father obviously" responded Anne.

"Well you haven't bothered for the last few years so I can't see why you're bothering now" came the reply.

"What are you talking about?" asked Anne.

"We've been looking after Alf for the last two years, feeding him, doing his washing because you couldn't be bothered" said Mr Brown folding his arms and now speaking with a slightly raised voice.

"What utter nonsense" said Anne "he couldn't stand the sight of either of you"

I couldn't quite believe what I was hearing and said that maybe this conversation could be had at a later date to which they both agreed and apologised to each other. But the truce was very short lived.

"Have you still got the key to dad's house?" asked Anne "because if you have I want it back".

Dennis Brown then got to his feet and came over and faced Anne from the other side of the trolley.

"Why are you pretending that you care, you haven't done for years so why the pretence now, you must be feeling guilty, is that what this is all about, you're feeling guilty"

"You two are a couple of gold diggers and dad knew that which is why I want his house key back before you strip the house of everything he ever possessed" shouted Anne.

Both of them were now leaning across the body and jabbing their fingers towards each others' face and shouting.

"Well there's nothing you can do about that" shouted Dennis Brown "because Alf has left everything to me and Jean in his will and I have a copy of it".

I shouted at them both to be quiet as this was neither the time nor the place but the arguments continued.

"Where were you on Christmas Day then" shouted Mr Brown "we looked after Alf all day, you were nowhere in sight"

"What are you talking about I looked after dad for the whole of Christmas week" shouted Anne.

It was time for me to intervene physically and after pulling them apart I ushered the Browns out of the side room and towards the front door of A&E. I gave them one of my cards and some legal advice concerning the next of kin and basically told them it was time for them to leave. I then saw Anne come storming down the corridor towards us and she deliberately barged into Mr Brown and then pointing a finger in his face shouted;

"You stay away from that house"

There was genuine anger etched all over her face as she continued walking at great pace out of the hospital closely followed by the nurse who was desperately trying to get her to come back inside. Without stopping Anne put up her hand and told the nurse to leave her alone.

"You can see the sort of woman we're with dealing with here can't you officer, that's just so typical of her" said a rather smug Mr Brown.

"I think you've said more than enough Mr Brown and as I said just now I think it's time you left" came my reply.

My obvious concern was for Anne. There are no rules remember when it comes to dealing with the death of a close relative and each of us reacts in a different way and this was clearly Anne's way of dealing with it. But I needed to talk to her and at least try to ascertain whether or not she wanted me to help her at this stage. By the time I'd got rid of the Browns Anne had disappeared out of the hospital entrance and was heading down Southwick Hill Road towards Cosham. I ran after her and caught her at the bottom of the hill by the traffic lights pleading with her to stop as I did so.

"Anne we need to talk, there are a few things we need to go through" I said huffing and puffing because I'd had to run.

"You just don't understand, none of you understand" Anne shouted back.

"I do understand, trust me I really do and I'm here to help you try and get through this" I said.

"Understand? Understand? Well understand this" she shouted "that bastard raped me when I was 12 and then I have to listen to that arse-hole Brown telling me that I didn't care and that I must be feeling guilty. I ended up in a children's home because of my father, now do you understand?"

Jesus Christ. Yes now I understand.

Anne refused my offer of a lift home or to get her a taxi and insisted that she wanted to walk and despite my reservations for her welfare I allowed her to continue. As I walked slowly back up to the hospital her shocking revelation was all I could think about. What must have been going through her mind as she stood looking at the body of her father, a man who had obviously inflicted so much pain upon her as a child only to hear Mr Brown basically telling her that she was a crap daughter and that she must have been feeling guilty? Oh how I wanted to tell Mr Brown but obviously couldn't.

I got back to the side room to find the staff nurse that had witnessed all of this in tears. She had never experienced anything like this before and I have to confess that neither had I. Between us we checked that both of Alf's rings were still on his fingers.

It was just past 6:30 pm as I got back into the patrol car and within seconds I found myself en route to another serious RTA at junction 10 of the M27 which kept us busy for the next three hours. By the time I got back to the office it was almost 10 o'clock and I was concerned for Anne's welfare. I rang her mobile but got no reply and so I phoned the house and spoke to her partner who said that he had picked her up from a cafe in Cosham earlier and that she was very emotional and that currently she was probably at her father's house. I left my details with him and said that I needed to talk to her again tomorrow to go through all the formalities.

It had been a long and rather difficult day once again and as I filled in the pages of my latest FLO log all I could hear was Anne's revelation.

The next afternoon I went to Anne's beautiful house in Gosport. We sat at her kitchen table and the first thing she did was apologise for her behaviour yesterday. I said that given the circumstances she had absolutely nothing to apologise for and that if anybody needed to apologise it was Mr Brown. She then went on to tell me that she had visited her father's flat that morning and that Dennis Brown had started on her again almost as soon as she got there telling her that he was in the process of buying Alf's car and that he had a copy of the will that left everything to him and his wife. I shook my head in disbelief. In spite of me telling him yesterday to go and obtain the proper legal advice he clearly couldn't help himself and had to stick his nose and his mouth into something that he had no right to do. Anne stated that she really couldn't care less about her father's possessions; she certainly didn't need the money or the car or anything else but was adamant, for obvious reasons, that the Browns were not entitled to any of it. I advised her that it would be in her interests to seek some proper legal advice from a solicitor as soon as possible.

I took all the necessary details for the G28, did the ID statement and talked about the press policy and as there were no other relatives Anne gave me permission for her father's details to be released. She declined the idea of writing a family statement and said that if the press turned up on her doorstep then her partner could deal with them and having seen the size of him they were more than welcome!

We sat and chatted for a while and it was clear that my role as Anne's FLO was going to be a fairly short lived affair. I gave her some further advice and basically insisted that she find herself a decent solicitor because I felt sure Mr and Mrs Brown would try their hardest to make life difficult for her. No sooner had I left the house than I received a call from Mr Brown asking me to visit him as soon as possible although he wouldn't say why. I didn't like Mr Brown or his attitude but I had to remain impartial and as professional as possible, although he was the sort of person that rubbed me up the wrong way as soon as he opened his mouth.

I'd barely walked through their front door when he literally shoved a copy of Alf's will under my nose, holding it in one hand and tapping it with the forefinger of his other hand as if to reinforce the fact that he and his wife were the sole benefactors of Alfred Morrison's estate. He went on and on and on about Alf's car and the fact that he had paid him £500, in two installments of £250 and that he had even got the car insured, which I found very strange. He didn't have a receipt though. He was convinced that Anne had already taken the car and probably sold it and I assured him that that was the least of her worries right now. He then started getting all personal about her again and I put my hand up in front of his face and told him to stop because it was unnecessary and I really didn't want to hear it. He insisted that we go out to the garage block to see if the car was in the garage. Just to shut him up I agreed. The garage door was unlocked and low and behold the car was still there, locked up and secure. He insisted that the car belonged to him and that if he saw Anne trying to drive it away then he wanted her arrested for theft. I advised him again to go back to his solicitor to seek further legal advice because this was not a police matter. However I also advised him that given the circumstances, if he in any way tried to block Anne from entering Alf's flat or taking the car or any of his possessions then that would become a police matter and he could find himself in serious trouble.

A couple of days later and the Portsmouth News ran a half page article on Alf's accident and it was obvious that as there had been no family statement that the press had gone knocking on the doors of Alf's neighbours and sure enough the two people most quoted were the Browns. He even supplied a photo of Alf allegedly taken just an hour before the accident. They went into great detail about how they looked after Alf and how they saw him on a daily basis but thankfully there was no mention of the animosity they felt towards Anne or any claims they were making about his estate. I felt sure that Mr Brown in particular would have mentioned this to the reporter who probably took the view that to print such things was probably not in his or the papers best interests.

That was basically the end of my involvement with Anne, other than to phone her in December to ask if she would be attending the inquest on the 14th. She declined to attend because that date was the third anniversary of her mother's death. She didn't mention anything else and I didn't ask and I didn't speak to her again.

Greed of course is a terrible thing and one of the 12 deadly sins. I don't think I can ever recall during my career a more inappropriate or callous approach by anyone to demand what they think is their right to a few basic possessions when the deceased is quite literally still warm. To physically fight over the body was abhorrent and distasteful and even though the Browns were not fully aware of the history involved there can still be no excuse for what they said and did.

LEE HASTINGS
(names changed to protect the family)

Operation GINGER
Category B
28th May 2006

2006 Hampshire fatalities = 72
2006 Nationally fatalities = 3047

It was a beautiful late spring afternoon, but of course it being the weekend meant that someone or something was bound to spoil the tranquillity of it all.

Charlie One for any Mike Charlie unit please for an RTA Hulbert Road, Waterlooville
Mike Charlie 08
Thank you Mike Charlie 08, getting several reports already about this one but it seems a motorcycle has collided with a lamp post and the road is blocked

Within a few minutes 08 had arrived at the scene and called it in as an all services. A motorcyclist had indeed collided with a lamp post on the central reservation of the dual carriageway that links the A3M with Waterlooville town centre. Although a dual carriageway it is subject to a 40 mph speed limit.

The office emptied and we headed north towards the scene. It was a bit chaotic to say the least with dozens of on lookers standing on the footpath desperate to see what was happening. There were now half a dozen RPU cars, a couple of Section vehicles and two ambulances at the scene. In the middle of it all was a yellow Triumph Sprint motorcycle laying on its side just past the damaged lamp post it had collided with and parked just behind that was a green, left hand drive Ford Mustang with a 30-something female sitting in the driver's seat with a Section officer crouched down by her side.

Mick Anderson took me to one side to state that this one needing dealing with very delicately because the driver of the Mustang was the wife of the motorcyclist and there was some evidence that they had been racing and also a possibility that they might have actually collided with each other prior to the bike hitting the lamp post. There was also strong evidence from the crew of one of the ambulances to suggest that a fairly large bag of cannabis fell out of the door pocket of the Mustang when they crouched down to talk to the lady to ascertain whether she was injured. They further stated that she put it back into the door pocket but within a couple of minutes it seemed to have disappeared. It was agreed that I would act as the FLO but take no part in the investigation at this stage in an effort to remain completely impartial during alcohol and drugs testing and in any subsequent arrest.

PC Jon Lansley who was one of the leading drugs recognition officers in the county was summoned to attend the scene to conduct a roadside drugs impairment test. Whilst we were waiting for him to arrive I crouched down beside the left hand drive Mustang to talk to the driver Sarah Hastings. She was an American and talked with a very slurred southern accent. At first I couldn't work out whether the slurred speech was due to alcohol or drugs but in the end decided that actually it was just her accent. She spoke very slowly and deliberately with that sort of southern country type droll. She didn't say much and just kept staring ahead towards the ambulance where I think they were still working on the motorcyclist.

Jon Lansley arrived and I briefed him about the circumstances and the fact that I would be acting as Sarah's FLO and taking no part in the investigation. However I would

241

be standing close by whilst he conducted the field impairment test. We got Sarah out of the car and took her about 200 yards away from the scene to an area that was reasonably quiet and away from the prying eyes of the public.

Field impairment testing was brought over from the United States to the UK in 2004 to give the police a tool to use at the roadside to test drivers who they suspected to be under the influence of drugs whether illegal or prescribed. Prior to field impairment testing it was incredibly rare for any motorist to be arrested for driving whilst under the influence of drugs because it was always down to the police officers opinion and nothing else which is neither scientific or technical. We've all seen American cops on TV doing the old finger to nose test or getting the motorist to walk in a straight line and perhaps laughed about it, I know I did, thinking it was all a bit prehistoric in comparison to the electronic devices that we use in the UK for alcohol testing. Surely something so basic looking couldn't prove anything? In Hampshire the only police officers eligible to undertake field impairment testing were Traffic officers and a large number of us undertook the course that was run by Jon Lansley and Nick Ellcombe after they brought the procedure back from the USA.

This roadside test consisted of a number of tests, undertaken by the motorist to establish their levels of concentration, balance, estimation of time, coordination and most important of all the size of the pupils in their eyes. As the old saying goes the window to the soul lies within the eyes, and that is never truer than when we are talking about drugs. Different drugs do different things to different parts of your body and your nervous system, but all drugs affect the eyes in one way or another, by making your pupils either dilate or constrict to the size of a pinhead and almost without exception causes the whites of your eyes to become bloodshot, sometimes severely so.

So the very first test a police officer will conduct will be to hold a calibrated chart with a number of different sized pupils along its edge which he will hold up to your face to gauge the size of your pupils. As a basic guide if your pupils are dilated, i.e. larger than normal, then that could indicate that you have taken cannabis. If your pupils are constricted, i.e. smaller than normal, then that could indicate that you have taken something like heroin.

The second test will require you to stand to attention with your arms by your sides and your feet together and your head tilted back with your eyes closed. You will then be asked to count 30 seconds quietly to yourself and at the end of the 30 seconds you will be asked how long that time was. If you say that your estimation of 30 seconds is only 20 seconds long (timed by the officer) that could indicate that you have taken some kind of accelerant drug like cocaine. If however your 30 seconds was say 40 seconds or more that could indicate that you have taken a drug like cannabis that slows your metabolism. Whilst you were counting the 30 seconds the police officer will be watching you to see if you're swaying from side to side or backwards and forwards as this is also one of the balance tests.

The next test is the old walking the line test, and as comical as it sometimes looks this is actually one of the most important and the most accurate. You are asked to stand with one foot in front of the other and heel to toe and you have to stand there in this position as the police officer gives you the rest of your instructions, this again being a balance test. You are then asked to walk the line, heel to toe whilst counting out nine steps, after which you turn in a certain manner and return along the line, heel to toe whilst counting out another nine steps. If you fall off the line or your heel and toe do not connect, or you lose count or fail to conduct the turn correctly then this could be deemed as a failure.

The next test will have you standing on one foot with

your other foot raised 6 inches from the ground whilst you count out loud from 20 to 30. You then change feet and conduct the test for a second time. This is obviously another balance and coordination test.

The final test will have you standing to attention again with both your arms outstretched in front of you at 45°. Then tilt your head back slightly, with your eyes closed and then follow the instructions that the officer gives you to touch the tip of your nose with the tip of either your right or left index finger. This is done seven times in a random manner and the officer will note whereabouts on your face your finger touched. This is another balance and coordination test.

The result of these tests will establish if the subject is under the influence of any kind of drug and is accurate enough to determine roughly what sort of drug the subject may have taken. A problem does arise where some drug users take more than one kind of drug which can confuse the issue. If the officer believes that the subject is under the influence of drugs then they can be arrested. However that is only part one of three parts of the process. The second part involves a doctor who will conduct a number of similar tests at the police station and if in his/her opinion the subject is still under the influence of those drugs then a sample of blood is taken for analysis. It is only then that medical proof is obtained to successfully prosecute the subject. Having conducted a large number of these tests myself I have to say they are incredibly accurate.

And so Jon started the field impairment process with Sarah. As I looked on I could tell that it wasn't going well and even after just three tests Jon looked over towards me and gave me a look that confirmed my suspicions. She failed every aspect of the test. She wouldn't stop talking, she didn't listen, she didn't take the test seriously, which given the nature of the accident she'd just been involved in you'd think she would have and Jon concluded that she was indeed under the influence of drugs. She was therefore arrested and taken to Waterlooville custody centre. She claimed she didn't know why she was being arrested and started to play the part of the victim. I now found myself in an extremely awkward position and not one that I had experienced before, for although I was her FLO I was also still a police officer and I found it incredibly hard to separate the two at this particular time.

Meanwhile back at the scene a full search was made of the Ford Mustang and the area where Sarah had conducted the field impairment test but no bag of cannabis was found. A drugs dog was then brought to the scene and he showed all the signs of drugs having been in the car but after another thorough search nothing was found.

News then filtered through from the hospital that the motorcyclist had died. His name was Lee Hastings and he was indeed Sarah's husband and I then had to break the news to her as she sat in the medical room at the police station. There were no tears, no outburst just a small sigh. I got her a cup of coffee and we sat there for a while waiting for the doctor to arrive.

After two hours there was no sign of the police surgeon and I was becoming somewhat concerned that so far the only person from the Hastings family who knew about Lees death was his wife who was currently being treated as a suspect. After consulting the custody sergeant and the SIO at the scene a decision was taken that we really couldn't wait any longer for two reasons. Firstly the influence of the drugs on Sarah appeared to have almost completely worn off and any test that a doctor may do now would probably be a negative test and secondly the rest of the family had a right to know sooner rather than later and we could be severely criticised for failing to notify them. So Sarah was released from custody and I drove her back to the family home in Cowplain.

Sarah seemed somewhat confused about the gravity of the situation she was involved in and spent most of the journey back to the house asking me when she was likely to get her car back. I explained in several different ways, as best I could, that any vehicle involved in a fatal RTA is seized by the police and fully examined by professional vehicle examiners to establish whether or not there were any faults on the vehicle that may have contributed to the accident. All she kept saying was that she hadn't been involved in an accident and I had to repeat several times that at the moment it did look as though she was involved and until the facts were fully established not only would we be keeping her car but she would remain a suspect until proved otherwise. She clearly wasn't happy about it and still didn't understand why the police had to keep her car. I was rather glad that the journey only took five minutes as the repetitive nature of the conversation was becoming somewhat tedious.

Sarah didn't know who was going to be at home and I gathered from what little information I had gleaned so far that Lee's teenage daughter from a previous relationship and one or two other hitherto unidentified people may also be there. We entered the house but it was empty so Sarah said that she would try to phone Lees daughter. She couldn't seem to get her head around her mobile phone or the daughter's number and must have spent a full 15 minutes trying to do this. I couldn't work out whether she was in shock or whether this was normal behaviour for her.

The house was a 1970s built semi-detached where the stairs come down into the lounge which is where we were sitting. My eyes were drawn to the cupboard under the stairs, you know the sort of thing the standard size under stairs cupboard with an almost triangular shaped door. Except this door was made of glass and not wood and above the door were the letters FBI. Given Sarah's accent I wondered if there may be a connection and for the first time she smiled.

"Take a look through the glass" she said

I peered through the door where I saw a couple of tree branches, some undergrowth and sawdust all over the floor. Then I saw something move. There was a two foot long lizard staring straight back at me. My head jumped back and I let out a sort of "whoa" noise which made Sarah smile again.

"So what does FBI stand for"? I asked.

"Fucking Big Iguana" came the reply.

I liked that, I liked that a lot.

The front door came flying open and in marched Lee's 15-year-old daughter.

"Before you say anything I know what's happened, I've been down there" she shouted at Sarah.

"Honey we need to talk" said Sarah.

"I don't wanna fuckin talk to you do I" shouted the girl "I'm going out for a fag" and with that she stormed out of the back door.

Sarah explained that the two of them didn't exactly get along and that she spent most of her time sleeping at a friend's house. She said she'd talk to her later.

We went through the G28 procedure but that was about it for now. I couldn't talk to her about the press because she was still a suspect and the ID had been done at the scene, so there wasn't much else to cover at this time. She said she had a few phone calls to make and I therefore left her to it.

I went back to the office, dug out a new FLO log and started writing. As I got to speak to the rest of the Relief it seemed from the witness accounts that the two of them had certainly been racing each other immediately before the bike collided with the lamp post.

The next day Sarah phoned me to ask when she could have her car back. I explained to her again that it was unlikely she would get it back until the police vehicle examiner had finished his detailed examination and pending further enquiries into the cause of the accident it may well be that the police would have to keep it even longer. I had to explain this to her three of four times before it finally sank in. Whilst I understood that yesterday she was very emotional and somewhat confused I couldn't quite get to grips with the fact that she still didn't understand the gravity of what was going on around her. She didn't ask me anything with regards to the investigation or how the accident may have happened in her eyes; she offered me nothing whatsoever and all she seemed to be concerned about was having her car returned. I was even more surprised when less than five hours later she phoned me again and asked exactly the same question; when can I have my car back? I gave her the same answers I'd given her earlier.

This pattern of behaviour continued almost daily for the best part of a fortnight. There was something very wrong and I couldn't help thinking that it was drug-related. None of us could get to grips with the fact that the ambulance man handed Sarah a bag of cannabis which she then put in the driver's door pocket and less than five minutes later it had disappeared. Then there was the fact that she was clearly under the influence of drugs and had failed the field impairment test miserably. Did she want her car back so desperately because there were drugs inside it? I put it to the SIO that before the car was returned to Sarah that it be fully searched by a drugs dog and by a search team. He agreed and arrangements were made for that to be done.

In the meantime I did some digging myself and made a startling discovery. Using Sarah's maiden name rather than her married name whilst undertaking certain police intelligence checks I discovered that Sarah had been deported from the United States several years ago because she was a twice convicted drug dealer. My suspicions concerning her were correct. However I couldn't quite get my head around the fact that she was an American subject and it was therefore not possible for her to be deported surely? It transpired that Sarah was actually born in Kent and only moved to the United States at the age of two and so she was never classed as a natural born American citizen, although she obviously had American citizenship. Because of her status the US authorities were given the perfect excuse to get rid of her. As a twice convicted drug dealer they had the power to deport her. It was an interesting development but what do I do with the information?

I spoke to Mike Batten about it and after his eyebrows had left his forehead and his jaw had hit the table we decided to go and seek further advice. Meanwhile the search of Sarah's Mustang had proved negative once again, so quite what she'd done with those drugs and why she was so desperate to get the car back were questions we were unlikely to get answers to.

There was good news and bad news with regards to the investigation itself. The good news was that three independent witnesses had seen the Triumph motorcycle and the Ford Mustang clearly racing each other between the A3M motorway, the Hulbert Road roundabout and the last few hundred yards before the crash itself. The bad news was that nobody saw any form of contact between the car and the bike prior to the bike hitting the lamp post and there was no physical or forensic evidence to prove that the two vehicles had come into contact with each other. This was clearly a setback. It basically meant that unless Sarah confessed to racing with her husband on the highway and then colliding with his bike and pushing it into the lamppost it was unlikely that she would face any form of prosecution. The toxicology report on Lee Hastings confirmed that he had a substantial amount of cocaine in his system.

It was decided to confront Sarah about her deportation from the USA prior to her interview which was due to take place in another month and that it would be me that asked the question. I wasn't entirely happy about this but at the same time I was very curious about what her reply might be. I went to the house and met her mother who had flown over from the USA to be with her daughter. I said I needed to talk to Sarah privately about something that was very personal, in other words I didn't really want her mother to be in the room. Sarah insisted that her mum stay and that she had no secrets. I then asked her about her convictions in the US and the fact that she had been deported because of them. She was surprised and angry at me and said it was none of my business. Her mother told her not to trust the police and not to say any more.

Sarah then reverted to type and switched the subject back to when she was going to get her car back again. I explained, yet again, the reasons why we were keeping her car and then she said that she didn't want me to act as her FLO any longer. I wasn't entirely surprised about this, after all I had confronted her about something that she didn't think I had any right to know about and she obviously felt cornered. Frankly I was somewhat relieved. I didn't like her, I didn't like her attitude, and I certainly couldn't understand why she placed more importance on getting her car back than on the fact that her husband was dead.

I left the house immediately and drove back to the office. My initial relief at being dumped quickly turned to anger, not because I'd been given the elbow but more because so far this woman had got away with far too much and I feared she was going to get away with a bit more yet. I told Mike Batten that Sarah and I were now divorced and whilst he was still laughing I told him that I'd given her his mobile number! Maybe he could come up with a reply about her Mustang that actually sinks in.

In the months that followed she was interviewed twice by the investigation team and in the end the CPS decided that there was insufficient evidence to charge her with anything. So how did Lee Hastings bike collide with a lamppost on the central reservation of a dual carriageway? I think the only person that knows the truth is Sarah.

NORMAN THURSTON

Operation SOUTHWELL
Category A
21st January 2007

2007 Hampshire fatalities = 94
2007 Nationally fatalities = 2946

January 2007 marked a milestone for me personally. It meant that I'd now completed 29 years' service and in less than 12 months' time I would be retiring. It was a daunting prospect and not one that I was looking forward to it has to be said. Whilst the job had changed beyond all recognition from my early days with much of those changes causing me untold misery, especially in the computing department, I did still enjoy my work and most of all the people I worked with and those I met.

Early turn in January is never a pleasant experience. The cold, dark mornings make the chore of getting out of a warm bed at 5am all the more daunting. But this morning it was reasonably bright, which always helps. Our Relief had been boosted by the arrival of some new faces and not before time either. A number of changes had taken place throughout the South Eastern Roads Policing Area and this included merging Fareham RPU with Cosham. Most of the guys at Fareham were ARV crews and a vast amount of money was spent at our place on a new armoury, office furniture and other essentials. Whilst we welcomed additional personnel onto our Relief the two Michaels and me were yet to be convinced that they were actually Traffic officers first and armed response officers second. There were definitely a number of them that fell into the latter category and this caused a certain amount of suspicion and resentment. Our three new boys would be watched very carefully.

We'd just finished breakfast and it was a little after 1040 am.

Charlie One to any Mike Charlie Unit please for an RTA Hambledon Road, Denmead
Mike Charlie 07
Mike Charlie 07 thank you, believed to be a hit and run involving a cyclist, we are getting further calls and it would appear to be serious
Mike Charlie 08 also attending

It being Sunday morning meant that we would be responsible for cleaning the patrol cars, sorting out all the equipment, replacing used or worn out items and generally making sure the car was fit for purpose for another week. I'd just started removing all the kit from the boot of the X5 when the first unit arrived at the scene of the RTA and immediately called it all services and that it was a confirmed fatal. I threw the kit back into the car and headed north up the A3 towards Waterlooville.

The B2133 Hambledon Road links the market town of Waterlooville with the outlying village of Denmead some three miles away. It's a busy single track road that is subject to the national speed limit in between its two restricted areas within the limits of each town. I'd been to a number of serious collisions there over the years.

I arrived some five minutes later. The road had already been closed by a local unit and I parked next to the two RPU units just as Pete Sarginson arrived with the crash tender. It was obvious that I would take on the FLO role as Adrienne appointed one of our new gun crew as the PIO.

I walked over to the scene itself where I found a man in his late 60s laying on the grass verge with some pretty horrific injuries despite the fact that he was wearing a decent cycle helmet. The paramedics had declared him dead at the scene and stated that he had died instantly. A few feet away in the ditch was a pedal cycle which had also sustained a substantial amount of damage to the rear. Part of my job is to search the body in order to ascertain any identity documents that might help in establishing who he was. I always try to do this with the utmost respect towards the person that I was now searching, it always felt so intrusive and I always found myself apologising to them as I did so.

I found a mobile phone but nothing else and so I took it back to the crash tender so that I could examine it further in private. There were very few numbers on the phone but the two that stuck out were the home number and one for Sandra. I contacted the force control room and asked them to instigate a subscriber check with BT and after half an hour they came back with the details that it belonged to Norman Thurston of Haslar Crescent, Waterlooville which was less than five minutes away. With this information I then conducted all the usual enquiries with the voters register and police intelligence checks which revealed that Jean and Norman Thurston were the residents at the address.

Whilst I was making these enquiries I was aware of some

frantic radio traffic concerning the vehicle that had allegedly collided with this cyclist. As I got back out of the crash tender so I saw that my colleagues were about 200 yards away past the scene talking to the driver of a white Vauxhall Corsa. I then saw him being placed in handcuffs and put into the back of a patrol car. Pete came back up to the crash tender to tell me that the driver had confessed to hitting the pedal cyclist before driving off from the scene and had just provided a positive breath test. At 10 o'clock in the morning?

"You should see the damage to the car" said Pete.

So I walked over to the car and was amazed to see quite a lot of damage to the front nearside headlamp and grille and a huge dent in the roof. When I say a huge dent I do mean huge, the entire roof was caved in and the interior light had been knocked out of its mounting and was hanging by the electrical cable. For forensic reasons I stood well back as I looked at the vehicle and a shudder went down my spine as I contemplated just how big an impact this had been.

It was time for me to go and knock on somebody's door once again. As I drove the short distance to the house my heart started to pound in the usual manner and as I got out of the car I could feel my legs starting to shake. I've lost count of the number of times I've had to do this I really have and it doesn't get any easier. Here I am about to deliver the worst news in the world and to shatter someone's life once more. I walked up the garden path towards the neat little bungalow, took a deep breath and rang the bell.

Mrs Thurston answered the door and she guessed immediately because Norman was overdue from his bike ride and she had already phoned the QA Hospital to see if he had been involved in an accident. We went into the lounge and we sat down and although she understood that Norman had been involved in an accident I don't think she had guessed that he was actually dead. Her first thoughts were to phone her daughter Sandra who lived in Southsea and would be up immediately. Jean and I sat back in the lounge and she started telling me about Norman and the fact that he had recently beaten bowel cancer and had just been given the all clear and had gone out on his bike on a celebration ride which was something he couldn't do all the time he was receiving his treatment. Yet again I felt an incredible anger towards the person responsible that they had snuffed out the life of an innocent human being in such circumstances.

The front door came flying open and in came Sandra.

"Tell me it isn't true, tell me it isn't true," she said towards her mum. She then turned to me.

"Did she tell you that dad had only just got over cancer?" followed by; "It's just so bloody unfair"

I couldn't agree with her more.

"Was the driver drunk?" she asked.

I then sat them down and gave them the briefest circumstances of the accident including the fact that the driver had failed a roadside breath test. It's always been my experience that telling a family all the facts as you know them at this time isn't always the best idea. It's often too shocking, partly because they won't take it all in and you find yourself repeating much of what you have said again later.

They then asked if they could go and see Norman and I had to tell them that his body was still at the scene of the accident and was likely to remain there until such time as the scenes of crime forensic officers had completed their detailed examination of both Norman, his bike and the offending car. I told them that although this is probably very difficult for them to comprehend right now but everything we were doing was geared towards justice for Norman in securing a successful prosecution against the person responsible and that any subsequent Crown Court case may be more than a year away. I then explained the seriousness of the circumstances concerning the driver in that he had allegedly collided with

Norman whilst under the influence of alcohol and had then failed to stop at the scene and that it was likely he would be facing a lengthy prison sentence when convicted, so it was essential that the police do their job properly in order to secure that. Sandra was incensed that somebody could leave her father to die at the roadside and just drive off and there was little or nothing I could say at this time that was going to pacify her.

I then had to leave the house and return to the scene. Part of my duty as the FLO is to escort the body from the scene to the mortuary at the Royal County Hospital in Winchester. This only happens in circumstances where there is likely to be serious charges laid against the alleged offender, whereby continuity in all aspects of the investigation are paramount and as I am the person who is likely to have the body identified I am also the person that will have to identify that body to the Coroner and to the Home Office forensic pathologist. If that continuity breaks down then this can give the defence team in Crown Court some leverage towards having the case dismissed. Norman's body was placed in an un-marked hearse and I escorted him to Winchester arriving there just before 4:30 pm. I formally handed the body over to the mortuary staff and was then told that the post mortem wouldn't be done until 2 o'clock on Tuesday 23rd January, some two days away and that formal identification by the family would have to take place after that.

By 5:30 I was back at the house and we sat down with a cup of tea which of course I stirred with my pen. I updated Jean and Sandra on the investigation so far and reiterated just how serious a Section 1 offence was and that it was basically only one down from manslaughter. I then had to explain to them that the defendant had the right to have a second independent post mortem carried out on his behalf after the initial post-mortem and that he had 30 days in which to lodge that request which would delay any funeral arrangements taking place. It goes without saying that the pair of them were obviously upset by this but were actually quite understanding and said that whatever it took to convict the man responsible then they would do their best to help. Sandra then asked again how the accident happened and although I couldn't give them the full circumstances because I didn't know them at this stage I did tell them that Norman had been hit from behind and that in the paramedic's opinion he had died instantly. We then went through all the usual formalities with regards to filling out the G28, the press policy and what my role as their FLO would mean to them. They obviously had other people to inform and we agreed that until such time as they had formally identified Norman then no name would be released to the press therefore giving them some breathing space in order to inform other friends and relatives.

I then left the house and was back in the office by about 7 o'clock where I updated the SIO and PIO who then told me that the driver Russell Swanton had provided a positive evidential breath test at the police station which put him almost twice the legal limit at the time of the crash. We discussed just how much alcohol you needed to consume the previous night in order to keep you at twice the limit the following morning; although various quantities were quoted we all agreed that it must have been a huge amount. I asked them to keep me updated on progress and I would them.

The next morning I phoned the Coroner's Office in Winchester to be told that the post mortem was unlikely to be held until next Thursday and not on Tuesday as originally planned because of a lack of Home Office pathologists. In the most serious cases, such as this, only a Home Office forensic pathologist can carry out the post-mortem and they were few and far between on a national level and therefore we had to wait until one became available. A couple of hours later I received a call confirming that the post-mortem would now take place on Wednesday 24th January and that the formal identification by the family could take place immediately afterwards.

I went to the house and informed Jean and Sandra about the revised post-mortem date, which they were obviously quite upset about but understood the police position. Jean then asked for some clarification over the press policy because she was a bit confused over what I'd said yesterday. This wasn't a surprise because as I have said on many occasions previously as a close relative of someone who has just died in a car crash you have a huge amount to take in during the initial stages and that it is almost impossible to retain all the information, which is why I always try and keep things as brief as possible. So we went through the press policy again and I gave them my usual spiel about controlling the press rather than the other way around. They decided that they would probably opt for the family statement and would try and have this ready by Wednesday.

One of the things I had learned about Norman whilst filling in the G28 form previously was that he had been a sub Mariner for 30 years and was immensely proud of his military service. In view of this Jean was keen to pursue the possibility that Norman receive a full Naval burial at sea and I said that I could probably assist with this because my wife had previously worked for the Royal Naval Chaplaincy within the Naval Dockyard at Portsmouth and could probably provide me with the necessary contact details and the procedure to facilitate her request.

Two days later on 24th January I attended the mortuary at the Royal County Hospital, Winchester where I formally handed over the body to the Home Office forensic pathologist Dr Hugh White. Later that afternoon I received a call authorising me to do the formal identification and so by 6 pm I had collected Jean and Sandra and driven them to Winchester where we met the Coroners Officer Barry Thomas. He was brilliant with the two ladies, explained the formalities to them and once they had composed themselves we all entered the viewing room where Jean made a positive identification. Barry and I then left to give them some privacy. It goes without saying that the emotion of it all can be quite overpowering and I felt myself becoming angry again that here I was trying to guide two lovely ladies through the trauma of doing a formal identification on a husband and father just because some piss head had decided to get behind the wheel and drive. How I hate drink drivers.

En route home they asked if we could stop at the scene of the crash so that I could explain and show them how it happened to give them some understanding. Scene visits always give some clarity to the relatives and helps them understand the circumstances that led up to the crash. We weren't there long and they didn't ask me too many questions. They spent most of the time just staring at that grass verge in silence. We went back to the house where Jean made us all a cup of tea and gave me a teaspoon and insisted that I didn't use my pen this time which provided some light relief! I then handed Jean an envelope which contained Normans wrist watch and glasses case. God how I hated handing over personal property in this way, it was just so impersonal but what was the alternative? She sat there opening and closing the spectacles case before carefully placing it on the coffee table. They then handed me the press statement they had prepared which read;

'Norman Thurston was born on 29 December 1934 in Woking, Surrey and brought up in Frensham. He joined the Navy on 27 January 1952 and was in the submarine service from 1961 to 1979 when he left the services. He was then a building safety officer working for Portsmouth building safety Association for 20 years when he retired at 65. He played golf up until last year when he gave up for health reasons and had many good friends at Waterlooville golf club. Latterly he became involved in raising funds for Macmillan Cancer support by growing and selling plants, which his family and friends will continue to do'.

Before I left Sandra asked what the latest position was regarding the second post-mortem and I said I would chase it up first thing tomorrow morning. It's a perverse situation and one that frankly should not be allowed to happen because it causes undue stress on a family already stressed beyond all recognition and it's caused by lawyers concerned only for their clients. It goes something like this;

Your lawyer suspects that you are likely to be charged with the most serious offences but until the police investigation is complete he will not know this for definite. If he suspects that you are facing a lesser charge then there is no need to have a second post-mortem and therefore the body can be released to the family for burial. The problem arises when the more serious charges are likely to be laid and this then gives the defendant the right, yes *the right*, to have an independent second post-mortem carried out. The lawyer will then ask the police "Is my client facing a section 1 death by dangerous driving or death by careless driving whilst under the influence of alcohol charge?" To which the police will reply that until their investigations are complete they cannot comment. The lawyer will then say that until such time as a decision is reached they reserve their right to hold a second post-mortem.

This ludicrous game of cat and mouse can go on for weeks, as was the case with Bridget Panormo. However since that time I understood that protocols had been put in place within Hampshire to prevent this from happening again, whereby the Coroner would authorise and pay for a second post-mortem, the results of which would be locked in his safe until such time as the defendant's lawyers requested the results. This second post-mortem could be carried out 24 hours after the initial post-mortem thus reducing the amount of time that the family would be kept waiting unnecessarily for the body to be released.

The mere thought that your loved one has to undergo a

post-mortem is abhorrent to most of us and causes many people a huge amount of anguish but it is generally understood that it is something that everyone has to go through. However having to come to terms with the fact that the person who caused your loved one's death, has the right to not only hold a second post-mortem but is allowed to delay it is surely too much for most of us to comprehend?

The next day I contacted the Coroner's office at Winchester only to be told that the second post-mortem should be completed by 9th February at the latest. The 9th February? That's another two weeks away. It became apparent that the agreed protocol instigated after Bridget Panormo's death was only a local one to the Portsmouth area and was not countywide which was ridiculous. I phoned Sandra who was obviously far from happy about this and I promised her that as soon as I knew a proper date I would inform her immediately.

A couple of days later I got a call from the Coroner's office to state that the post-mortem would now definitely take place on 7th February and as promised I phoned Sandra, who was still clearly unhappy about the idea but was now resigned to the fact that this had to be done.

On 8th February I was off sick but took a call from Barry Thomas at the Coroner's office at Winchester to state that the second post-mortem had been completed yesterday and that the body could now be released to the family. Because I was off sick Barry said he would phone Sandra and the undertakers on my behalf to let them know and he phoned me back later that day to tell me that had been done. I felt somewhat relieved that at least now Jean and Sandra could lay Norman to rest.

Swanton was due to answer his bail on 21st April.

However the police enquiries weren't yet complete due in part to mobile phone data that they required to prove or disprove certain phone calls that were made in the aftermath of the crash and until that data was made available by the phone company that it was impossible to question Swanton further. He was therefore re-bailed to 4th May. By a strange quirk of coincidence there was a second fatal RTA at almost exactly the same spot involving a motorcyclist and a car that same day. This crash occurred less than 50 metres from where Norman had lost his life but was in no way a repeat set of circumstances. However I knew as soon as I heard this that the press would have a field day and try linking the two.

I phoned Sandra the next day concerning Swanton's bail date and again she became somewhat frustrated but understood the need for the police to be as thorough as possible and again I promised her that I would phone once he returned on bail in May. We also discussed yesterday's fatal accident on Hambledon Road and I explained to her that the media would likely try to make a big issue out of it even though there is absolutely no connection between the two.

Two days later whilst off duty I received a very angry call from Sandra concerning an article she had just read in last night's Portsmouth News where it wrongly stated that the case papers had now been sent to the CPS for a decision about whether or not they prosecute Swanton. I hadn't read the article myself but quickly grabbed my copy of the paper and I knew as soon as I read it that the information was clearly wrong. I told Sandra that I was due to go into work in an hour's time and that I would investigate it further and let her know. In the meantime she said she was going to contact The News to ascertain who had written the article.

Sandra phoned me back an hour later to tell me that the journalist was Colin McNeal and that she had spoken to him and he had insisted that he had obtained the information from Adrienne Jerram. I could only repeat what I'd said earlier in that he had obviously misinterpreted what Sgt. Jerram had said because the procedure he quoted didn't exist. Sandra was now pretty angry and said that it seems that the police are telling her one thing and telling the press something else which she was far from happy about. I could only apologise and said that I would investigate further. Sgt. Jerram wasn't on duty at this time because she was currently on night shift, so I e mailed her telling her that my position as the FLO had been compromised somewhat and that I was far from happy about it. I then asked her to contact The News to speak to the journalist concerned. It was a few days before I saw her but she basically said that it was a breakdown in communication between her and Colin McNeal and that she had suitably advised him over the charging procedures.

My eldest daughter suffered a series of epileptic seizures and was admitted to the QA Hospital in Cosham. It has to be said at this point in time that my workload as an FLO was way past the saturation point and that my sponge had been overflowing for months. I had been trying to balance my duties towards Jean and Sandra together with eight other FLO commitments on a daily basis and I was close to cracking. Having my daughter in hospital was the tipping point for me and some of my colleagues; in particular the two Michaels were seriously concerned for my welfare. I was told in no uncertain terms that I was to take a term of compassionate leave and that I wasn't to return until my daughter had been released from hospital. I wasn't happy about this because I didn't want to leave any of the families that I was dealing with in the lurch, which is how it felt. I basically got booted out of the office and told not to come back until she was at home. In hindsight obviously they were right but I was never going to admit that.

On 4th May having just visited by daughter in hospital I decided to pop into the office to see if Swanton had answered his bail and what charges had been laid against him. I spoke to the PIO who said he had just returned from the custody unit at Waterlooville police station after charging Swanton with Section 3A of the Road Traffic Act, causing death by careless driving whilst over the prescribed drink drive limit and for failing to stop at a road traffic accident. My blood started to boil when I was told that Swanton came across as the most arrogant and non-caring person they had ever come across and that during his formal interview he went "no-comment" to every question and stated that he would give his version of events in court. He showed absolutely no remorse for his actions. This definitely had shades of the Bridgette Panormo and David Nunn cases.

I sat by the phone for almost half an hour trying to pluck up the courage to phone Jean and tell her. But what do I tell her? Yes I could tell her the good news that at last Swanton had been charged but could I really tell her just how arrogant he apparently was? What would that do to her? Was it even necessary at this stage for her to know? Should I tell Sandra first so that she could tell her mum? All these questions and many more whizzed around inside my head before I finally bit the bullet and picked up the phone. I gave her the good news first and tried to explain the procedures that were to follow regarding court appearances and the likelihood that this was going to be a not guilty plea at Crown Court at some time in the future. She got somewhat confused about all this and could not understand why Swanton couldn't plead guilty to what he had done when he appeared before the Magistrate's Court. This seemed like the ideal opportunity to tell her what I had just been told about his attitude towards it all. This confused her even further because Sandra had apparently had a phone call from Adrienne last week concerning the article that was in The News only to be told that Swanton was apparently a broken man and very remorseful. I then had to tell her that wasn't my understanding having just spoken to the two officers that had dealt with Swanton tonight. She understandably became very upset about this and asked why there was so much confusion between us all? It was a good question and one that I was unable to answer. I was livid and Jean was right, why was there so much confusion? I told her I would investigate further and asked her to get Sandra to call me tomorrow. Before I left the office I left a note for Adrienne, who was currently out at yet another fatal RTA to ring me as soon as possible at home.

Just before 11 o'clock she phoned me and confirmed that yes she had spoken to Sandra last week and that during their conversation she had told her that Swanton appeared to be upset on the day of the crash, although she had not actually met him or even seen him. Although she didn't actually say so I got the distinct impression that she was trying to be kind to Sandra, perhaps knowing that the bereaved often feel better about the situation if they think that the person responsible is being genuinely remorseful. I told her that my position as the FLO had been seriously compromised yet again and that all contact with the family should be done through me, if only to prevent further confusion. She said she had made the call in good faith as I was currently off on compassionate leave and that they didn't want to involve me as I had problems of my own. However I pointed out that although I understood her sentiments it had in fact caused me more problems than it solved.

I was at QA the next day with my daughter when my mobile phone rang and it was Sandra. I left the room and found somewhere quiet because I knew that this was likely to be a lengthy conversation and so it proved. We talked about charging procedures, bail, initial court appearances and the likelihood of Swanton pleading guilty or not guilty. In my opinion it was likely that Swanton would be pleading not guilty given his attitude when charged. Just when I thought I had cleared things up with Sandra she then told me that during the same conversation she'd had with Adrienne that she had told her not to bother attending the first court appearance which was set for 21st May because there was no point, it was just an initial hearing to set a trial date or a date for sentencing depending on Swanton's plea. I told her that I totally disagreed with this because it is the family's right to attend every court hearing no matter how trivial and that if it was Sandra and Jeans wish to attend each and every court case, no matter how many there may be, then not only should they attend but I would come and collect them personally and guide them through the whole procedure.

There was a palpable sigh of relief from the other end of the phone and she stated that both of them wanted to be there on every occasion. Whilst on the phone I broached the idea of them supplying a victim impact statement, which had recently been renamed as a victim personal statement, although I preferred the former name because that is what it was designed to do, have an impact on the courts and the defendant. Sandra stated that her and mum had kept notes over the last few months which will help me when it actually came to writing their statement. I said I would drop off a copy of a previous statement that I had written to give them some idea of what was required. I then told her that I would contact her nearer the time of the first court appearance on 21st May to make arrangements to collect them and convey them to court. She seemed much happier with the way things were going now and I reminded her that one of the first things I told them way back in January was that they were in for one hell of a rollercoaster ride and so it was proving.

On 21st May I picked them both up and drove them to South East Hants Magistrates Court in Portsmouth where for the first time they saw the man responsible for killing

Norman. We sat at the back of the court and as Swanton entered the dock so Jean and Sandra held hands and stared intently at him. I feel certain that he could feel their eyeballs burrowing into the back of his head from where he was stood. His court appearance was very brief and it was immediately adjourned to the Crown Court on 29th May.

A couple of days later I spent the best part of three hours sitting at Jeans dining room table helping them write their victim personal statement. I'd written a fair few of these by now and it was important to keep it brief but to make it as hard-hitting as possible so that the court and the defendant were left in no doubt as to the impact this incident had had on them.

On 29th May it was time to attend Portsmouth Crown Court for the first time. It was here that we were likely to find out for definite whether Swanton would plead guilty or not guilty. I arrived at Jeans house and she was clearly very nervous and apprehensive about the whole thing. We then drove a few miles to collect Sandra from work and then drove down into the city to face Swanton once more. I parked the BMW X5 in the rear yard at Portsmouth Central Police Station and we walked around the side of the police station, across the front of the Magistrates Court building and around the corner to the Crown Court. I stopped dead in my tracks because the big steel doors at the entrance to the Crown Court appeared to be shut. I quite literally stood there staring at them. I looked at my watch and it said 9:40 am so we weren't late or particularly early. I then asked Sandra what the date was and she confirmed it was 29th May. I then got my diary out to double check that today was the day and there it was in black and white as I'd written it only a week before whilst at the Magistrates Court that Tuesday the 29thMay was Swanton's Crown Court date. I ran up the steps to the doors and banged on them as hard as I could but there was no reply. I then went back down the steps and walked along the side of the building to where the police office is located and when I looked through the window the office was in darkness and there was nobody there. I was now completely and utterly confused, doubly so because there was nobody else here, no other court personnel, nobody at all. What the hell is going on? I felt such an idiot, this must be my fault surely and I must have got something wrong? I needed to make a phone call and so headed across the courtyard to the adjacent CPS office. That was also empty which only added to my confusion, but eventually I got a reply from a CPS solicitor who was working in a back office. I explained the situation to her and she said that the Crown Court was closed for a 'privilege day'.

"A privilege day? What the hell is a privilege day? I asked in a rather high pitched voice.

She went on to explain that both the Magistrates Court and the Crown Court were traditionally closed on the Tuesday after the May bank holiday as a privilege day for the staff.

"Well aren't they the lucky ones" I exclaimed.

I was furious. What really bothered me was that everybody else had been told about an adjourned date except me and the family. Unbelievable.

Jean and Sandra sat down in a chair as the CPS solicitor made them a cup of tea which was the least they deserved. I started to make various phone calls to try to get to the bottom of what had occurred and every now and again I glanced at Sandra who was looking at the floor shaking her head in disbelief. They had obviously been working up to this and had psyched themselves up to face Swanton and had literally had the door slammed in their face. Everybody I spoke to back at the office had never heard of a privilege day or anything like it but the bottom line was the case had been adjourned until tomorrow and nobody had thought to inform me or the family. I swear I'm going to have someone's head over this. I drove Sandra back to work and she cut a dejected figure as she left the patrol car and walked towards her workplace. Jean was more upset than angry and couldn't understand how such a mistake could be made. She wasn't the only one.

So the next day we repeated the exercise and thankfully this time the Crown Court doors were open. We made our way upstairs to the plush corridors outside number four court. Swanton arrived with his father and his lawyer. They went into a small meeting room whilst Jean, Sandra and myself met the lawyer from Biscoes solicitors who was acting on Jeans behalf in a civil capacity. As we came out of our meeting so the door from Swanton's meeting room opened and out breezed his lawyer. As he passed us I was surprised to see him wink at the Biscoes solicitor. It did look a bit odd but then I suppose they all know each other as the legal profession is a tightly knit community and I didn't think any more of it.

Swanton entered a not guilty plea, which was no real surprise and his case was adjourned back to the Crown Court on 7th September.

After dropping Sandra at work I took Jean home and she asked me to come into the house. We sat down with a cup of tea and I knew there was something on her mind. She then showed me a letter from Biscoes solicitors and there at the bottom amongst all the names of the directors and partners was the name Barry Swanton (Consultant). Jean was concerned enough to phone Biscoes to ascertain whether Barry Swanton was related to Russell Swanton and was horrified to learn that Barry Swanton was in fact the defendant's father. Maybe that wink meant more than I originally thought? I told Jean in no uncertain terms to drop Biscoes immediately and that I would help her obtain new representation.

I had used a firm of solicitors recently with another fatal accident I had been dealing with and was quite impressed with the manner in which they went about their business. I therefore phoned the solicitor I had been dealing with on that occasion, Paul Fretwell and asked him if he would represent Jean and Sandra in the future. I gave him a basic outline of all the terrible things that had happened to them including details about the crash and I felt confident that he would do his utmost to help them in the future and that he would contact them immediately.

A couple of weeks later I received a letter from Sandra berating me because of a letter that she had received from Paul Fretwell that gave intimate details of the collision and the injuries that her father had sustained. These details had come from the conversation that I'd initially had with Mr Fretwell and I had no idea that he was likely to repeat them in a letter to the family. Quite why he did this or what he was hoping to achieve I have no idea but suffice to say it caused Jean and Sandra yet more pain. She went on to accuse me of hiding things from her and was fearful of what else I might not have told them and what else might come out in court that they weren't aware of. I phoned Paul Fretwell and he was extremely apologetic and stated that he didn't think before writing the letter. Oh just brilliant. He promised me that he would write to them again offering his sincere apologies which I think was the least he could do.

Despite leaving a number of messages I couldn't contact Sandra that day but she phoned me the next morning whilst I was at home and she was still obviously very angry about this latest situation. I apologised first of all but stated that I hadn't hidden anything from either of them and would never do so but I did reiterate that in the days following the crash I asked them exactly how much they wanted to know and that Sandra had replied "just the basics at this time" which is what I gave them. I told her it was a very difficult judgment call for me to understand exactly how much to tell them having only just met them. Whilst she fully understood my position she was now concerned that graphic detail about her father's injuries would come out in court and upset her mum even further. I stated that I thought that was unlikely to happen, as the judge would have the technical medical details in writing prior to the hearing and would not put a family through the trauma of having to hear exactly what injuries had been sustained. I then told her that prior to the trial I would sit her and Jean down and go through all the evidence so that they knew exactly what was coming their way and that there would be no nasty surprises for them. She seemed happy with this although still somewhat concerned for her mother's welfare. We both agreed, that difficult though that may be, it would be better hearing it from me rather than from a stranger in open court. Whilst we were on the phone I then told her that I would have to miss the next court appearance on 7th September because I was on annual leave and out of the country, but that I had made arrangements for another officer to collect her and Jean in the usual manner and convey them to and from court which she was very happy with.

I returned from my leave on 18th September and almost as soon as I walked through the office door I was greeted by the two colleagues I had tasked with the taxi duty on 7th September. It transpired that they were half an hour late in picking them up and didn't get them to Crown Court until 10:10 am by which time the case had already started and they missed Swanton changing his plea to guilty. I sat on the edge of the table looking at the floor. Their grovelling cut no ice with me and I let them know it in no uncertain terms. They'd let me down but worse than that they'd let Jean and Sandra down and that after everything that they had been through, that was unforgivable. They went on to tell me that en route home Sandra was so angry and distressed that she asked them to stop the car and she got out and walked. Could it get any worse?

The only good news in this was that Swanton was told by Judge Richard Price that; "The offence was an extremely serious one and it is almost inevitable that you will receive a prison sentence. You must not hold out any hope that because you are being allowed to go home today that you will be allowed to go home on October 5th."

So the case was adjourned again for sentencing on October 5th so at least I would be there for that. All I had to do now was phone Sandra which I was dreading. Thankfully she'd had time to calm down and was fine with me and we agreed to meet on October 2nd to go through the file in full as we had previously discussed.

We met at Jean's house and I went through the file with them. I've dealt with many cases during my career but there weren't many that were as bad as this and I knew that I had to tell them the full circumstances in a manner that was as painless as possible.

It is a truly awful story and starts with Norman leaving the house on Sunday morning to go out for something as simple as a bike ride. Russell Swanton had been with a friend at a pub in Portsmouth the previous evening and had consumed three pints of Stella lager before they left by taxi to attend a party at Fort Southwick on Portsdown Hill where he consumed a further five or six cans of lager and three vodka and orange drinks. These drinks were not pub measures but had been poured free hand into half pint glasses so it was difficult to ascertain exactly how much alcohol he had consumed. He left the party at around 3 am and returned to his friend's house to stay the night. He woke up at around 9:30 am feeling groggy and hung over, but got into his car to drive home to Denmead. As he drove along Hambledon Road so he saw Norman on his bike up ahead and as he approached from behind he stated that Norman appeared to be steering around something in the road or had maybe been blown slightly by the wind. Swanton's car hit the rear of the cycle which Swanton described as "a minor incident". He failed to stop and continued to drive down the road. He then turned right into Soake Road but then reversed back into Hambledon Road and headed back towards the scene of the accident. However he then turned right into Closewood Road which was literally only 20 yards from where Norman Thurston was now laying on the grass verge. Instead of rendering Norman some assistance he continued down Closewood Road where at some point he stopped and phoned his father Barry Swanton who was on holiday in France. His father told him to contact the emergency services but Swanton didn't do this and then carried on driving down the road before going around the block, coming back through Forest Road to the roundabout with Hambledon Road before finally returning to the scene of the crash and pulling up in a lay by some 200 yards from the scene. He had driven a total of 2.2 miles since the crash. He then dialled 999 but was put on hold and then cut off so decided to walk back to the scene itself where the police and paramedics were already in attendance having been called by other people. He was arrested at the scene for providing a positive breath test and taken to Waterlooville police station where he gave brief details of the crash as already outlined. However when it came to his formal interview some months later he refused to answer any police questions and conducted what is commonly referred to as a no comment interview.

There were several issues concerning this incident that I wasn't happy with. In my experience with people who drink and drive they invariably lie about the amount of alcohol they have consumed even when confronted with scientific proof and I was certain that Swanton had done exactly this. For a 35-year-old well-built male to be twice the legal limit almost 8 hours after his last alcoholic drink, would in my opinion indicate that he had consumed far more than he was prepared to admit to but of course the only person that can tell us the whole truth regarding that is Swanton himself. His description of the collision being a minor incident is nothing short of an attempt by him to reduce the force of the impact to something close to a bump in a car park, to place into people's minds that actually it could have happened to anyone of us and that accordingly he didn't really need to stop and help Norman because he was probably OK. Whilst the damage to the front nearside headlight and grille area was relatively minor, the damage to the bonnet and the roof in particular was not and showed quite clearly the massive impact that took place and without doubt he knew straight away just how serious the situation was. Why else did he almost go back to the scene? Because he knew. And when he saw Norman laying on that grass verge he lost his bottle because he knew he was over the drink drive limit. He stated that he panicked and drove off. I've become sick to my back teeth over the years about people who panic when involved in such incidents. Why do they panic? Simple. They panic because they are bloody guilty and they don't want to get caught. And that's why they drive off. During the course of his formal police interviews his arrogance really rose to the surface when he refused to answer any police questions stating that he would tell the court his version of events during the trial.

I think Jean and Sandra took it all rather well but Sandra in particular was incensed by the fact that Swanton didn't stop to render her father some kind of assistance, even to dial 999 to get an ambulance, how could anybody be so callous? I had to warn them that no matter what sentence Swanton received it would not bring Norman back obviously and not to build their hopes up too much that he might receive the maximum sentence which was ten years in prison. I suggested that he would be extremely lucky to get less than three years given the circumstances but fingers crossed he would get a whole lot more. They both nodded their heads.

The next day I was at home when I received a phone call from Sgt. Paul Diamond who told me that he had just received a phone call from Jean saying that she had received a call from the witness care unit at the Crown Court advising her that Swanton's case had been brought forward 24 hours to 2:15 pm tomorrow. I told him that my daughter was still currently in hospital and could he phone Jean back to tell her that I would collect her and Sandra tomorrow at 1:30 and take them to the court.

I walked into the office the next afternoon to be told by the PIO that he had just received a phone call from CPS stating that Judge Price who had been presiding over the case had only just realised that he knew Swanton's father Barry and had therefore just excused himself from the case with no new adjournment date set. I slumped down onto a chair. I really don't believe this, it sounds so bent.

I phoned Sandra and she was absolutely furious and who could blame her. She said she would phone Jean whilst I phoned the CPS in an effort to get some answers, which I couldn't. I phoned Sandra back and she said that mum was now hysterical and Sandra now intended going to the press.

Within a matter of hours I received a phone call from Elise Brewerton, a journalist at the Portsmouth News who I had spoken to on a number of occasions in the past concerning other cases and whom I trusted. She wanted my opinion on this latest twist so I gave it to her and in the next day's edition there was a full page article about the case and Judge Price's connection to it. The article quoted from the Code of Conduct issued by the Judges Council and a section of which reads 'a Judge shall, in his or her personal relations with individual members of the legal profession who practice regularly in the judges court, avoid situations which might reasonably give rise to the suspicion or appearance of favouritism or partiality'.

A Crown Court manager was quoted as saying that "the

court was given information on the name of the defendant's father and on seeing that name Judge Price realised he knew the defendant's father some 20 years ago. He knew him only on a professional level and he was not a close friend, simply someone he had known in a professional manner".

Elise had quoted me word for word and I stated that "The family has been through hell since Norman's death in January and I am frankly sick of having to apologise for other people's mistakes" which kind of summed up how I felt.

The following afternoon Sandra phoned me to state that she had just received a phone call from the Portsmouth News telling her that the adjournment date was now 12th October. Again she was upset and asked the question why has the media told her the new date and not the CPS? I couldn't answer her but said I would make my own enquiries to ascertain whether this information was correct, which sadly it was.

A couple of days later I took a call from Jean who'd just had a call from the witness care unit confirming the adjournment date as 12th October at 10:30 am in front of Judge Hetherington. She was still quite upset, not at me or the police in general, but at CPS and the court system itself because it seemed to have a completely non-caring attitude towards the victim. I couldn't agree with her more and knew that they weren't the first and certainly wouldn't be the last such people to be treated in this manner.

At lunchtime on 11th October I received a call from Jean who'd just had another call from the witness care unit telling her that tomorrow's court case had now been put back until 11 am. I smelt a rat and the cynical side of me was under no illusion that somebody somewhere was pulling a lot of strings in an effort to ensure that the minimum number of people and in particular the press would be present at Swanton's hearing. I told Jean that I would pick her and Sandra up at the previously agreed time and that we would be there in good time for 10 am just in case my suspicions were correct. I then contacted the Portsmouth News to tell them to ignore any such postponement and to ensure that their reporter was also there at 10 am. I did not want them to miss the opportunity to splash Swanton all over the front page of the local paper.

I really felt this was it, we were finally going to see some justice for Jean and Sandra and I had butterflies in my stomach as I collected them from home and drove them the few miles south to Portsmouth Crown Court. We walked up the stairs to court six and arrived there just before 10 am. However we were kept waiting until 11:30 am because of another case that was in court before ours. I spoke to the prosecuting barrister and told him that Jean and Sandra wanted me to read out their victim personal statement to the court rather than anybody else. He rather snootily looked down his nose at me and said it wasn't my place to read such statements and that he was quite capable of doing so. I reiterated that it was the family's request that I read it out but he stood his ground, told me that I had written an excellent statement and that he was more than capable of putting across Jean and Sandra's feelings to the court.

Swanton was called into court and entered the dock. We all filed in behind him and took our places in the public gallery and you could cut the atmosphere with a knife. My heart was pounding and I so hoped that justice would finally be done today.

As usual there was much to-ing and fro-ing, much pontificating by those in wigs and gowns as us mere mortals sat and observed proceedings. The prosecuting barrister outlined the circumstances to the court and didn't pull any punches. He seemed pretty good at delivering the facts in a manner that left nobody in any doubt as to the seriousness of Swanton's actions and I felt quite confident that he would deliver the victim personal statement, which was so important to Jean and Sandra in an effective manner.

However, when it came to reading out that statement Swanton's lawyer rose to his feet and objected very strongly to it being read to the court. When asked by Judge Hetherington why he didn't want it read out he stated that it was too emotive and would upset his client. Upset his client? Who gives a shit about that? There then followed a good ten minutes of argument between Swanton's barrister, the prosecuting barrister and the Judge in what would and would not be allowed to be read out and in the end it was agreed that all of the statement would be read except the last three paragraphs because they would be too upsetting. The Judge stated that he had a copy of the statement in front of him and that he was fully aware of all its content and that he would take this into consideration when passing sentence. I sat there with clenched fists. Of course it would be upsetting, that was the whole point of a victim personal statement, to convey to all those gathered in the court just how big an impact such a violent and unnecessary death has on the relatives left behind.

And so the prosecuting barrister started to read Jean and Sandra's statement and for the purpose of this book I have included the full statement including the last three paragraphs so that you can judge for yourself whether it would have been too upsetting for Russell Swanton to hear.

'My name is Jean Thurston and I'm writing this statement in conjunction with my daughter Sandra. Sunday, 21st January 2007 was the worst day of our lives. To be told that the man you had been married to for over 50 years had been killed in such appalling circumstances was absolutely devastating. Before I tell you just how much Norman's death has affected us, allow me just for a moment to give you some idea of the man he was.

Norman was a wonderful, loving husband and father. He served his country for 27 years in the Royal Navy, 19 of those on board submarines. After retiring from the Navy he worked for another 20 years in the building trade as a safety officer for Portsmouth Building Association before retiring for a second time. He was a natural leader and was highly respected by his peers and those who worked for him. In his leisure time he enjoyed golf and gardening. But three years ago he was diagnosed with bowel cancer. Some people might have withered upon being given such news but Norman was a strong man, he was a fighter and he was determined to beat it. And he did just that. After three years of chemotherapy and radiotherapy he was given the all clear. He had always been a keen gardener and decided to help other cancer victims by growing hundreds of pop plants every year to raise much-needed funds for the Macmillan Cancer Support charity. He also helped to raise other charitable funds for the Rachael Maddocks School. He was always helping others and rarely considered his own plight, in fact our neighbours had no idea he was suffering from cancer for a long time and were staggered when they found out. He was a strong man, a caring and thoughtful man, who always put others before himself.

It's been four months now since Norman's death, but it seems like a lifetime. I am totally lost without him by my side. I cannot sleep and when I do I have nightmares and wake up crying. I always think he's there and talk to him. When I pass the spot where he died, which I have to do quite regularly, I can picture him laying there. Can you imagine how that feels? Try picturing one of your loved ones laying at the roadside and it might give you some idea about how we are feeling.

Apart from the obvious grief that we are suffering over the loss of Norman, we are also overwhelmed by a sense of incredible anger. He was a good, honest and decent human being, who had survived the ravages of cancer, who was suddenly and brutally killed by a selfish, arrogant and spineless man who broke the golden rule of society and drove a car whilst under the influence of alcohol.

Russell Swanton you did this. You killed Norman Thurston, not in some freak accident but because you were arrogant enough to think that *you were okay to drive. But you did something even worse than that. Having obviously hit Norman on his bike what did you do? Did you stop and render him some assistance? Did you stop and phone for an ambulance? Did you do any of the things a decent human being would have done? No. You didn't do any of these things. Thinking only of yourself you drove off, leaving Norman for dead at the roadside. And have you showed us, his family, the slightest remorse since? No you haven't and I sincerely hope you don't think that a belated apology to the court might help us now, so please don't bother on our account, as it will be seen by everyone as completely hollow and worthless.*

You Mr Swanton will never really be held accountable for your actions and no matter what sentence you receive, it will never compensate us for our loss. There is a huge difference between you and Norman. Had the roles been reversed he would have stopped and done everything he could to help you. We hope you can live with your conscience, because we have to live with your actions for the rest of our lives'.

The court room was completely silenced and stayed that way for a few moments after that statement had been read as those present absorbed what they had just heard. The defence barrister then had the audacity to tell the Judge that Swanton was indeed sorry and that he wished to convey that to Norman Thurston's family. As Jean had said so succinctly in her statement that any apology received now would be seen as a hollow gesture and not to bother. But he obviously couldn't help himself and I think it was seen by all as a pathetic attempt to again make himself feel somewhat better about what he had done.

Judge Hetherington then told Swanton to stand. This is it. Once again I saw Jean and Sandra hold hands. Swanton was sentenced to 12 months in prison and received a two-year driving disqualification. There was a sharp intake of breath from many of those present and I heard Sandra whimper "no".

12 months in prison? 12 months. I must have heard it wrong; surely he didn't just sentence Russell Swanton to 12 months imprisonment? I looked at the prosecuting barrister as he turned towards us and I saw his eyebrows raised so even he seemed surprised. My immediate thoughts were that the old boy's network had been at play here and that yet more strings had been pulled which resulted in Swanton receiving an incredibly lenient sentence for taking the life of another man in a drink drive related incident.

As we left the court everybody appeared to be shaking their heads in disbelief and I quickly ushered Jean and Sandra into one of the small meeting rooms at the side of the court where the prosecuting barrister came straight in and said;

"I'm so sorry but the Judge got it all wrong and was unduly lenient"

Not for the first time Sandra was incensed at the injustice of the system and just kept asking.

"Was that all my fathers' life was worth? 12 months" whilst Jean seemed to be in a state of shock, not so much at the sentence but more that the Judge had allowed Swanton's defence team the opportunity not to have the most important part of her statement read out to the court. Despite the fact that I had warned them on more than one occasion prior to today not to be disappointed with Swanton's sentence, whatever it might be, even I was taken aback by just how lenient the Judge had been towards him.

There seemed to be people swarming about all over the corridor outside the court seemingly incredulous at what they had just witnessed. I was approached by Simon Jones, a journalist from the Portsmouth News who asked me for a quote on my feelings about the sentence. I said a lot of things that maybe I shouldn't have done but frankly I didn't care any more, the manner in which Jean and Sandra had been treated by the judicial system was disgusting, with no compassion shown towards them or towards Norman in any way whatsoever. Although the 12 month prison sentence was poor in itself the fact that Swanton only got a two-year driving disqualification just proved to me that there was something seriously wrong here. I have dealt with countless drink drivers in my career and the mandatory sentence for a first-time offender who has merely been stopped at the roadside by the police is a 12 month ban. A second time offender would receive a minimum of 18 months up to around three years depending on the level of intoxication. So how come Russell Swanton who was twice the legal limit, had killed somebody and driven off, only received a two-year disqualification? By the time he gets out of jail which would be in a little over six months, he will only have 18 months left in which to catch a bus. In my opinion, at the very least he should have received a five-year disqualification and ordered to resit an extended driving test before getting his licence back.

The Saturday edition of the Portsmouth News is their biggest seller with a readership of over 300,000 so I was very pleased to see that Russell Swanton's face was splashed all over the front page together with the headline;

3 PINTS OF STELLA
5 CANS OF LAGER
2 VODKAS AND
7 HOURS SLEEP
… YET HE STILL
THOUGHT HE'D
BE SAFE TO DRIVE

Family fury as drunken motorist is jailed for just 12 months over cyclist's death.

As a front page headline it was pretty good and Simon Jones and Elise Brewerton had followed that up with a full page article about the crash and the court case together with a full editorial comment column which pulled no punches. There were of course a number of quotes within the article, the most poignant of which came from Sandra;

"I think it is absolutely disgusting. My mother and I are both totally devastated by this. When the judge gave the sentence I felt like I had been kicked in the stomach. This is not justice. We thought today would be the day that we could begin to get on with our lives but how can we when we are so bitter that he can take a life and be out of prison within six months".

I think my quote was almost as forthright;

"Most law-abiding people would not put themselves in this position. The vast majority of people know that if you have a skin full the night before it takes more than a few hours' kip to get it out of the system. For the amount of alcohol that he had drunk it would have taken 24 to 36 hours and I think he would have felt drunk still at the time of the accident. He admitted that he felt groggy and tired. Being hung over does not mean you're sober, it means you're still feeling the effects of alcohol. A few hours' sleep having consumed that much alcohol is not enough. My heart goes out to the family. I'm completely gutted, it is nowhere near the sentence we were hoping for. What sort of message does that convey?"

Lorna Jackson from the road safety charity BRAKE was quoted as saying;

"One year for a man's life, there is no sense of justice there. This is significantly less than the maximum sentence and I can clearly see why the family is devastated by this. Drivers must be aware if you're going out and you know you are going to be driving the next morning you should not be drinking alcohol the night before because you can still be over the limit. That is not a mitigating factor at all. Drivers have to be aware and take responsibility".

The editorial comment was placed beneath a subtitle that read;

THE PAIN OF FAMILY'S LOSS WILL NEVER DISAPPEAR

'The decision to drive with alcohol still in his system from the night before is one that Russell Swanton will regret for the rest of his life. But it is the family of Norman Thurston, the pensioner whose life was needlessly lost in the accident caused by Swanton, who will suffer the most. The heart-rending statement from Mr Thurston's wife, which detailed the pain caused by his loss and was read to the court at Swanton's trial, is testament to that. Swanton may not have known the precise extent to which his body would still be affected in the morning from his drinking session the previous night. But common sense would have told him that three pints of strong lager, five or six cans of beer and three shots of vodka would have left him seriously in danger of still being over the limit. He was given a 12 month prison sentence and there will be many who feel that is lenient considering the devastating impact of his actions. Thankfully, the dangers of drink-driving are now firmly ingrained in the public consciousness, thanks to a string of effective and often shocking publicity campaigns. It is now socially unacceptable to drink alcohol and then get behind the wheel.'

It was now time for me to leave Jean and Sandra in peace but not before Sandra had told me that she intended writing to the Home Office in the strongest possible terms about the manner in which her family had been treated by the judicial system. As we said our goodbyes to each other I still found myself apologising to them, because I was after all part of that judicial process and felt guilty, angry and embarrassed by this whole affair. But most of all I felt let down by a system that I had generally held in very high regard.

A few days later I received a thank you card from Jean and amongst some of the kind comments she had written were the words;

"Sandra and myself would like to thank you and your colleagues so very much for your help and support. You all did your very best and could not have done more. We will see what reply Sandra receives from the Home Office"

It took a while but Sandra did eventually receive a response from the Home Office. It was a very brief, standard letter stating that her complaint had been investigated (although it didn't say by whom!) and that there was no case for the Judge or the system itself to answer.

THE LEGACY

As an FLO I had a close personal relationship with many of the families I came into contact with and I was therefore privy to just how much the death of their loved one affected them. Or at least I thought I did. It wasn't until I started re-contacting them to seek their permission to use the details of their relatives accident in this book that they gave me further information on the long term affects upon them and their family and even with my experience I found much of what they told me both shocking and upsetting.

I always knew that you don't just "get over it" and that time is supposedly a great healer (although I've never really believed in that one) but I had no real idea just how far reaching and long lasting the affects can be. The ripple effect from a road death touches many people from the immediate next of kin, other relatives, friends, neighbours, work colleagues, nursing staff and the emergency services who deal with the aftermath. But the real suffering, the long term legacy, is only really felt by the victim's closest family.

All of them it seems have suffered a variety of issues from mental health and emotional problems, work related stress, failures in relationships, financial worries, off-spring struggling at school or college with exams and general behavioural issues, even refusing to learn how to drive because it reminds them of the accident, all of which have manifested themselves months or even years later. But the most common long term problem is guilt. Guilt that they are still alive and not their loved one. Guilt that they weren't there at the time to protect them. Guilt when they laugh. Guilt if they re-marry or move onto form new relationships. Guilt that they can carry on with their own lives. And there's no getting over that either, for most it remains a constant feeling, gnawing away at them through their sub conscious every single day.

Some of those feelings manifest themselves in ways that some people who have never experienced such grief might not be able to understand. One father I know couldn't stand looking at the arm chair I'd sat in as I told him that his daughter had died and several days later he took it out into the garden and set fire to it. His son couldn't get to grips with all the sympathy cards they were sent, he'd always associated greeting cards with happy occasions like birthdays and Christmas. The fact that concerned friends and relatives had sent cards just made him angry.

Carole Miller and Dean Foster although truly grateful that they survived their ordeal are still suffering in a huge way. When I visited Carole to talk to her about this book (in September 2014) she explained that she still has at least two more major operations to undergo including a complete knee replacement. She cannot walk un-aided for more than about 200 yards, can't kneel down to play with her young grandson and still has regular nightmares. That's eight years after the crash.

Even my favourite reporter Jeff Reines was so affected by some of the things he had reported that he gave up journalism and moved to Cornwall for a much quieter life.

There are more public legacies that we all see from time to time; road side shrines. They can be as simple as a bunch of flowers tied to a lamppost or as permanent and elaborate as small memorial gardens or even fully engraved head stones with photographs of the deceased attached to them, all lovingly tended by their respective families. There has been a lot of debate about these shrines with some local authorities trying to ban them, stating that they are a distraction to other drivers or an eye sore. I read an article once where a local council had cited the lack of planning permission in its efforts to have one road side shrine removed. Personally I think they are a good thing and for two reasons. First and foremost it gives the family left behind a bit of focus, an attachment to the place where their loved one lost their life. By attending 'that' place it's a lot more personal to them, it's not some anonymous grave yard, this is their very personal spot and no-one can take that away from them. And secondly I think they help to remind all of us just how many lives are lost in our locality and just for a second as you drive past one they do make you think. And if that makes us all drive more carefully then that is a good legacy.

In the United States road side shrines are actively encouraged on condition that the only permanent fixture is a two foot high metal pole with a small disc placed at the top with the words 'Drive Safely' on it.

I have to say at this point that three of the biggest FLO commitments I undertook i.e. Bridgette Panormo, David Nunn and Norman Thurston all had one thing in common; in that had the offending driver had the decency to apologise and say sorry for getting it wrong at the earliest opportunity and certainly within the first week after the crash, it would have made all the difference to the families concerned and I cannot emphasise too strongly just how important that apology can be. But then some people, no matter how guilty they are both legally and morally just can't find it within themselves to do that can they?

But even if they did apologise the family still has to go through the trauma of a trial if there is a defendant being prosecuted over the death of their relative. And it's here that much of the good work that the police and FLO's in particular do is completely undone. You only have to read this book to understand that the judicial system just doesn't seem to have the same empathy towards the bereaved that the police service has strived for over the last few years. The whole system is seemingly geared towards protecting the rights of the accused rather than the victim. Court staff from Judges to Barristers are not trained to think about the feelings of the bereaved because they only deal in cold facts. Sure, when it suits them to turn on a speech directed at a Jury they'll lay on a thick pile of sympathy to help their cause (whether prosecutor or defender) but rarely have I ever come across a member of the judiciary that really took the family into consideration.

Towards the latter part of my career victim impact statements (later renamed victim personal statements) were introduced in an effort to get the Courts to understand the long term consequences for the victim and/or their family. It's a brilliant concept and really helps the family to get across how they feel. It's a vital component for them to make the Court and most importantly the defendant fully understand how the death of their relative has affected them. So when a CPS lawyer unilaterally decides that he won't read out the victim impact statement because he thinks the Judge has heard enough do you think that helps the family concerned? No it didn't, because their voice wasn't heard. And when the defence Barrister for Russell Swanton successfully pleaded that three paragraphs in Jean Thurston's statement were too emotive and might upset his client, do you think that helped Jean and Sandra? No it didn't, because not only was their voice not heard but it was callously censored to protect the feelings of the man held responsible for killing a husband and father.

The CPS, lawyers, barristers, Judges and everyone else who works within the judicial system need a major rethink when it comes to dealing with victims of crime. Because that's what the victims of road death are when a third party is criminally culpable; they are victims of crime just as those who are victims of murder are. It's a violent, unnatural and unnecessary death but the punishment rarely reflects this.

I always briefed my families about the possible (and probable) outcome at Court. For those convicted of careless driving the penalty was likely to be a £200 fine and maybe a six month driving ban at best. For those convicted of Section 1 death by dangerous driving the very least sentence imposed should be two years imprisonment and a five year driving ban with an extended driving test. It should be even higher if alcohol or drugs are involved. It didn't always pan out that way of course but my briefing to them stipulated that it wasn't the sentence that was important but the conviction itself. This was legal proof that their loved one wasn't responsible but that a third party was; that was the really important aspect and that whatever fine or driving disqualification was imposed was secondary.

As I said at the beginning of this book, being an FLO was, without question, the best thing I ever did during my career. Yes it was the hardest, most challenging, demanding, emotionally draining, frustrating commitment I'd ever undertaken but the one thing that drove me to continue doing it for over six years were the families I dealt with. Almost without exception they were amazing people. We were flung together at the very lowest point in their lives and I'm quite sure there were times when they couldn't face me intruding into theirs. But their strength and fortitude gave me the will to do my best for them.

There were and probably still are a number of police officers within the service that don't agree with the FLO role. One of them once said to me "you're a copper not a bloody social worker," and to some extent I suppose he was right but my reply to him was quite simple and it was something I highlighted at the start of this book. We all join 'the job' to help make a difference, to protect the vulnerable and those who cannot help themselves at that particular moment in time. It's not all about catching criminals, big car chases, pub fights and policing football matches. It's the little things that police officers do every day of the week that make the work we do so worthwhile. But very little of it ever gets recognised by management, the public or the media, who are all too quick to judge at times.

As an FLO I spent a lot of my time just sitting in someone's house, drinking their tea (after stirring it with my pen!) and just listening to a mother, a father, a wife, a son talk about the person they had just lost. Sometimes that would be two hours or more; sometimes it happened during a number of visits over several weeks or even months. It didn't matter to me and I know other FLO's did/do exactly the same thing. It's a vital part of the role and stems from the very best traditions of being a British Police officer.

But it wasn't all tea and sympathy. You may recall that during my FLO course we got told in no uncertain terms that we would not be allowed to take on more than five FLO commitments at any one time. That's all very well if you have enough FLOs to share the work load but if you haven't what then? The answer is you pile more and more onto the ones you do have. In 2005 my Relief was down to the bare bones, there were only three of us working full time; myself and the two Michaels and it came at a time when we were being hammered with work, it seemed that everything we got sent to was either a confirmed fatality or a potential.

Although I have highlighted a number of cases in this book I've barely scratched the surface on what we actually dealt with in total. In late 2005 I had no less than nine FLO commitments on my plate with five of those being Section 1's. On top of that I was the PIO for another fatal and I took responsibility for most of the probationers that came onto our Relief for their two week RPU attachments, which meant me showing them how the motorway worked, how to deal with minor RTA's, issuing tickets to errant motorists, dealing with drunk or drugged drivers, disqualified drivers and other criminals who use cars and a whole host of other responsibilities. All these things inter-twined with being an FLO, because it wasn't ever supposed to be a full time role. We were still Traffic Cops first and FLO's second.

I was sitting at my desk when Sgt. Jerram came over and asked if I could take on yet another FLO commitment in the north of the county somewhere. At that very moment something inside of me snapped, I felt myself welling up and the tears just rolled down my face. I didn't say anything, I just got up and went outside and sat on the wall. I'd never felt pressure like it ever before. I felt embarrassed, weak, ashamed even, but deep down I knew my sponge was now full and was currently over flowing. It was time for me to say 'no' I can't take on anymore.

The two Michaels came out to join me a few minutes later. They were pretty close to cracking themselves but at least they didn't have to take on the emotions of each family, they could remain fairly detached from that side of things for which they were very grateful. Adrienne apologised and said that she had found another FLO to take on the latest commitment and that she thought I needed a break from it all. Well I couldn't just phone all the families and say "hey, I'm having a break from being your FLO, I'll be back in a month or two" so we agreed that I would come off the FLO list for the time being which meant no new deployments but I would continue to help out the families I was already committed to.

Before I knew it I was sitting in front of Quita Jones the force psychiatrist and FLO welfare coordinator. I was off the road for at least two months after that, which we had basically agreed to anyway but her job was to protect both me and the organisation I suppose.

I didn't really need to see her because I had my own rock at home. Without Trish and my family I doubt I could have coped with any of it. I could off-load all my thoughts onto her and it was so important to have that stability at home, it's not a job for a young or single person in my opinion, it's vital to have good support at home. What got me the most though was that I didn't see it coming. I genuinely thought that with all my knowledge and experience that I would recognise within myself the symptoms of suffering from stress. But I hadn't noticed and was really quite angry with myself. It had crept up on me unnoticed until I reached that tipping point when I was simply asked to take on another FLO commitment. It was a valuable lesson and one that I wasn't ever going to allow a repeat of. This was my legacy.

In March 2007 my wife successfully applied for a new job as a Service Manager with a local company providing social housing for the vulnerable. On her first day she had to attend a 'bean-bag' session with a couple of other new candidates plus several other people already working within the organisation whose roles were being reorganised so there were about a dozen people in the room. After all the usual formalities it was time for the modern take on the 'getting-to-know-you' type of questions whereby Trish and one of the other new candidates were dragged out to the front of the class and told to sit back to back and then give a potted history about themselves. Trish said she was married, had three kids, lived locally and then for some inexplicable reason said that she was married to a police officer and that as a Traffic cop I sometimes had to go and tell families that their loved one had been killed. There was a sharp intake of breath from the lady she was sat back to back with.

"I know your husband," she said. "He was my family liaison officer"

They both turned to face each other and Trish recognised the name.

"Not Bridgette?" asked Trish.

"Yes" replied Tania and with that they both burst into tears.

I doubt the others in that room really understood what was happening in front of them. Trish and Tania had never met before obviously, although they had talked on my mobile a couple of times when I wasn't in the room or was having a shower or something. Just what the odds were on them meeting in such circumstances I've no idea but I suspect they are pretty high and they have remained good friends ever since.

A few weeks later Trish suggested that we invite Mick and Tania over for dinner. I'd always liked them as you know but felt uneasy about crossing the line between the professional me, and the off duty, social me. And what about their feelings? I felt pretty sure that Mick in particular would always associate me with that awful day in February 2004 and probably didn't want to meet me again anyway. Trish talked me into it and I can almost hear Tania persuading Mick to do the same and so they arrived at our house one evening for dinner. My heart was doing its usual heavy pounding and I could feel myself shaking as I opened my front door to them, which made a change from it happening the other way around!

It was a bit awkward to start with, probably because we were all nervous and maybe a bit wary about saying the wrong thing but the pair of them made me feel rather relaxed about it all in the end. We have met many times since and they even came to my retirement 'do' which I was particularly chuffed about.

I retired from the Police service in 2008. In truth I didn't actually want to go, my heart was telling me to stay but my head was screaming 'get out' whilst you can. Even though I'd left the job itself I actually continued in my role as an FLO for about six months afterwards because I was still dealing with a couple of families that had inquests and a court case to go through. I should have handed them over to another FLO but had built up such a good relationship with them that frankly I didn't feel able to. No-one within my old department ever knew and I didn't get paid for any of it either.

Writing this book has been one of the hardest things I've ever done, even though I've had two books published prior to this one. It has taken me the best part of three years to write and always with the family's feelings uppermost in my mind. I hope I have managed to convey just how big an impact a road death has on the family left behind and of the huge roller coaster ride they have been on. I no longer have to undertake the long, short walk as I called it towards someone's front door but right now, somewhere in the country there is an FLO who is doing just that. Spare a thought for all those involved.

If you enjoyed this book then why not seek out Steve Woodward's previous works?

'Kilo Sierra Five One' (Policing Portsmouth in the 1980s)

'From T Ford to T5' (One Hundred Years of Hampshire Constabulary Transport)